FROM OLD ENGLISH TO STANDARD ENGLISH

Other books by Dennis Freeborn

Varieties of English
A Course Book in English Grammar

FROM OLD ENGLISH TO STANDARD ENGLISH

A COURSE BOOK IN LANGUAGE VARIATION ACROSS TIME

Dennis Freeborn

First published 1992 by
THE MACMILLAN PRESS LTD
Houndmills, Basingstoke, Hampshire RG21 2XS
and London
Companies and representatives
throughout the world

ISBN 0–333–53767–X hardcover
ISBN 0–333–53768–8 paperback

A catalogue record for this book is available from the British Library.

Printed in Hong Kong

Reprinted 1992, 1993

Contents

Preface

Language change

The English language, like all living languages, is in a continuous state of variation across time. The language of one generation of speakers will differ slightly from another, and at any one time there are 'advanced' and 'conservative' forms, whether they belong to regional, educational or class dialects. Change takes place at every level of language. New words are needed in the vocabulary to refer to new things or concepts, while other words are dropped when they no longer have any use in society. The meaning of words changes – *buxom* once meant *obedient*, *spill* meant *kill*, and *knight* meant *boy*. A word-for-word translation of some Old English will probably not read like grammatical contemporary English, because word order and grammatical structure have also changed. Pronunciation in particular is always being modified and varies widely from one regional or social group to another. Since the spelling of words in writing has been standardised, changes in pronunciation are not marked in the spelling, the orthography of the language.

Standard English

One variety of English today has a unique and special status – Standard English. Its prestige is such that, for many people, it is synonymous with the English language. This book sets out to show what the origins of present-day Standard English were in the past. It is concerned principally with the forms of the language itself, and makes reference to the historical, social and political background in the establishment of Standard English in outline only.

Levels of study

It is helpful to consider three levels of study which may be followed according to students' needs, or to the amount of time available for study. At the first, **observational** level, features of the language can be simply noted and listed as interesting or different; at the second, **descriptive** level, such features are identified more specifically, using appropriate descriptive terms from a model of language; at the third, **explanatory** level, they are placed in their relation to general processes of language change, and in their social, political and historical context.

The 'texts'

The core of the book is a series of 151 texts which exemplify the changes in the language from Old English to the establishment of Standard English. The texts have been selected for a number of reasons. The Old English texts are almost all from the *Anglo-Saxon Chronicle*, and so provide something of the historical context of the language a thousand years ago. Some texts have aspects of language itself as their subject. As we have no authentic records of the spoken language before the invention of sound recording, letters and diaries of the past are included, because they are likely to provide some evidence of informal uses of English in the past. Some literary texts have been chosen, but the series does not constitute a history of English literature.

Activities

The activities are designed to encourage students to find out for themselves – to consider possible reasons for what they observe, and so to study data at first hand and to consider hypotheses, rather than to accept the answers to problems of interpretation that others have given. The process of analysing the texts demonstrates how our knowledge of earlier English has been arrived at. The surviving corpus of Old and Middle English texts is all the evidence we have about the language as it was then. There are no grammar books, descriptions of pronunciation, spelling books or dictionaries of English before the sixteenth century. The tasks in the activities are no more than suggestions, and teachers can omit, modify and add to them as they think useful.

Facsimiles

The facsimiles are an essential part of the book, not just decorative additions to the 'texts', for they are the primary sources of our knowledge of the language, and give students at least some idea of the development of spelling and writing conventions. Literary texts are generally printed with modern spelling and punctuation, and although editions of Old and Middle English retain the older spelling, they usually add present-day punctuation.

Commentaries

Analytic commentaries are provided for some of the texts in the book. Each commentary is a 'case study' based on the text itself, which provides some of the evidence for change in the language.

The *Text Commentary Book* and *Word Book*

Two supplementary books in typescript published by the author are available for teachers and advanced students. The *Text Commentary Book* contains detailed explanatory analyses of the linguistic features of many of the texts. The *Word Book* provides a complete word list, in alphabetical order, for each Old and Middle English text. The lists for the Old English texts give the base form of inflected words and a translation, so that you can refer to an Old English dictionary or grammar more easily. Those for the Middle English texts include the derivation of each word. The *Word Book* also contains selected lists of words in present-day English which are derived from Old English, Old French, Old Norse or Celtic.

Cassette tape

A cassette tape containing readings of some of the Old English, Middle English and Early Modern English texts is also available from the author. For details of the cassette tape and supplementary books write to: Dennis Freeborn, PO Box 82, Easingwold, York YO6 3YY.

Aims

The aims and layout of the book are therefore different from those of the established textbooks on the history of English, or Old and Middle English, which are listed in the bibliography. The empirical study of English which is exemplified in *Varieties of English* (Macmillan, 1986) is here applied to historical texts. The essential method is the same.

Dennis Freeborn
July 1991

Acknowledgements

The author and publishers wish to thank the following for permission to use copyright material:

Guardian News Services Ltd for an extract from the *Guardian*, 24.8.89;
Newspaper Publishing plc for letters to *The Independent* by Daniel Massey, 14.11.87, and Carol Clark, 25.11.87.

Every effort has been made to trace all the copyright holders, but if any have been inadvertently overlooked the publishers will be pleased to make the necessary arrangement at the first opportunity.

Texts and facsimiles

The texts consist of extracts from the following sources:

Chapter 1

1 Peterborough chronicle for AD 443
2 Peterborough chronicle for AD 449
3 Peterborough chronicle for AD 455
4 Peterborough chronicle for AD 519
5 Peterborough chronicle for AD 611
6 Peterborough and Parker chronicle for AD 614
7 St Luke's Gospel 15: 11–13

Chapter 2

8 Peterborough chronicle for AD 628
9 Peterborough chronicle for AD 595
10 Peterborough and Parker chronicle for AD 601
11 Cædmon's hymn
12 Peterborough and Parker chronicle for AD 787
13 Peterborough chronicle for AD 793
14 Peterborough and Parker chronicle for AD 878
15 *The Phoenix*
16 The Battle of Brunanburh – Parker and Peterborough chronicle for AD 937
17 OE inscription, St Gregory's Minster, Kirkdale, N Yorks
18 Parker chronicle for 1066
19 Peterborough chronicle for 1066

Chapter 3

20 Short metrical chronicle (14th century)
21 Robert of Gloucester's chronicle (c.1300)
22 Peterborough chronicle for 1140
23 Peterborough chronicle for 1137
24 *Ormulum* (i) (late 12th century)
25 *Ormulum* (ii)
26 *The Fox and the Wolf* (early 13th century)
27 *Cursor Mundi* (c.1300)
28 The Eagle, from the *Bestiary* (13th century)

Chapter 4

29 John of Trevisa on the English language (i) (1385)
30 John of Trevisa on the English language (ii)
31 Michael of Northgate, *Ayenbite of Inwyt* (i) (1340)
32 Michael of Northgate, *Ayenbite of Inwyt* (ii)

Chapter 5

33 John Barbour, *Bruce* (i) (c.1375)
34 John Barbour, *Bruce* (ii)
35 York proclamation (1415)
36 York potters' 'Pentecost Play' (c.1470)
37 *The Lay Folks' Catechism* (1357)
38 John Wyclif's version of *The Lay Folks' Catechism* (c.1360)
39 Geoffrey Chaucer, *The Reeve's Tale* (late 14th century)

Chapter 6

40 *Sir Gawayn and þe Grene Knyȝt* (i) (late 14th century)
41 *Sir Gawayn and þe Grene Knyȝt* (ii)
42 William Langland, *Piers Plowman* (i) (c.1370)
43 William Langland, *Piers Plowman* (ii)
44 William Langland, *Piers Plowman* (iii)
45 William Langland, *Piers Plowman* (iv)
46 Edited version of Text 45

Chapter 7

47 *The Travels of Sir John Mandeville* (i)
48 *The Boke of Mawndevile* (verse)
49 *The Travels of Sir John Mandeville* (ii)
50 Geoffrey Chaucer, 'The Tale of Melibeus'
51 Geoffrey Chaucer, 'The Parson's Tale'
52 Geoffrey Chaucer, 'The Friar's Tale' (Harley MS)
Geoffrey Chaucer, 'The Friar's Tale' (Hengwrt MS)
53 Thomas Usk's appeal (i) (1384)
54 Thomas Usk's appeal (ii)

Chapter 8

55 *The Boke of Margery Kempe* (i) (c.1420)
56 *The Boke of Margery Kempe* (ii)
57 *The Boke of Margery Kempe* (iii)
58 *The Boke of Margery Kempe* (iv)
59 Agnes Paston's letter to William Paston (1440)
60 Margery Brews' letter to John Paston (1477)
61 John of Trevisa (1385)
62 William Caxton's printing of John of Trevisa (1482)
63 William Caxton on the diversity of English (1490)
64 William Caxton's advertisement (1478)
65 Sir Thomas Malory, *The Tale of King Arthur* (c.1460–70)
66 George Cely's letter to Richard Cely (1478)
67 Richard Cely's letter to his family (1479)
68 Memoranda by George Cely (1483)

Chapter 9

Chapter 10

Chapter 11

Chapter 12

Symbols

OE	Old English
ME	Middle English
EMnE	Early Modern English
MnE	Modern English
OF	Old French
ON	Old Norse
WW	Word-for-word translation
m	masculine (gender)
f	feminine
n	neuter
nom	nominative (case)
acc	accusative
gen	genitive
dat	dative
sg	singular (number)
pl	plural
n	noun
vb	verb
adj	adjective
cj	conjunction
neg	negative
NP	noun phrase
VP	verb phrase
PrepP	prepositional phrase

S	subject (in clause structure)
P	predicator
C	complement
O	object
A	adverbial
< >	e.g., <e>, refers to written letters of the alphabet
/ /	e.g., /e:/, refers to the spoken sound, using the symbols of the International Phonetic Alphabet (IPA)

The IPA symbols can be found in:

Freeborn, D., French, P. and Langford, D.
Varieties of English
(Macmillan, 1986) Chapter 4, pp. 75–6.

Gimson, A.C.
An Introduction to the Pronunciation of English, 3rd edn
(Edward Arnold, 1980) pp. 328–9.

1. The English language is brought to Britain

1.1 How the English language came to Britain

English in the 1990s is an international language. It is spoken as a mother tongue by nearly 400 million people, in the British Isles, Canada, the United States of America, Australia and New Zealand. It is a second language for many others in, for example, India and Pakistan and some African states, where it is used as an official language in government and education. Many different regional and social varieties of English have developed and will continue to do so, but there is one variety which is not related to any one geographical region, but is used in writing, and generally also in educated speech.

> Educated English naturally tends to be given the additional prestige of government agencies, the professions, the political parties, the press, the law court and the pulpit – any institution which must attempt to address itself to a public beyond the smallest dialectal community. It is codified in dictionaries, grammars, and guides to usage, and it is taught in the school system at all levels. It is almost exclusively the language of printed matter. Because educated English is thus accorded implicit social and political sanction, it comes to be referred to as STANDARD ENGLISH ...
>
> (*A Comprehensive Grammar of the English Language,* R. Quirk *et al.*, Longman, 1985, p.18)

This book tells in outline how present-day Standard English developed from the English of the past.

Four hundred years ago, in the 1590s, English was spoken almost exclusively by the English in England, and by some speakers in Wales, Ireland and Scotland, and this had been so for hundreds of years, since the language was first brought to Britain in the fifth century.

To give you a first impression of the changes in the language since it was brought to Britain, here are two short texts in **Old English** (OE), with their word-for-word (WW) translations, which were written down in the ninth century. The first is the beginning of a description of the island of Britain, while the second tells how the Britons were conquered by the Romans in AD 47. The texts are printed with their original punctuation. The sign <⁊> was used in manuscript writing for *and*, like <&> today.

rittene igland is ehta hund mila lang.
7 twa hund brad. 7 her sind on þis
iglande fif geþeode. englisc. 7 brit
tisc. 7 wilsc. 7 scyttisc. 7 pyhtisc. 7
boc leden. Erest weron bugend þises
landes brittes.

OE

Brittene igland is ehta hund mila lang.
7 twa hund brad. 7 her sind on þis
iglande fif geþeode. englisc. 7 brittisc. 7 wilsc. 7 scyttisc. 7 pyhtisc. 7
boc leden. Erest weron bugend þises
landes brittes.

WW

of-Britain island is eight hundred miles long.
& two hundred broad. & here are in this
island five languages. english. & british. & welsh. & scottish. & pictish. &
book latin. First were inhabitants of-this
land britons.

The scribe wrote *five languages* and then listed six. He had divided into two what should have been one language – *Brito-Welsh*. The Old English words *brittisc* and *wilsc* referred to the same people.

OE

xlvii. Her Claudius romana cining gewat mid here on brytene. 7 igland geeode. 7
ealle pyhtas. 7 walas underþeodde romana rice.

WW

47. Here Claudius romans' king went with army in britain. & island over-ran. &
all picts. & welsh made-subject-to romans' empire.

The following account (Texts 1–3) in OE from the *Anglo-Saxon Chronicle* tells us why the language was first brought to Britain in the fifth century.

The *Anglo-Saxon Chronicle* has survived in several manuscripts, and most of the extracts and facsimiles of the original writing which follow in this chapter are taken from the copy known as the *Peterborough Chronicle* (see Section 3.3). Sometimes other manuscript versions are quoted, in particular the *Parker Chronicle*, because the differences between them provide some interesting evidence for changes in the language.

If you compare the facsimiles with the printed reproduction of the texts, you will find some marked differences in letter shapes, and some OE letters which are no longer used. The OE alphabet and modern conventions for printing are described in Section 2.2.4, but in the meantime you could work out for yourself what the differences are.

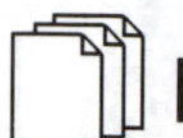

Activity 1.1

The account in Text 1 from the *Peterborough Chronicle* was copied in the twelfth century from an earlier copy first written down in the ninth century. The WW translation is followed by a paraphrase in Modern English (MnE). Abbreviated words in the manuscript have been filled out, but the punctuation is the original.

(i) Compare the WW translation of Text 1, the chronicle for AD 443, with the text of the Old English.
   (a) List some OE words that are still used in MnE (some will be different in spelling).
   (b) List some OE words that have not survived into MnE.
   (c) List any letters of the alphabet that are not used in MnE.
   (d) Comment on the punctuation.

(ii) Read the MnE version and consider some of the reasons why the WW translation does not read like present-day English.

(iii) Repeat the assignment for Texts 2 and 3.

TEXT 1 – Chronicle for AD 443

OE

cccc.xliii. Her sen-
don brytwalas ofer sæ to
rome. 7 heom fultomes
bædon wið peohtas. ac hi
þær nefdon nænne. forþan
þe hi feordodan wið ætlan
huna cininge. 7 þa sendon
hi to anglum. 7 angel cynnes æðelingas ðes ilcan
bædon.

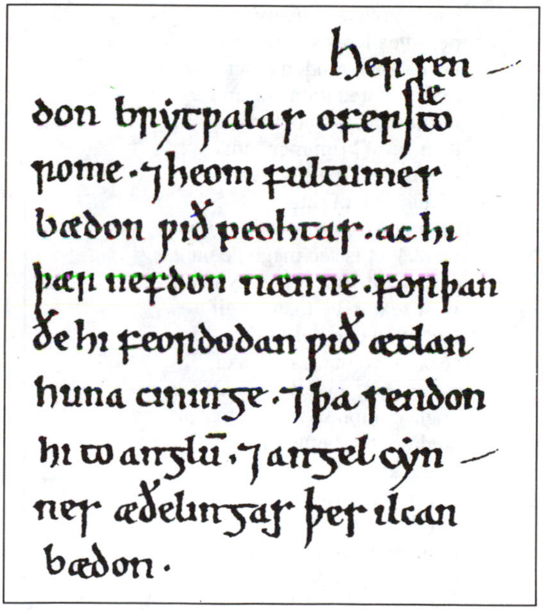

WW

443. Here sent
britons over sea to
rome. & them troops
asked against picts. but they
there had-not none. because
they fought against attila
huns king. & then sent
they to angles. & angle
-peoples princes the same
asked.

443. In this year the Britons sent overseas to Rome and asked the Romans for forces against the Picts, but they had none there because they were at war with Attila, king of the Huns. Then the Britons sent to the Angles and made the same request to the princes of the Angles.

TEXT 2 – Chronicle for AD 449

cccc. xlix. Her martia-
nus 7 ualentinus onfengon
rice. 7 rixadon .vii. wintra.
7 on þeora dagum gelaðode
wyrtgeorn angel cin hider.
7 hi þa coman on þrim ceo-
lum hider to brytene. on
þam stede heopwines fleot.
Se cyning wyrtgeorn gef
heom land on suðan eas-
tan ðissum lande. wiððan
þe hi sceoldon feohton wið
pyhtas. Heo þa fuhton
wið pyhtas. 7 heofdon si-
ge swa hwer swa heo co-
mon. Hy ða sendon to
angle heton sendon mara
fultum. 7 heton heom sec-
gan brytwalana nahtsci-
pe. 7 þes landes cysta.
Hy ða sona sendon hider
mare weored þam oðrum
to fultụme. Ða comon
þa men of þrim megðum
germanie. Of ald seaxum.
of anglum. of iotum. Of
iotum comon cantwara. 7 wiht-
wara. þæt is seo megð þe nu
eardaþ on wiht. 7 þæt cyn on
west sexum þe man nu git
hæt iutna cyn. Of eald
seaxum coman east seaxa.
7 suð sexa. 7 west sexa. Of
angle comon se a syððan
stod westig. betwix iutum
7 seaxum. east angla. middel angla. mearca. 7 ealla
norþhymbra. Heora he-
retogan wæron twegen
gebroðra. hengest. 7
horsa.

WW

449. Here martia-
nus & valentinus took
kingdom. & reigned 7 winters.
& in their days invited
vortigern angle people hither.
& they then came in three ships
hither to britain. at
the place heopwinesfleet.
The king vortigern gave
them land in south east
of-this land. provided
that they should fight against
picts. They then fought
against picts. & had victory
wherever they came.
They then sent to
anglen ordered send more
help. & ordered them say
britons' cowardice.
& the land's goodness.
They then at-once sent hither
greater force to others
as help. Then came
these men from three nations
germany. From old saxons.
from angles. from jutes. From
jutes came kent-people. & wight-people.
that is the race which now
dwells in wight. & the race among
west saxons that one now still
calls jutes' race. From old
saxons came east saxons.
& south saxons. & west saxons. From
anglen came it ever since
stood waste. between jutes
& saxons. east angles. middle
angles. mercians. & all
northumbrians. Their leaders
were two
brothers. hengest. &
horsa.

MnE

449. In this year Marcian *(Eastern Roman Emperor)* and Valentinian *(Western Roman Emperor)* came to power and reigned seven years. In their days Vortigern invited the Angles here and they then came hither to Britain in three ships, at a place called Ebbsfleet *(in Kent)*. King Vortigern gave them land in the south-east of this country, on condition that they fought against the Picts. They fought the Picts and were victorious wherever they fought. Then they sent to Anglen, and ordered the Angles to send more help, and reported the cowardice of the Britons and the fertility of the land. So the Angles at once sent a larger force to help the others. These men came from three Germanic nations – the **Old Saxons**, the **Angles** and the **Jutes**. From the **Jutes** came the people of **Kent** and the **Isle of Wight** (that is, the people who now live in the Isle of Wight, and the race among the West Saxons who are still called Jutes). From the **Old Saxons** came the men of **Essex**, **Sussex** and **Wessex**. From **Anglen** (which has stood waste ever since, between the Jutes and Saxons) came the men of **East Anglia**, **Middle Anglia**, **Mercia** and the whole of **Northumbria**. Their leaders were two brothers, Hengest and Horsa.

TEXT 3 – Chronicle for AD 455

OE

cccc.lv. Her hen-
gest 7 horsa fuhton wiþ
wyrtgerne þam cininge
on þære stowe þe is cwe-
den ægelesþrep. 7 his broþor horsan man ofsloh.
7 æfter þonn feng to
rice hengest. 7 æsc his
sunu.

Her hen
gest 7 horsa fuhton wiþ
wyrtgerne þā cininge
on þære stowe þe is cwe_
den ægelesþrep. 7 his broþor horsan man ofsloh.
7 æfter þonn feng to
rice hengest. 7 æsc his
sunu.

WW

455. Here hen-
gest & horsa fought against
vortigern the king
in the place that is called
aylesford. & his bro-
ther horsa one slew.
& after that came to
kingdom hengest. & æsc his
son.

MnE

455. In this year Hengest and Horsa fought against king Vortigern at a place called Aylesford, and Hengest's brother Horsa was killed. Then Hengest became king and was succeeded by his son Æsc.

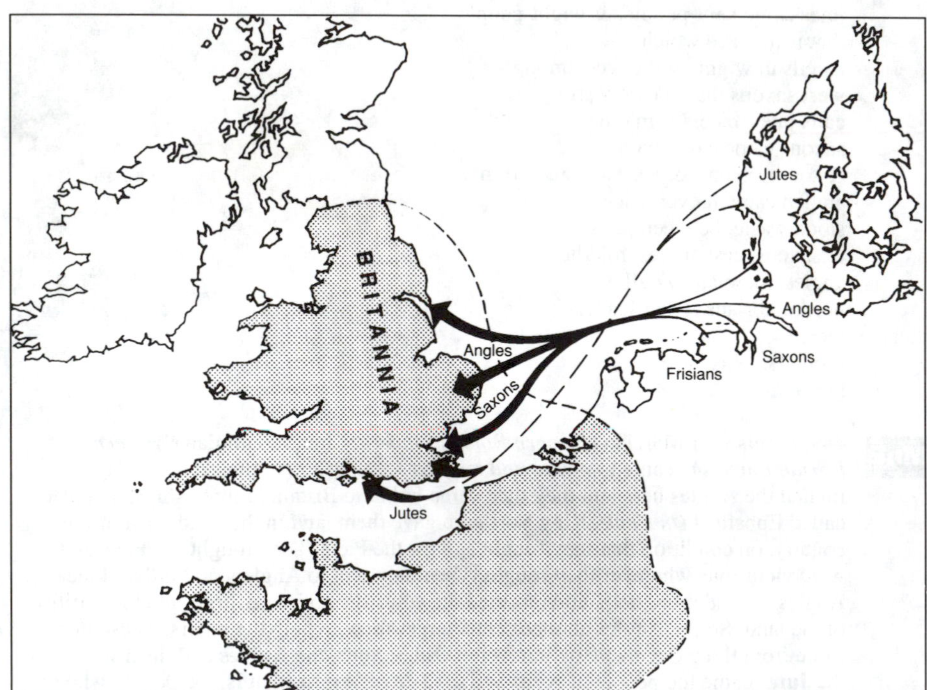

Map 1. The invasions of the Angles, Saxons and Jutes

1.2 Roman Britain

In the middle of the fifth century, Britain had been a province of the Roman Empire for over 400 years, and was governed from Rome. The official language of government was **Latin**. It would have been spoken not only by the Roman civil officials, military officers and settlers, but also by those Britons who served under the Romans, or those who needed to deal with them. The term **Romano-British** is used to describe those 'romanised' Britons and their way of life.

The native language was **British**, one of a family of **Celtic** languages. Its modern descendants are **Welsh**, and **Breton** in Brittany (Britons migrated across the Channel in the sixth century to escape the Anglo-Saxon invasions). There were also speakers of **Cornish** up to the eighteenth century. Irish and Scottish **Gaelic** come from a closely related Celtic dialect. None of these languages resembles **English**, which comes from the family of **West Germanic** languages.

The Saxons had been raiding the east coast of Roman Britain for plunder since the early third century, and a military commander had been appointed to organise the defence of the coastline. He was called, in Latin, *Comes litoris Saxonici*, the 'Count of the Saxon Shore'. But Roman power and authority declined throughout the fourth century, and we know that a large-scale Saxon raid took place in AD 390.

By AD 443, the Roman legions had been withdrawn from Britain to defend Rome itself, so when the Romano-British leader Vortigern invited the Angles Hengest and Horsa to help to defend the country, they found Britain undefended, open not only for raiding and plunder, but also for invasion and settlement.

This was not a peaceful process. Bede describes what happened in his *History of the English Church and People*, which was written in Latin in the eighth century (see Section 2.2.3).

> It was not long before such hordes of these alien peoples crowded into the island that the natives who had invited them began to live in terror. ... They began by demanding a greater supply of provisions; then, seeking to provoke a quarrel, threatened that unless larger supplies were forthcoming, they would terminate the treaty and ravage the whole island. ... These heathen conquerors devastated the surrounding cities and countryside, extended the conflagration from the eastern to the western shores without opposition, and established a stranglehold over nearly all the doomed island. A few wretched survivors captured in the hills were butchered wholesale, and others, desperate with hunger, came out and surrendered to the enemy for food, although they were doomed to lifelong slavery even if they escaped instant massacre. Some fled overseas in their misery; others, clinging to their homeland, eked out a wretched and fearful existence among the mountains, forests and crags, ever on the alert for danger.
>
> (Translation from the Latin by Leo Sherley-Price, Penguin, 1955)

There is no surviving evidence of the British or Celtic language as it was used in the fifth century, and practically no Old Celtic words are to be found in MnE, except a few like *ass*, *bannock* and *crag* (see the Celtic-derived word list in the accompanying *Word Book*), and a larger number of Celtic place names of rivers, forests and hills. The reasons for this must lie in the lack of integration between the British and the Anglo-Saxon invaders. As Bede records, the British were in time either driven westwards into Wales and Cornwall or they remained a subject people of serfs. The dominant language would therefore have been English.

The complete conquest of 'Englaland' – the land of the Angles – in fact took another two centuries. There are tales of a Romano-British king called Arthur who led successful resistance in the 470s, winning several battles that were recorded in Welsh heroic legends. He must have been a Romano-British noble, and was probably a commander of cavalry. Twelve victories against the Saxons are recorded, and much of the country remained under British rule for some time. But Arthur's name does not appear in the *Anglo-Saxon Chronicle*, and his historical existence is still disputed, although the chronicle does tell of other battles that took place, as in the following example.

TEXT 4 – Chronicle for AD 519

.dxix. Her certic ⁊ kynric onfengon
west seaxna rice. ⁊ þy ilcan geare hi gefuhton wið
bryttas. ðer man nu nemnað certices ford. ⁊ siððan
rixadon west seaxna cynebarn of þam dæge.

her certic ⁊ kynric onfengon
west seaxna rice · ⁊ þi ilcan geare hi gefuhton wið
bryttas · ðer man nu nemnað certices ford · ⁊ siððan
rixadon west seaxna cynebarn of þam dæge ·

519. Here certic & cynric took
west saxons' kingdom. & the same year they fought against
britons. where one now names certic's ford. & afterwards
ruled west saxons' princes from that day.

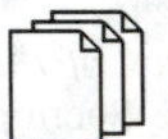

Activity 1.2

(i) Use the WW translation to write an acceptable version of Text 4 in MnE.
(ii) Compare the *Peterborough Chronicle* text for AD 519 (Text 4) with the following version from the *Parker Chronicle*. What differences are there?

dxviiii. Her cerdic ⁊ cynric west sexena rice onfengun. ⁊ þy
ilcan geare hie fuhton wiþ brettas. þær mon nu nemneþ
cerdices ford. ⁊ siþþan ricsadan west sexana cynebearn of þan
dæge.

519. Here cerdic & cynric west saxons' kingdom seized. & the
same year they fought against britons. where one now names
cerdic's ford. ⁊ after ruled west saxons' princes from that
day.

Similar entries about fighting against the Britons were recorded throughout the sixth century and into the seventh and eighth centuries, by which time they would have been driven as a fighting force from England. They are often referred to by the name *Wealas*, or *Walas*, meaning *foreigners*. This is the origin of the modern words *Wales*, *Welsh* and *Cornwall* (*Cornwalas*).

The singular noun *wealh* is also used to mean *slave* or *serf*, which is an indication of the status of the Britons under Anglo-Saxon rule. For example, the entry for AD 755 in the *Parker Chronicle* tells of Cynewulf, King of Wessex:

⁊ se Cynewulf oft miclum gefeohtum feaht wiþ bretwalum.

& that Cynewulf often great battles fought against brito-welsh.

It mentions in passing how a Welsh hostage became caught up in a local fight against Cyneheard, a prince of Wessex:

> hie simle feohtende wæran oþ hie alle lægon butan anum bryttiscum gisle.
> 7 he swiþe gewundad wæs.
>
> they continuously fighting were until they all lay (dead) except one british hostage.
> & he badly wounded was.

Here are two typical short entries in the *Peterborough Chronicle*, followed by the *Parker Chronicle* text. The annal for AD 614 is evidence of continued British resistance.

TEXT 5 – Chronicle for AD 611

dc.xi. Her kynegils feng to rice. on weast
seaxum. 7 heold .xxxi. wintra.

Her kynegils feng to rice. on weast
seaxum. 7 heold .xxxi. wintra.

WW 611. Here cynegils took to kingdom. among west
saxons. & held 31 winters.

MnE 611. In this year Cynegils succeeded to the West
Saxon kingdom and reigned for 31 years.

TEXT 6 – Chronicle for AD 614

Œ dc.xiiii. Her kynegils 7 cwichelm ge fuhton
on beandune. 7 ofslogon .ii. þusend walana. 7 lxv.

Her kynegils 7 cwichelm ge fuhton
on beandune. 7 ofslogon .ii. þusend walana. 7 lxv.

WW 614. Here cynegils & cwichelm fought
at beandune. & slew 2 thousand welsh. & 65.

MnE 614. In this year Cynegils and Cwichelm fought
at Beandune and slew two thousand and sixty-five Welsh.

Parker Chronicle annals

dc.xi. Her cynegils feng to rice on wesseaxum. 7 heold .xxxi. wintra.

dc.xiiii. Her cynegils 7 cuichelm gefuhton on bean dune. 7 ofslogon .ii. þusend wala. 7 lxv.

1.3 Studying variety in language across time

As speakers of present-day English, we recognise many different dialects and dialectal accents, but usually we identify differences by labelling them with a geographical region – Scottish, Welsh, Northern, West Country, Liverpool, Cockney, Geordie – or by making some kind of personal judgement, like 'he's talking posh' or 'she speaks good English', 'they've got a dreadful/beautiful accent' or 'that's bad grammar'.

Students of language are interested in finding out what people's attitudes to language use are, but they also try to be objective in studying all varieties of the language, not only Standard English. They identify different **levels** which can be separately examined: **meaning** (**semantics**) is conveyed through **words** (**vocabulary** or **lexis**) in a particular **order** in sentences (**grammar**).

In speech, each of us has an individual **pronunciation**, which belongs to a particular **accent** of English. The study of pronunciation is called **phonology**. In writing, we are not allowed any variation in spelling (**orthography**), which has not changed since the mid-eighteenth century (with the exception of a few words, for example, *musick*), and can be checked in any dictionary. But our handwriting (**graphology**) and pronunciation cannot be regulated like this: we write English in an individual way and speak it with a personal variety of an accent. Different accents are liked or disliked by different people: some accents have prestige, while others are stigmatised. The accent with the most prestige in England is called **Received Pronunciation** (RP) by linguists. Its popular name is 'BBC English'. Some refer to it as 'standard' pronunciation. Your attitude towards it will depend on a variety of reasons personal to you.

The English language consists of the sum of all its **dialects**, of which the most prestigious is **Standard English** – it has such prestige that many people think of it as 'correct English', and regard other dialects as substandard. Linguists prefer to classify Standard English as one dialect among many, and refer to the others as **non-standard dialects**. Each regional dialect has its own range of accents.

This description seems to suggest that dialects and accents are clearly identifiable as separate varieties with marked boundaries. This is in fact not true. They merge and blend with each other, but we have to pretend that they are separate in order to make sense of the obvious differences between dialects that are geographically far apart. We can clearly hear small differences between speakers of our own dialectal accent, even within the same town, but lump together speakers of unfamiliar dialects. To Southerners, all Northerners talk alike, and vice versa.

To study the dialects of a language, we therefore focus our attention on the following:

- Meaning (semantics): the **semantic** level.
- Vocabulary (lexis): the **lexical** level – loss of old words, gain of new words.
- Word structure: the **morphological** level – prefixes and suffixes, internal changes in words.
- Grammar (syntax): the **syntactic** level – word order in sentences and phrases.

The object of this book is to provide an outline of how the English language, and Standard English in particular, has developed into its present form. The texts that illustrate this development make up a series of 'case studies' which can be studied in greater or lesser detail. Some record historical events in the language of the time at which they happened.

1.4 How has the English language changed?

It is interesting to observe successive changes in the language in versions of the same text. The most useful source is the Bible, because translations have been made in every period from Old English to the present day.

Activity 1.3

Discuss some of the differences you can observe in the following texts, which are the beginning of the parable of the Prodigal Son from St Luke's Gospel, Chapter 15 (the verses of the chapter are numbered). Look at vocabulary, spelling, word structure and word order. (OE words that have changed in meaning, or are no longer in the language, have been translated.)

TEXT 7 – Parable of the Prodigal Son, Luke 15: 11–13

Late West Saxon OE, c.1050

11 He cwæð. soðlice sum man hæfde twegen suna. 12 þa cwæð
se gingra to hys fæder. fæder syle me mynne dæl mynre æhte.
þe me to gebyreð. þa dælde he hym hys æhta. 13 þa æfter feawa dagum ealle hys
þyng gegaderode se gingra sunu ⁊ ferde wræclice on feorlen ryce. ⁊ þær
forspylde hys æhta lybbende on hys gælsan.

Word-for-word version in MnE

11 He quoth (*spoke*). soothly (*truly*) some (*a certain*) man had two sons. 12 then quoth
the younger to his father. father sell (*give*) me my deal (*part*) of-my property.
that me to belongs. then dealed (*gave*) he him his property. 13 then after few days all his
things gathered the younger son & fared abroad in far-off country. & there
spilled (*wasted*) his property living in his luxury.

Late fourteenth century ME, S. Midlands

11 And he seide, A man hadde twei sones; 12 and the ȝonger of hem seide to the fadir,
Fadir, ȝyue me the porcioun of catel, that fallith to me. And he departide to hem the
catel. 13 And not aftir many daies, whanne alle thingis weren gederid togider, the
ȝonger sone wente forth in pilgrymage in to a fer cuntre; and there he wastide hise
goodis in lyuynge lecherously.

EMnE, 1582

11 And he said, A certaine man had tvvo sonnes: 12 and the yonger of them said to
his father, Father, giue me the portion of substance that belongeth to me. And he
deuided vnto them the substance. 13 And not many daies after the yonger sonne
gathering al his things together vvent from home into a farre countrie: and there he
vvasted his substance, liuing riotously.

1.5 How can we learn about OE and later changes in the language?

The evidence for changes in the language lies in the surviving manuscripts of older English going back to the eighth century, and in printed books since the end of the fifteenth century. A lot of older English texts have been reprinted in modern editions, and so can be readily studied.

All our knowledge of pronunciation, however, has to be worked out from *written* evidence. So we can never reproduce for certain the actual pronunciation of English before the invention of sound recording in the late nineteenth century, but we try to make a reasonable guess by building up different kinds of evidence.

1.6 Changes of meaning – the semantic level

Some people believe that words have 'real meanings' and object to evidence of change in current usage. For instance, *aggravate* and *disinterested* have taken on the meanings of *annoy* and *uninterested*, in addition to those of *make worse* and *impartial*. It is argued that the new meanings are wrong, and an appeal is made to the **derivation** or **etymology** of a word – that is, what its original meaning was in the language it came from. Here is an example from the 'Letters to the Editor' column of a newspaper. The first writer is arguing that Latin should be taught in schools; the second letter is one of the replies that were printed later.

First letter

It is demonstrably more easy to explain the function of a word when you know what it means. The very word 'education' provides me with a wonderful example. In Latin *e* from *ex* meaning 'out' and *ducare* 'to lead' – literally, therefore, *to lead out*. To lead out of ignorance into the light of knowledge.

(The *Independent*, 14 Nov 1987, writer – Daniel Massey)

Second letter

Knowing the derivation of the word *education* is of as much help to us in deciding how children should be educated as knowing the derivation of, say, 'hysteria' would be in choosing a treatment for that condition.

May I suggest that your etymologically minded correspondents look up 'treacle' in a good dictionary? They will then know what to do if ever bitten by a snake.

(The *Independent*, 25 Nov 1987, writer – Carol Clark)

Activity 1.4

(i) Discuss the argument and the response. It would help if you were to check the recorded meanings of *educare* in a Latin dictionary, and *education* in an English dictionary.

(ii) Look up the original meanings of *hysteria* and *treacle* in a dictionary containing details of the derivation and successive meanings of words.

To understand that words do change their meaning is to understand that words like *aggravate* and *disinterested* can have two meanings. Many words have changed so much that their original meaning seems quite remote; it is interesting to use a good dictionary to trace the sequence of meanings and to see how one leads to another.

For example, the earliest written record of the word *buxom* in the *Oxford English Dictionary* (*OED*) is dated 1175 and is spelt *buhsum*. It is recorded in a modern dictionary of Anglo-Saxon as *bocsum*, meaning *flexible*, *obedient*, and its first syllable *boc-/buh-* came from the OE word *bugan*, meaning *to bow down* or *bend* – that is, *bocsum/buhsum* means 'bow-some', 'pliable'. Its present-day meaning is defined in the *Concise Oxford Dictionary* as 'plump and comely'. How did this come about and what then is its 'true meaning'?

Its meaning changed in the following stages (details from the *OED*):

I **easily bowed or bent**

1 **morally**

a **obedient**

Beo **buhsum** toward gode (1175) – Be **obedient** to God

This meaning survives into the nineteenth century:

To be **buxom** and obedient to the laws and customs of the republic ...
(1843, George Borrow)

b **submissive, humble, meek**

Þat lauedi til hir lauerd lute
Wit **buxum** reuerence and dute
The lady bowed to her lord
With **humble** *and fearful reverence*
(c.1300, *Cursor Mundi*)

c **amiable, courteous, kindly**

Meek and **buxom** looke thou be
And with her dwell
(c.1460, Mystery Play, *The Annunciation*, Angel to Joseph)

d **ready, willing**

And many a beggere for benes **buxum** was to swynke
And many a beggar was **willing** *to toil for (a meal of) beans*
(1377, Langland, *Piers Plowman*)

2 **physically**

flexible, pliant, unresisting

Then gan he scourge the **buxome** aire so sore
That to his force to yielden it was faine
(1596, Spenser, *The Faerie Queene*)

II **blithe, jolly, well-favoured**

3 **bright, lively, gay**

A Souldier firme and sound of heart, and of **buxome** valour
(1599, Shakespeare, *Henry V*)

4 **full of health, vigour and good temper; well-favoured, plump and comely, 'jolly', comfortable-looking (in person): (chiefly of women)**

She was a **buxom** dame about thirty
(1823, Scott, *Peveril of the Peak*)

These meanings overlapped for centuries in the course of the development of the present-day meaning of the word, which is confined to references to women as 'comfortable-looking in person'. It cannot be said that the 'real meaning' today is 'obedient'.

Activity 1.5

The words in the following list have all changed their meaning in time.

(i) Choose some words from the list and look up their original meanings in the word lists in the *Word Book* or in a dictionary that provides the etymology of words.
(ii) Use the dictionary to trace the successive changes of meaning.

bachelor
beam
booty
boy
build
can (vb)
career
castle
chore
cloud
coin
control
dairy
danger
deal (n)
deer
delicate
dizzy
dreary
dull
eerie
faint
false
fear
flour
fowl
gentle
giddy
girl
glance
harlot
harvest
heap
holiday
honest
horrid
kind (n)
knave
knight
lady
left (-hand)
lewd
loft
lord
lose
may (vb)
meal (to eat)
meat
medley
mess
mood
mole (mark)
moss
must (vb)
naughty
nerve
nice
organ
parliament
pastor
pen (writing)
pester
pharmacy
pond
Pope
prestige
pretty
pudding
quell
rather
read
rid
sad
saucer
sell
sergeant
shall
share (n)
shroud
shut
silly
sincere
skill
sky
sleuth
slogan
smite
soft
solve
spill
spoon
starve
stomach
stool
team
toil
town
toy
truth
try
very
walk
want
weird
whine
win
womb
worm

If you wish, try to match the words to their original meanings, which are listed below in alphabetical order, before looking them up:

advise
agreeable
animal
autumn
be able to
be allowed to
belly
bird
birth, origin
blood-stained
boy 1
boy 2
bread-guardian
bread-kneader
bristling
charming
child
chip of wood
clean
clear (vb)
cloud
condiment-dish
conflict (n)
cunning (adj)
danger
destroy
die
discharge a debt
dispute (vb)
distinction
distinguish
division
enclosure 1
enclosure 2
encourage
encumber
exchange
fate
father
feather
feigned
fettered
finest part of ground meal
food
foolish 1
foolish 2
fraud
garment
give
have to
having nothing
illusion
insane
instrument (music)
jest
keep copy of accounts
kill 1
kill 2
knight
know
lack
lay(man)
loyalty
maidservant's place
marsh
medicine
more quickly
offspring, family
part (n)
portion (of food)
power
race-course
respectable
rock (n)
roll (vb)
sausage
serpent
servant 1
servant 2
shepherd
simple
sinew
sky
slip (vb)
smear
speaking
spot (n)
strive
stupid
Sunday
thought
throat
throne
time, occasion
timid
trail (n)
tree
troop
true
turn (n)
unfasten
village
war-cry
weak
weary
wedge
well-born
whizz (of an arrow)

2. Old English

We call the language of the Anglo-Saxon period and up to about 1100 to 1150, after the Norman Conquest, **Old English** (OE). Our knowledge of OE is based on a number of manuscripts that have survived from OE times, from which the grammar and vocabulary have been reconstructed by scholars, working from the sixteenth century onwards (for a sixteenth century example see Section 2.2.5), but especially in the nineteenth and twentieth centuries. They have provided us with the dictionaries and grammars of OE, and the editions of OE texts, to which we can refer.

2.1 Dialects and political boundaries

The English were not a politically unified nation until late OE times, and as they originally came from different parts of western Europe (see Text 2 and Map 1), they spoke different dialects of West Germanic. They settled in different parts of Britain, but they were able to communicate with each other. Dialects are varieties of a language that differ in pronunciation, vocabulary or grammar, but are not different enough to prevent understanding.

The country as it existed during the seventh and eighth centuries is sometimes referred to as the **heptarchy** – that is, the country of seven kingdoms: Northumbria, Mercia, East Anglia, Essex, Kent, Sussex and Wessex (see Map 2).

Wars were frequent in the country during Anglo-Saxon times, in which one or other of the kingdoms might dominate the others. For instance, the following example tells of a battle between Wessex and Mercia in AD 628.

TEXT 8 – Chronicle for AD 628

Œ dc.xxviii. Her kynegils 7 cwichelm ge fuhton
wiþ pendan æt cirnceastre. 7 geþingodon þa.
(*Peterborough Chronicle*)

her kynegilr 7 cpichelm ge fuhton
pið pendan æt cirnceastre. 7 ge þingodon þa.

WW 628. Here cynegils & cuichelm fought
with penda at cirencester. & settled then.

MnE 628. In this year Cynegils (*King of Wessex*) and Cwichelm fought against Penda (*King of Mercia*) at Cirencester, and then they agreed terms.

Œ dc.xxviii. Her cynegils 7 cuichelm gefuhtun
wiþ pendan æt cirenceastre. 7 geþingodan þa.
(*Parker Chronicle*)

The fact that there were seven kingdoms does not mean, however, that there were seven different dialects. The evidence from OE manuscripts suggests that there were in fact three or four: **Northumbrian** and **Mercian**, which together are called **Anglian**, from the West Germanic dialect of the Angles; **Kentish** and **West Saxon**, developing from the dialects of the Jutes and Saxons (see Map 3).

Map 2. The seven Anglo-Saxon kingdoms

Map 3. The dialects of Old English

All living languages are in a continuous state of change and development, and OE was no exception between the fifth and twelfth centuries. So any mention of the forms of OE words, or features of pronunciation, illustrates one dialect of the language at one stage of its development in a generalised way. It is usual to use the late West Saxon dialect of the tenth and eleventh centuries to describe OE, because West Saxon was by then used as a standard form for the *written* language, and most surviving manuscripts are written in West Saxon.

2.2 Written OE

2.2.1 Runes

The writing system for the earliest English was based on the use of signs called **runes**, which were devised for carving in wood or stone. Few examples have survived in Britain, the most famous of which can be found on an 18-foot cross now in the church at Ruthwell, Dumfriesshire. On the Ruthwell Cross are some runic inscriptions in the Northumbrian dialect which are part of a famous OE poem called *The Dream of the Rood* (*rood* comes from the OE word *rod* meaning *cross*), in which the 'cross' relates the events of the Crucifixion. The Ruthwell Cross probably dates from the eighth century.

Activity 2.1

(i) Use a dictionary or the OE word list in the *Word Book* to look up the original meaning of the words *rune*, *write* and *read*.

(ii) Use the chart of runic symbols to transcribe the following extract from the Ruthwell Cross. It appears at the top of the SW face of the Cross.

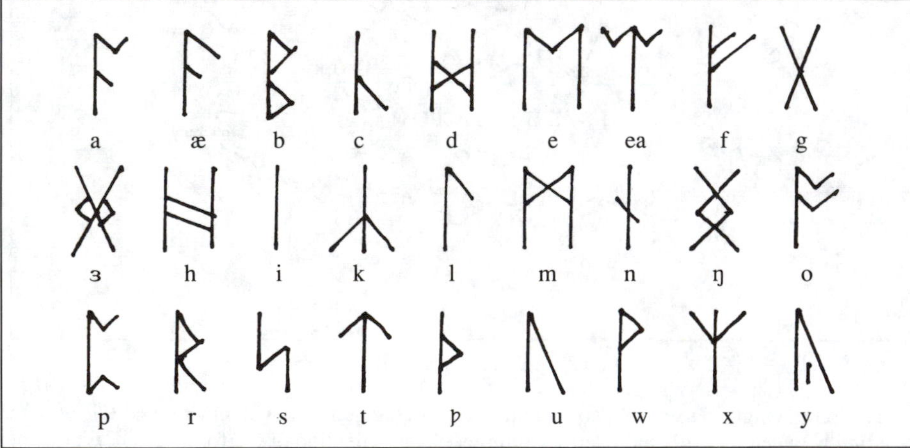

(A transcription and translation of the runes, with a short commentary, can be found in the *Text Commentary Book*.)

2.2.2 Early writing

Written English as we know it had to wait for the establishment of the Church and the building of monasteries, at which time the monks wrote manuscripts in Latin, the language of the Church. This did not begin to happen until the seventh century. In that century, much of the north of England was converted to Christianity by monks from Ireland, while Augustine had been sent by the Pope to preach Christianity to the English, which began in the south, in Kent. Here are the *Peterborough Chronicle* records of the event.

TEXT 9 – Chronicle for AD 595

d.xcv. Hoc tempore monasterium sancti bene-
dicti a longobardis destructum est. Her gregorius papa sende to brytene augustinum mid wel manengum
munucum. þe godes word engla þeoda godspellodon.
(*The first sentence is in Latin*)

Hoc tempore monasteriū sc̄i bene
dicti a longobardis destructū ē. Her gregorius papa sende to brytene augustinū mid wel manengum
munucum. þe godes word engla þeoda godspellodon.

595. At-this time monastery of-saint benedict by longobards destroyed was. Here gregory pope sent to britain Augustine with very many
monks. who god's word to-english nation preached.

595. At this time the monastery of St Benedict was destroyed by the Lombards. In this year Pope Gregory sent Augustine to Britain with very many monks, who preached God's word to the English nation.

TEXT 10 – Chronicle for AD 601

dci. Her sende gregorius papa augu-
stine arcebiscope pallium on brytene. 7 wel manege
godcunde larewas him to fultume. 7 paulinus biscop ge-
hwirfede eadwine norðhymbra cining to fulluhte.

Her sende gregorius papa augu-
stine arcebiscope pallium on brytene. 7 wel manega
godcunde larewas him to fultume. 7 paulin' biscop ge
hwirfede eadwine norþhymbra cining to fulluhte.

601. Here sent gregory pope augu
stine archbishop pallium in britain. & very-many
religious teachers him for help. & paulinus bishop
converted edwin northumbrians' king to baptism.

601. In this year Pope Gregory sent the pallium to archbishop Augustine in Britain, and very many religious teachers to help him; and bishop Paulinus converted Edwin King of Northumbria and baptised him.

Parker Chronicle annals

.dxcv. Her Gregorius papa sende to brytene Augustinum. mid wel manegum munecum. þe godes word engla ðeoda godspelledon.

dci. Her sende gregorius papa augustino. ærce biscepe pallium in bretene. 7 welmonige godcunde lareowas him to fultome. 7 paulinus biscop gehwerfde edwine norþhymbra cyning to fulwihte.

The monks adapted the **Roman alphabet** from Latin to write English, which means that the spelling of OE gives us a good idea of its pronunciation. We know the sounds of Latin represented by the Roman alphabet, because there has been a continuous tradition of speaking Latin to the present day. This also provides the evidence for the different OE dialects, because different spellings for the same words would indicate differences of pronunciation or word form.

2.2.3 Evidence of dialectal variation

Here are two versions of the earliest known poem in English. It is found in the OE translation of Bede's *History of the English Church and People*, which was written in Latin and finished in AD 731. Bede's history was translated into English in the late ninth century as part of a great revival of learning under King Alfred. The poem, a hymn to God the Creator, is all that survives of the work of the poet Cædmon, who lived in the seventh century. (For a brief discussion of OE verse, see Section 2.4.)

TEXT 11 – Cædmon's hymn

West Saxon dialect

Nu we sculan herian heofonrices Weard
Metodes mihte and his modgeþonc
weorc Wuldorfæder; swa he wundra gehwæs
ece Dryhten, ord onstealde.
He ærest gesceop eorðan bearnum
heofon to hrofe, halig Scyppend;
ða middangeard, moncynnes Weard,
ece Dryhten, æfter teode
firum foldan, Frea ælmihtig.

Northumbrian dialect

Nu scylun hergan hefænricæs Uard
Metudæs mæcti end his modgidanc
uerc uuldurfadur; sue he uundra gihuæs
eci Dryctin, or astelidæ.
He ærist scop ælda barnum
heben til hrofe, haleg Scepen;
tha middungeard, moncynnes Uard,
eci Dryctin, æfter tiadæ
firum foldu, Frea allmectig.

Now we must praise heaven-kingdom's Guardian
Creator's might and his mind-thought
work Glory-father's; as he of-wonders each
everlasting Lord, beginning established.
He first shaped of-earth for-children
heaven as roof, holy Creator;
then middle-earth, mankind's Guardian,
everlasting Lord, after determined
for-men earth, Ruler almighty.

Activity 2.2

(i) Use the WW translation of the West Saxon poem to write a version in MnE.
(ii) List the dialectal variations.

2.2.4 The OE alphabet

Facsimiles of original OE writing are hard to decipher at first because some of the letters look different from the shapes familiar to us. In printing and writing OE today, present-day shapes of Roman letters are used, with three additional non-Roman letters which were devised for writing OE. These were necessary because some sounds in OE did not have an equivalent in Latin, and so no Roman letter was available. They were:

<æ> – a vowel pronounced /æ/ and called *ash* – derived from Latin. It is today popularly known as 'short a', as in MnE *cat*.

<þ> – a consonant pronounced /θ/ or /ð/; the letter is called *thorn* from its runic name – now replaced by <th>.

<ð> – a consonant also pronounced /θ/ or /ð/; the letter is called *eth* – derived from Irish writing and now replaced by <th>. (These two letters tended to be interchangeable, and did not separately represent the voiced or voiceless <th> consonant.)

These letters are usually retained in printing and writing OE today.

Another non-Roman letter used in writing was:

<ƿ> – pronounced /w/ and called *wynn* from its runic name. This letter is usually not used in printing OE today but is replaced by <w>. Letter <w> was not part of the OE alphabet. The consonant /w/ was represented in the earliest OE writing by <u> or <uu> ('double-u') and was then replaced by <ƿ>.

The roman letter <g> was written <ȝ> (called *yogh*) and pronounced /g/, /j/ or /ɣ/, depending on the sounds that preceded or followed it (see Commentary 1 of the *Text Commentary Book*, Section 1.2.7, iiid). Modern reprints of OE usually use letter <g>, not <ȝ>.

<k>, <q> and <z> were less commonly used; <j> and <v> were not yet in use.

The OE alphabet therefore consisted of:

Vowel letters: a æ e i o u y
Consonant letters: b c d f g (*written* <ȝ>) h (k) l m n p (q) r s t þ/ð w (*written* <ƿ>) x (z)

Here is a list of the letters of the OE alphabet with a brief indication of pronunciation. Some letters in OE represented more than one sound, but pronunciation and spelling were much closer in OE than in MnE. You will notice that the spelling of the same sound in MnE is often different from that in OE. OE vowel letters represented both long and short OE vowels (see Commentary 1 of the *Text Commentary Book*, Sections 1.2.3 and 1.2.4). Long vowels are conventionally marked by a macron, for example, ē, in modern printed texts, although in this book long vowels are only marked when the information is necessary.

This list will need some explanation from a teacher or tutor, but there is a more detailed introduction to the pronunciation and spelling of OE in Commentary 1 of the *Text Commentary Book*.

Letter	**OE word and MnE translation**	**OE sound (IPA symbol)**	**MnE word with same sound (RP)**
Vowels			
<i>	bringan *bring*	/ɪ/	bring
	rīdan *ride*	/i:/	machine
<y>	hyll *hill*	/y/	German schütten
	hȳf *hive*	/y:/	German grün
<e>	elm *elm*	/ɛ/	elm
	fēdan *feed*	/e:/	German gegen
<æ>	æsc *ash*	/æ/	ash
	clǣne *clean*	/æ:/	French être
<a>	sacc *sack*	/a/	American English sock
	gāt *goat*	/a:/	cart
<o>	fox *fox*	/ɔ/	fox
	gōs *goose*	/o:/	German wohnen
<u>	ful *full*	/ʊ/	full
	fūl *foul*	/u:/	fool
<ea>	earnian *earn*	/ɛə/	–
	ēast *east*	/ɛ:ə/	–
<eo>	eorþ *earth*	/eə/	–
	prēost *priest*	/e:ə/	–

Letter	OE word and MnE translation	OE sound (IPA symbol)	MnE word with same sound (RP)
Consonants			
<p>	pullian *pull*	/p/	pull
<b>	brid *bird*	/b/	bird
<t>	tægl *tail*	/t/	tail
<d>	dogga *dog*	/d/	dog
<c>	col *coal* or	/k/	coal, king
	cirice *church*	/tʃ/	church
<g>	gift *gift* or	/g/	gift
	geong *young* or	/j/	young
	bog *bough*	/ɣ/	–
<cg>	hecg *hedge*	/dʒ/	hedge
<x>	æx *axe*	/ks/	axe
<f>	fot *foot*	/f/	foot
	lufu *love*	/v/	love
<þ> or <ð>	þæc or ðæc *thatch*	/θ/	thatch
	feþer or feðer *feather*	/ð/	feather
<s>	sendan *send* or	/s/	send
	ceosan *choose*	/z/	choose
<sc>	sceap *sheep*	/ʃ/	sheep
<h>	sihþ *sight* or	/ç/	German nichts
	boht *bought*	/x/	German nacht
<l>	leþer *leather*	/l/	leather
<m>	mona *moon*	/m/	moon
<n>	niht *night*	/n/	night
<r>	rarian *roar*	/r/	roar
<w>	wæter *water*	/w/	water

2.2.5 *A Testimonie of Antiquitie*

A small book called *A Testimonie of Antiquitie* was printed in London in 1567. Its purpose was to provide evidence, in a contemporary religious controversy, about the Church sacraments. It reproduced, with a translation, a sermon 'in the Saxon tongue' by Ælfric, who was Archbishop of Canterbury in AD 995. He was a famous English preacher and grammarian.

The book is of interest to students of language because the translation provides an example of sixteenth century Early Modern English (EMnE) both in style and spelling and printing, while the Old English sermon is reproduced in a type face that copies OE manuscript letter forms. Just as <u> and <v> were two shapes of the same letter, so there were two forms for /s/, <s> and <ʃ> (not to be confused with <f>), which were used into the eighteenth century. These letter shapes derive from manuscript writing.

Here is the beginning of Ælfric's sermon in *A Testimonie of Antiquitie*, with its sixteenth century translation, and the list of 'The Saxon Caracters or letters, that be moste straunge', which are printed at the end of the book. The WW translation of the OE in the facsimile is also given.

The epiſtle beginneth thus in the Saxon tonge.

Ælꝼꞃıc abb. ᵹꞃeꞇ Sıᵹeꝼeꞃþ ꝼꞃeondlıce; Me ıꞅ ᵹeꞅæꝺ ꝥ ðu ꞅæꝺeꞅꞇ beo me ꝥ ıc oþeꞃ ꞇæhꞇe on Enᵹlıꞅcen ᵹeƿꞃıꞇen. oþeꞃ eoƿeꞃ ancoꞃ æꞇ ham mıꝺ eoƿ ꞇæhþ. ꝼoꞃþan ðe he ꞅƿuꞇelıce ꞅæᵹþ ꝥ hıꞇ ꞅıe aleꝼꝺ. ꝥ mæꞅꞅe pꞃeoꞅꞇaꞅ ƿel moꞇan ƿıꝼıᵹen. anꝺ mın ᵹeƿꞃıꞇen ƿıþcƿeþeþ ðyꞅen.

That is, Elfricke abbot doth ſend frendlye ſalutation to Sigeferth. It is tolde me that I teach otherwyſe in my Engliſh writynges, thē doth thy anker teach, which is at home wyth thee. For he ſayth playnly that it is a lawfull thing for a prieſt to marye, and my wrytynges doth ſpeake agaynſt thys.&c-

¶ *The Saxon Caracters or letters, that be moſte ſtraunge, be here knowen by other common Caracters ſet ouer them.*

d. th. th. f. g. i. r. ſ. t. w.
¶ ꝺ. ð. þ. ꝼ. ᵹ. ı. ꞃ. ꞅ. ꞇ. ƿ.
y. z. and. that.
ẏ. ȝ. ⁊. ꝥ.

¶ Æ. Æ. Th. Th. E. H. M.
¶ Æ. Æ. Ð. Þ. Є. Ƕ. M.
S. W. And.
Ꞅ. Ƿ. ⁊.

¶ *One pricke ſignifieth an vnperfect point, this figure; (which is lyke the Greeke interrogatiue) a full pointe, which in ſome other olde Saxon bookes, is expreſſed wyth three prickes, ſet in triangle wyſe thus* :·

WW

Ælfric abbot greets Sigeferth
friendlily; to-me is said that
thou saidest about me that I other
taught in English wri-
tings. than your anchorite (= *religious hermit*) at
home with you teaches. because
he clearly says that it
is permitted. that mass priests
well may wive. and my
writings against-speak this.

oþer ... oþer = otherwise ... than = differently from

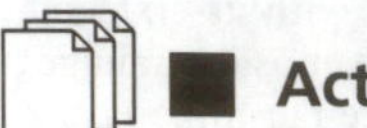

Activity 2.3

(i) Copy the list of letters used in the OE alphabet and compare the letter shapes in the *Peterborough Chronicle* facsimiles with the printed versions in the 1567 book.

(ii) Compare the modern and OE forms for similarities and differences.

2.3 Danish and Norwegian Vikings

The *Anglo-Saxon Chronicle* records an event in AD 787 which proved to be an ominous portent of things to come.

TEXT 12 – Chronicle for AD 787

Peterborough Chronicle

OE

dcclxxxvii. Her nam breohtric cining
offan dohter eadburge. 7 on his dagum comon
ærest .iii. scipu norðmanna of hereða lande. 7 þa se gerefa þær to rad. 7 he wolde drifan to ðes ciniges tune
þy he nyste hwæt hi wæron. 7 hine man ofsloh þa. Ðæt
wæron þa erestan scipu deniscra manna þe angel cynnes land gesohton.
(*Peterborough Chronicle*)

WW

787. Here took breohtric king
offa's daughter eadburh. & in his days came
first 3 ships of-northmen from hortha land. & then the reeve
there to rode. & he wished drive to the king's manor
because he knew-not what they were. & him one slew there. That
were the first ships danish men's that Angle-people's
land sought.

Parker Chronicle

Activity 2.4

(i) Use the WW translation to write a version of this chronicle in MnE.
(ii) Compare the *Peterborough Chronicle* text with the facsimile of the *Parker Chronicle* version. What differences can you find between them?

By the end of the eighth century the Angles, Saxons and Jutes had finally occupied and settled almost the whole of England. The *Anglo-Saxon Chronicle* continued to record battles for supremacy between the kings of the seven Anglo-Saxon kingdoms, as in the following example in the annal dated AD 827.

> 827. In this year there was an eclipse of the moon on Christmas morning. And the same year Egbert conquered Mercia, and all that was south of the Humber, and he was the eighth king to be 'Ruler of Britain': the first to rule so great a kingdom was Ælle, king of Sussex; the second was Ceawlin, king of Wessex; the third was Æthelbert, king of Kent; the fourth was Rædwald, king of East Anglia; the fifth was Edwin, king of Northumbria; the sixth was Oswald who reigned after him; the seventh was Oswy, Oswald's brother; the eighth was Egbert, king of Wessex.
>
> (Translated by G. N. Garmonsway, *Everyman Classics*, 1972)

But by AD 827 the three ships which the king's reeve had ridden to meet in AD 787 had already been followed by greater numbers of Norsemen, who began to make annual attacks for plunder on the coasts and up the rivers of England and northern France. The *Peterborough Chronicle* annal for AD 793 records the first Norwegian Viking attack on the monasteries of Lindisfarne and Jarrow on the NE coast.

TEXT 13 – Chronicle for AD 793

dccxciii. 7 litel æfter þam þæs il-
can geares on .vi. ides ianuarium earmlice heðenra manna
hergung adiligode godes cyrican. in lindisfarena ee
þurh reaflac. 7 mansleht.

7 litel æfter þam þæs il-
can geares on · vi · id' ianr earmlice hedenra manna
hergung adiligode godes cyrican · in lindisfarena ee
þurh reaflac · 7 man slehte ·

793. & little after that the
same year on 6 ides january miserably of-heathen men
raid destroyed god's church. on lindisfarne isle
by robbery. & murder.

793. and a little after that in the same year on 8th January God's church on the island of Lindisfarne was miserably plundered and destroyed by the heathen, with great slaughter.

Another chronicle annal

dcclxxxxiii. ðes ylcan geares earmlice hæðenra hergung adyligodan godes cyrican in lindisfarena ee. þurh reaflac 7 manslyht.

Norsemen from Norway were soon to raid the NW coast of England, the north of Ireland, the western islands and coast of Scotland, and the Isle of Man.

Danes began to attack the east coast of England in AD 835. By the middle of the ninth century, large Danish armies regularly ravaged the land and began to occupy and to settle permanently in parts of the country. The most famous of the Saxon English kings, Alfred, King of Wessex, after years of continuous war, negotiated treaties with the Danes. By the time of Alfred's death in AD 899, at the end of the ninth century, only Wessex remained independent. The rest of England, north and east of the old Roman road called Watling Street (from London to Chester), was shared between the English and the Danes, and became known as the **Danelaw**. Here is a typical entry in the *Anglo-Saxon Chronicle* describing the ravages of the Danish armies during King Alfred's reign.

TEXT 14 – Chronicle for AD 878

dccclxxviii. Her hiene bestæl se here on midne winter ofer
twelftan niht to cippanhamme. ⁊ geridan west seaxna land ⁊
gesetton. ⁊ mycel þæs folces ofer sæ adræfdon. ⁊ þæs oðres
þone mæstan dæl hi geridon butan þam cynge ælfrede (. ⁊ he)
litle werede yðelice æfter wudum for. ⁊ on morfestenum.

⁊ þæs on eastron wrohte ælfred cyning lytle werede
geweorc æt æþelinga ige. ⁊ of þam geweorce wæs winnende
wið þone here. ⁊ sumer setena se del þe þær nehst
wæs. þa on ðere seofeðan wucan ofer eastron he gerad to
ecgbrihtes stane be easton sealwudu. ⁊ him comon þær ongean
sumorsæte ealle. ⁊ willsæte. ⁊ hamtun scyr se dæl þe
hire beheonan sæ wæs. ⁊ his gefægene wæron. ⁊ he
for ymb ane niht of þam wicum to æglea. ⁊ þæs ymb
ane niht to eðan dune. ⁊ þær gefeaht wið ealne here ⁊
hiene geflymde. ⁊ him æfter rad oð þet geweorc. ⁊ þær
sæt .xiiii. niht. ⁊ þa sealde se here him gislas. and mycele
aðas. þet hi of his rice woldon. ⁊ him eac geheton
þet heora cyng fulwihte onfon wolde.
(*Peterborough Chronicle*)

878. Here it(self) stole-away the host in mid winter after
twelfth night to chippenham. & overran west saxons' land &
occupied. & much of-the folk over sea drove. & of-the other
the most part they subdued except the king alfred (. & he)
with-small band with-difficulty through woods went. & in moor-fastnesses.

& after at easter built alfred king with-little company
fortress at athel-ney. & from that fortress was fighting
against the host* . & of-somerset the part that there nearest
was. then in the seventh week after easter he rode to
egbertstone by east of-selwood. & to-him came there back
of-somerset-men all. & wiltshire. & hampshire the part that
of-it on-this-side-of sea was. & of-him glad they-were. & he
went after one night from those camps to iley. & later after
one night to edington. & there fought against all the host &
it put-to-flight. & it after rode up-to the fortress. & there
sat 14 nights. & then gave the host him hostages. and great
oaths. that they from his kingdom wished. & him also promised
that their king baptism receive would.

*The OE word *here* (*host*) was always used for the Viking armies.

Œ

dccclxxviii. Her hiene bestæl se here on midne winter ofer tuelftan niht to cippanhamme. ⁊ geridon wesseaxna lond ⁊ gesæton. ⁊ micel þæs folces ofer sæ adræfdon. ⁊ þæs oþres þone mæstan dæl hie geridon buton þam cyninge Ælfrede ⁊ he lytle werede unieþelice æfter wudum for. ⁊ on morfæstenum.

⁊ þæs on eastron worhte Ælfred cyning lytle werede geweorc æt eþelinga eigge. ⁊ of þam geweorce was winnende wiþ þone here. ⁊ sumursætna se dæl se þær niehst wæs. þa on þære seofoðan wiecan ofer eastron he gerad to ecgbryhtes stane be eastan seal wyda. ⁊ him to com þær ongen sumorsæte alle. ⁊ wilsætan. ⁊ hamtun scir se dæl se hiere behinon sæ wæs. ⁊ his gefægene wærun. ⁊ he for ymb ane niht of þam wicum to iglea. ⁊ þæs ymb ane to eþan dune. ⁊ þær gefeaht wiþ alne þone here ⁊ hiene gefliemde. ⁊ him æfter rad oþ þæt geweorc. ⁊ þær sæt .xiiii. niht. ⁊ þa salde se here him fore gislas. ⁊ micle aþas. þæt hie of his rice uuoldon. ⁊ him eac geheton þæt hiera kyning fulwihte onfon wolde.
(*Parker Chronicle*)

Activity 2.5

(i) Rewrite this chronicle in MnE.

(ii) Compare the forms of the OE and MnE words. List the OE words that have not survived into MnE and specify the changes to MnE words which derive from OE.

(iii) List the differences between the two chronicle versions and discuss the possible reasons for them.

Scandinavian attacks continued throughout the first half of the tenth century and were recorded in the *Anglo-Saxon Chronicle*. One of them, dated AD 937 in the annal, is in the form of a poem celebrating the Battle of Brunanburh in Scotland (the exact site is not known). Æthelstan, King of Wessex, defeated the Norsemen attacking from Ireland.

2.4 The Battle of Brunanburh – OE poetry

The lines of OE poetry divide into two half-lines, each with two main stresses. Stress in OE was usually on the first syllable of a word (see Commentary 1 of the *Text Commentary Book*, Section 1.1). Words seldom contained more than three syllables, so there was a strong natural 'falling' rhythm in ordinary speech which was exploited in poetry. There was no rhyme or regular metre, so the sound of verse was a 'heightened' form of ordinary speech, but the two parts of each line were linked by the **alliteration** of two or three words in each line. These words were stressed lexical words – nouns, adjectives, verbs or adverbs – not function words like pronouns or prepositions. The following example is from the poem *The Phoenix*.

TEXT 15 – *The Phoenix*

Œ

hæbbe ic gefrugnen þætte is **f**eor heonan
eastdælum on **æ**þelast londa
firum gefræge. nis se **f**oldan sceat
ofer **m**iddangeard **m**ongum gefere
foldagendra ac he **a**fyrred is
þurh **m**eotudes **m**eaht **m**anfremmendum

WW

have I heard that is far hence
east-lands in noblest of-lands
to-men famous. not-is that of-earth region
throughout world to-many accessible
of-earth-possessors but it removed is
through creator's might from-evil-doers

MnE

I have heard that far from here
in eastern lands is the noblest of lands
famous among men. That region of earth is not
accessible to many earthly rulers throughout the world
but through the might of the Creator
it is far off from evil-doers.

In OE manuscripts, poetry was set out like prose, not in separate lines in the way we are used to. Lines and half-lines were often clearly marked with a dot like our full-stop, as in the manuscript poem of the Battle of Brunanburh. The following three short extracts from the poem, taken from the *Parker Chronicle*, show how poetry was written down.

TEXT 16 – The Battle of Brunanburh, Chronicle for AD 937

Œ

dcccxxxvii. Her æþelstan cyning. eorla dryhten. beorna
beahgifa. 7 his broþor eac. eadmund æþeling. ealdor langne tir.
geslogon æt sæcce. sweorda ecgum. ymbe brunnanburh.

þær læg secg mænig. garum ageted. guma norþerna.
ofer scild scoten. swilce scittisc eac. werig wiges sæd. wesseaxe forð.
ondlongne dæg. eorod cistum. on last legdun. laþum þeodum. heowan
here fleman. hindan þearle. mecum mylen scearpan.

ne wearð wæl mare. on þis
eiglande. æfer gieta. folces gefylled. beforan þissum. sweordes
ecgum. þæs þe us secgað bec. ealde uðwitan. siþþan eastan hider.
engle 7 seaxe. up becoman. ofer brad brimu. brytene sohtan.
wlance wig smiðas. weealles ofercoman. eorlas ar hwate. eard
begeatan

WW

937. Here athelstan king. of-earls lord. of-men
ring-giver. & his brother also. edmund prince. life long honour.
won in battle. of-swords with-edges. by brunanburh.

there lay man many-a. by-spears killed. man northern.
over shield shot. also scots too. weary of-battle sated. west saxons forth.
throughout day. troops in-companies. on trail pursued. loathed people. hacked
from-army fugitives. from-behind harshly. with-swords millstone sharp.

not happened slaughter more. in this
island. ever yet. of-folk felled. before this. of-sword
with-edges. as to-us say books. ancient scholars. since from-east hither.
angles & saxons. up came. over broad seas. britain sought.
proud war smiths. welshmen overcame. earls for-honour eager. country
conquered

Activity 2.6

(i) Rewrite the extracts in lines of verse and mark the alliterating words. (The second and third extracts both begin with the *second* half-line of a line.)

(ii) Use the WW translation to write an acceptable version in MnE. You will need to add words to the original and paraphrase some of it.

The *Peterborough Chronicle* entry is in complete contrast:

Œ

M.dcccc xxxvii. Her æðelstan cyning lædde fyrde to brunanbyrig.

A n̄. dccc. xxxvii. Her æðelstan cyning lædde fyr
de to brunanbyrig.

WW

937. Here athelstan king led troops
to brunanburh.

A period of 25 years of peace after AD 955 was once again broken when more attacks by Norsemen began in the 980s. Some came from Normandy across the Channel, where Norsemen (the Normans) had also settled, as well as from Denmark and Norway. In 1017, the Danish king, Cnut, became 'King of All England'; the line of Danish kings was not ended until 1042, when the English Edward the Confessor became king.

2.5 Effects on the English language

The settlement of the Norsemen and the occupation of the Danelaw had important effects on the English language.

Old Norse (ON) is the name now given to the language spoken by the Norsemen – Danish and Norwegian Vikings. It was **cognate** with OE; that is, they both came from the same earlier Germanic language. It seems likely that the two languages were similar enough in vocabulary for OE speakers to understand common ON words, and vice versa, so that the English and Norsemen could communicate. An Icelandic saga says of the eleventh century, 'there was at that time the same tongue in England as in Norway and Denmark'. But speakers simplified their own language when talking to the other, and OE dialects spoken in the Danelaw in time became modified in ways which were different from the Wessex and Kentish dialects. Present-day northern and East Anglian dialects show ON features, particularly in vocabulary.

Many OE words therefore have a similar cognate ON word, and often we cannot be sure whether a MnE reflex has come from OE, ON or from both. In the OE word list in the *Word Book*, the ON cognate of an OE word is given where it is known. If the word is marked *fr. ON*, it means that the OE word has derived from ON, which is proof of the close contact between the two languages.

Activity 2.7

(i) Use the OE word list to look up those ON words that are cognate with OE words spelt with <sc> (see Commentary 1 of the *Text Commentary Book*, Section 1.2.6, 3f). Does it seem likely that an OE speaker would have recognised the ON words?

(ii) Look up in the *Word Book* or a dictionary the MnE words beginning with <sk> which derive from ON. Does it seem likely that the pronunciation of ON <sk> had changed to /ʃ/ like OE <sc>?

(iii) OE *scyrte* and ON *skyrta* both have reflexes in MnE. What has happened to the meaning of the two words?

(iv) Make a selection of other OE words from the *Word Book* or a dictionary that have ON cognates. Write down the ON cognate word and compare it with the OE. Does the evidence support the claim that OE and ON speakers could communicate with one another?

So one important result of Danish and Norwegian settlement in the Danelaw was its effect on the English language. English and Norse speakers lived in communities that were close enough for contact to take place, and sometimes within the same settlement, or family after inter-marriage. A large number of proper names of Scandinavian origin can be found in late OE and early ME documents. In time, the communities merged and Norse was no longer spoken, but the English dialects spoken in different parts of the Danelaw had been modified –

in pronunciation, in vocabulary and to some extent in grammar. The earliest evidence, however, does not appear in writing until much later, during the ME period, because most late OE was written in the West Saxon dialect, which had become a standard. The long-term effects are still with us, in the present-day dialects and accents of East Anglia, the Midlands, northern England and southern Scotland.

Unlike the English, the Danes and Norwegians had not at this time developed a system of writing other than runes, and no evidence of the dialects of the Norse language spoken in the Danelaw is available. Norse must have been spoken throughout, but was gradually assimilated with English.

Some evidence of this assimilation can be seen in the porch of a small church in Kirkdale, North Yorkshire, called St Gregory's Minster. A sundial dating from about 1055 has been preserved, which has the following inscription carved in stone.

TEXT 17 – Inscription, St Gregory's Minster, Kirkdale, North Yorkshire

Transcription

ORM GAMALSUNA BOHTE SCS (= SANCTUS) GREGORIVS MINSTER
ÐONNE HIT WES ÆL TOBROCAN ⁊ TO FALAN ⁊ HE HIT LET MACAN
NEWAN FROM GRUNDE XPE (= CHRISTE) ⁊ SCS GREGORIVS IN EADWARD
DAGUM CNG (= CYNING) ⁊ IN TOSTI DAGUM EORL ⁊ HAWARÐ ME
WROHTE ⁊ BRAND PRS (= PREOSTAS)

Translation

ORM GAMALSON BOUGHT ST GREGORY'S MINSTER WHEN IT WAS ALL
BROKEN & FALLEN DOWN & HE CAUSED IT TO BE MADE ANEW FROM
THE GROUND TO CHRIST AND ST GREGORY IN KING EDWARD'S DAYS &
IN EARL TOSTI'S DAYS & HAWARTH & BRAND PRIESTS MADE ME

Tosti, or Tostig, was Earl of Northumberland and brother to Harold Godwinson, who became King of England in 1066, on King Edward's death (see also Texts 18 and 19 in Section 2.8). Orm and Gamal are Norse names, but the language is OE.

2.5.1 OE and Scandinavian surnames

The name *Orm Gamalson* looks familiar to us as the usual way of referring to people by their forename and surname, as in *David Williamson*. This name no longer literally means *David, son of William*, and there is nothing strange today about the name *Marion Johnson*, which is unlikely to mean *Marion, son of John*. But *Orm Gamalsuna* (*Orm Gamalson*) did mean *Orm, son of Gamal*, and this way of creating personal names, by adding *-suna/-son* as a **patronymic suffix** (name derived from the father), was in fact a Scandinavian custom, which was in time adopted throughout the country.

The Anglo-Saxon patronymic suffix was *-ing*, as in *Ælfred Æþelwulfing*, *Alfred, son of Athelwulf*, and was used to name families or peoples as descendants from a common ancestor.

2.5.2 OE and Scandinavian place names

These names were also incorporated into place names, as in *Walsingham*, *Billingham* and *Kidlington*, although the *-ing* suffix tended to be used in a more general way as well, so must not always be taken literally to mean *son of* or *the family of*. Some place names consist of the patronymic alone, for example, *Woking*, *Tooting*, *Malling*.

The suffixes that indicate place names in OE included *-hyrst* (*copse*, *wood*), *-ham* (*dwelling*, *fold*), *-wic* (*village*), *-tun* (*settlement*) and *-stede* (*place*), as in present-day *Wadhurst*, *Newnham*, *Norwich*, *Berwick*, *Heslington* and *Maplestead*.

The detailed study of place names provides much of the historical evidence for the settlement of Danes and Norwegians in England.

Activity 2.8

Use an atlas and atlas gazetteer of England to identify towns and villages with place names ending in the following Scandinavian suffixes:

(a) *-by* (town, farm)
(b) *-thorp(e)* (village)
(c) *-thwaite* (piece of land)
(d) *-toft* (piece of land)

If you find a sufficient number, and mark them on a blank map, you should find good evidence of the extent of the Danelaw.

2.6 Latin vocabulary in OE

A great deal of 'Latinate' vocabulary was adopted into English from the sixteenth century onwards, during the Renaissance, or revival of learning, when both Latin and Greek were generally considered to be languages superior to English. These words are often long and learned, and contrast with shorter Anglo-Saxon words in their use in formal speech and writing. But OE also contained words of Latin origin, some of which are still common words in MnE, and are in no way learned or obscure.

2.6.1 Latin words adopted before the settlement in England

Some words of Latin origin had already been adopted in the language brought over with the Angles and Saxons. This was because OE was a Germanic language, and the Germanic people were in continuous contact with the Romans. There are no written records from this period, so the evidence for the early adoption of Latin words lies in an analysis of known sound changes.

In the following assignment, only words that have survived into MnE have been listed. Many OE words derived from Latin have not survived, for example, *cylle* from Latin *culleus* (leather bottle), *mese* from *mensa* (table) and *sigel* from *sigillum* (brooch).

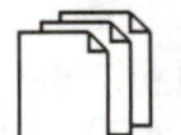

Activity 2.9

(i) Use the word list of Latin-derived words in the *Word Book* or a dictionary to find out the OE and original Latin forms of the following words.
(ii) Divide the words into sets according to their meanings (for example, domestic, household articles, etc.). Consider what these sets of adopted words might suggest about the relationship between the Germanic tribes and the Romans.

belt
bin
bishop
butter
cat
chalk
cheese
copper
cup
dish
fork

inch
kettle
kiln
kitchen
line
mile
mill
mint
-monger
mortar (vessel)
mule

pan
pea(se)
pepper
pillow
pin
pipe (musical)
pit
pitch (tar)
plum
poppy
pound

purse
Saturday
sickle
street
tile
toll
wall
-wick
wine

None of the words listed is polysyllabic or learned, and their Latin origin cannot be guessed from their form or meaning.

Although Latin would have been spoken in Britain during the Roman occupation up to the fifth century by educated Britons, hardly any Latin words were passed on from this source to the Anglo-Saxon invaders. An exception was the *-caster/-chester* suffix for place names like *Doncaster* and *Manchester*, from the Latin *castra*, meaning *camp*.

2.6.2 Latin words adopted during the OE period

Other Latin words were adopted into the language at different periods of the Anglo-Saxon settlement, many as a result of the conversion to Christianity and the establishment of the Church. Latin was the language of the Bible and church services, and of learning and scholarship.

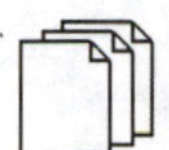

Activity 2.10

(i) Use the word list of Latin-derived words in the *Word Book* or a dictionary to find out the OE and original Latin forms of the following words.

(ii) Divide the words into sets according to their meanings; for example,
  (a) religion and the Church
  (b) education and learning
  (c) household and clothing
  (d) plants, herbs and trees
  (e) foods.

You will also need an additional category, (f), for miscellaneous words that do not fall into sets easily.

abbot	circle	lobster	priest
alms	cloister	martyr	psalm
altar	cook (n)	mass (church)	radish
anchor	coulter	master	sabbath
angel	cowl	mat	sack
apostle	creed	minster	school
ark	crisp	mussel	shrine
balsam	disciple	myrrh	silk
beet	fan	nun	sock
box	fennel	organ	sponge
candle	fever	palm	synod
cap	fig	pear	talent
cedar	font	pine	temple
chalice	ginger	plant	title
chest	lily	pope	verse

2.7 OE grammar

We have to speak in sentences to convey meanings. **Words** are grouped into **phrases**, and phrases into **clauses**, and in written English one or more clauses make up a **sentence**. There are two principal ways in which words are related to form phrases and clauses to give meanings. One is using an agreed **word order**. The other is changing the form of words, either by adding **inflections** (prefixes or suffixes) or altering part of a word.

In OE, the order of words in a clause was more variable than that of MnE, and there were many more inflections on nouns, adjectives and verbs.

2.7.1 Word order

Today, the order of the elements in a declarative clause (one making a statement) is SP(C/O)(A); that is, the subject comes first, followed by the predicator (or verb), then the complements or objects, and last the adverbials, if any. This pattern was already common in OE, as the following examples illustrate. (Examples in this and the following section are from the OE versions of the Garden of Eden (Adam and Eve) and the Flood (Noah) stories in the book of Genesis from the Old Testament.)

S P A
seo næddre cwæþ to þam wife
the serpent said to the woman

S P O
hi gehyrdon his stemne
they heard his voice

S P O & S P
seo næddre bepæhte me and ic ætt
the serpent deceived me and I ate

But there were also different orders of words. For example, after a linking adverb the verb came before the subject:

A P S A A
þa cwæþ seo næddre eft to þam wife
then said the serpent after to the woman

A P S cj S P C
þa geseah þæt wif þæt þæt treow wæs god to etenne
then saw the woman that the tree was good to eat

or the verb might sometimes come last in a subordinate clause:

S P A cj S C P
hi oncneowon þa þæt hi nacode wæron
they knew then that they naked were

OE word order in asking questions and forming the negative also differed from MnE:

A P S O cj S neg P
Hwi forbead God eow þæt ge ne æton?
Why forbade God you that you not eat?
(= *Why did God forbid you to eat?*)

Other examples can be found in the OE texts in Chapters 1 and 2 by reading the WW translations.

Activity 2.11

Identify the clause elements and the order of the subjects and predicators in the following clauses (phrases are bracketed in the first set).

Text 12

(Her) (nam) (breohtric cining) (offan dohter eadburge)
7 (on his dagum) (comon) (ærest) (.iii. scipu norðmanna) (of hereða lande)
7 (þa) (se gerefa) (þær to) (rad)
7 (he) (wolde drifan) (to ðes ciniges tune)

ðy (he) (nyste)
(hwæt) (hi) (wæron)
7 (hine) (man) (ofsloh) (þa)
(þæt) (wæron) (þa erestan scipu deniscra manna)
(þe)(angel cynnes land) (gesohton)

Text 14

Her hiene bestæl se here on midne winter ofer twelftan niht to cippanhamme
7 Ø geridan west seaxna land
7 Ø gesetton
7 mycel þæs folces ofer sæ adræfdon
7 þæs oþres þone mæstan dæl hi geridon butan þam cynge ælfrede
7 he litle werede yðelice æfter wudum for 7 on morfestenum

2.7.2 Number, case and gender – inflections on nouns and adjectives

Number

There are only a few inflections in MnE today which mark the grammatical functions of nouns. We show the **number** of a noun, that is, whether it is **singular** (sg) or **plural** (pl), by adding /s/, /z/ or /ɪz/ in speech, and <s> or <es> in writing, as in:

cat / cats　　dog / dogs　　church / churches

There are a few irregular plurals that have survived from OE, like *men*, *geese* and *mice,* which show plural number by a change of vowel, and *oxen*.

Case

In MnE today, only the personal pronouns (except *you* and *it*) are inflected to show whether they are the subject or object in a clause.

MnE			**OE**		
S	P	O	S	P	O
I	saw	**it**	**ic**	seah	**hit**
you (sg)	saw	**her**	**þu**	sawe	**hi**
he	saw	**me**	**he**	seah	**me**
she	saw	**him**	**heo**	seah	**hine**
we	saw	**you** (pl)	**we**	sawon	**eow**
you (pl)	saw	**us**	**ge**	sawon	**us**
they	saw	**them**	**hi**	sawon	**hi**

Adjectives are not inflected to agree with nouns in MnE, nor is the **definite article** (*the*), but they were in OE. The feature of the grammar that marks these functions is called **case**.

subject	**nominative case** (nom)
direct object	**accusative case** (acc)
indirect object	**dative case** (dat)

In a **prepositional phrase** (PrepP) in OE, the noun was in either the accusative or dative case, according to the preposition.

The only other MnE inflection on nouns is the <'s> or <s'> in writing to show possession – called the possessive or **genitive case** (gen). This is the only grammatical case in MnE that survives from OE in nouns. In OE, the genitive noun usually preceded the noun head of the phrase, as illustrated in the following examples.

godes cyrican (Text 13)	God's church
sweord**a** ecgum (Text 16)	(by the) swords' edges
sweord**es** ecgum (Text 16)	(by the) sword's edges

Place names often began as genitive + noun constructions:

certic**es** ford (Text 4)	Cerdic's ford (*not identified*)
æþeling**a** ige (Text 14)	Etheling's isle = Athelney
heopwin**es** fleot (Text 2)	Ypwine's fleet (river) = Ebbsfleet

Phrases of measurement also contained a genitive, as in:

.iii. scipu norðmann**a** (Text 12)	3 ships of-Norsemen
.xl. wuc**ena** (Text 18)	40 of-weeks
.xxxi. wintr**a** (Text 6)	31 of-winters = 31 years

Gender

In MnE, we have to select the correct pronoun *he*, *she* or *it* according to the sex, or lack of sex, of the referent – he is **masculine** (m), *she* is **feminine** (f) and *it* is **neuter** (n). This is called **natural gender**. In OE, nouns for things that today are all neuter, and nouns for a male or female person, might be masculine, feminine or neuter. For example, *sunne* (*sun*) was feminine, *mona* (*moon*) was masculine, and *wif* (*woman*) and *cild* (*child*) were neuter in gender. This is called **grammatical gender**.

So nouns and adjectives in OE, including the equivalent of MnE *the*, were marked by a complex system of inflections for number, case and gender. Here are a few examples. Notice that sometimes the inflection is zero (Ø), like the MnE plural of *sheep*, or past tense of *cut*. The inflections are shown after a hyphen.

seo næddr-**e** cwæþ the serpent said	sg	nom	f
God-Ø cwæþ to **þære** næddr-**an** God said to the serpent	sg	dat	f
þæt wif-Ø andwyrde the woman answered	sg	nom	n
God-Ø cwæþ to **þam** wif-**e** God said to the woman	sg	dat	n
se hræfn-Ø fleah þa ut the raven flew then out	sg	nom	m
he asende ut **þone** hræfn-Ø he sent out the raven	sg	acc	m
hi gehyrdon **his** stemn-**e** they heard his voice	sg	acc	f
he genam hi in to **þam** arc-**e** he took her into the ark	sg	dat	m
heora beg-**ra** eag-**an** wurdon geopenede their both eyes became opened	pl	nom	n
ofer **þære** eorþ-**an** bradnyss-**e** over the earth's broadness (= surface)	sg	gen	f
þa wæter-**u** adruwodon the waters dried up	pl	nom	n
he abad oþr-**e** seofan dag-**as** he waited (an)other seven days	pl	acc	m

Proper nouns were also inflected: *ælfred cyning* (Text 14) is subject and so nominative case; in the PrepP *butan* ***þam*** *cyng-***e** *ælfred-***e**, *except king Alfred* (Text 14), all three words in the noun phrase (NP) are in the dative case, following *butan*.

2.7.3 Verbs

In MnE, there are different ways of forming the **past tense** and **past participle** of verbs.

MnE regular verbs – OE weak verbs

The majority of verbs are **regular**, and we add /t/, /d/ or /ɪd/ in speech and <ed> (usually) in writing to the verb to form both the past tense and past participle.

MnE	**OE**
kiss – kissed – kissed	cyssan – cyste – cyssed
fill – filled – filled	fyllan – fylde – fylled
knit – knitted – knitted	cnyttan – cnytte – cnytted

MnE regular verbs derive from a set of OE verbs whose past tense was marked with /t/ or /d/ in a **dental suffix**, which are now called **weak verbs**.

MnE irregular verbs – OE strong verbs

There is another set of common verbs in MnE whose past tense and past participle are marked by a change of vowel, while the participle has either an <en> suffix (not <ed>) or none. These are called **irregular verbs**. Here are a few examples, to which you could add many more.

MnE	**OE**
ride – rode – ridden	ridan – rad – riden
choose – chose – chosen	ceosan – ceas – coren
drink – drank – drunk	drincan – dranc – druncen
come – came – come	cuman – com – cumen
speak – spoke – spoken	sprecan – sprac – sprecen
see – saw – seen	seon – seah – sewen
fall – fell – fallen	feallan – feoll – feallen

The irregular verbs in MnE derive from a much larger set of verbs in OE, marked by changes of vowel, which linguists have called **strong verbs**.

(This is an outline only – the verb systems in both OE and MnE are more varied than shown here.)

Inflections for person and tense

OE verbs were also marked by different suffixes to agree with their subject – either 1st, 2nd or 3rd person, and singular or plural number. In MnE, the only present tense inflection is <s>, to agree with the 3rd person singular subject:

I/you/we/they drive   he/she/it drive-**s**

In OE, this verb would have a variety of suffixes:

ic drif-**e**   þu drif-**st**   he/heo/hit drif-**þ**   we/ge/hi drif-**aþ**

In MnE, there are no additional suffixes to mark agreement in the past tense:

I/he/she/it/we/you/they drove

In OE, the past tense had some suffixes to mark agreement:

ic draf   þu drif-**e**   he/heo/hit draf   we/ge/hi drif-**on**

(These examples illustrate only some of the forms of inflection in OE verbs.)

2.7.4 Evidence of changes in word endings in OE

One of the important differences between OE and MnE is that MnE has lost most of the inflections of OE. We can observe the beginnings of this loss of word suffixes from evidence in the manuscripts. If you compare the spellings of the same words in the *Anglo-Saxon Chronicle* texts in Chapters 1 and 2, you will sometimes find differences in the vowel letters that mark case in nouns and tense in verbs. Here are some examples, where the text words are followed by the form with the 'correct' OE suffix (there are other differences in spelling in other words, but these are not discussed here).

	Peterborough Chronicle	***Parker Chronicle***	**Regular OE form**
Text 1	nefdon	næfdan	næfdon = ne hæfdon
	feordodan	fyrdedon	feordodon or fyrdedon
	cininge	cyningæ	cyninge
	bædon	bædan	bædon
Text 2	coman	comon	comon
	feohton	feohtan	feohtan (*infinitive*)
	sendon	sendan	sendan (*infinitive*)
Text 3	broþor	broþur	broþor (*unstressed syllable, not a case ending*)
Text 4	onfengon	onfengun	onfengon
	nemnaþ	nemneþ	nemnaþ
	rixadon	ricsadan	ricsodon
Text 8	gefuhton	gefuhtun	gefuhton
	geþingodon	geþingodan	geþingodon

Such spelling irregularities became frequent, so we can assume that the vowel sound of these suffixes was no longer, for example, a clear /o/ or /a/, but was 'reduced' to the vowel /ə/. This is the commonest vowel in present-day English, the one we use in most unstressed syllables, but we have never used a separate letter of the alphabet for it. The scribes of OE therefore began to use vowel letters in these unstressed syllables at random. Eventually, letter <e> came to be generally used, as discussed in Chapter 3 (see also Commentary 1 of the *Text Commentary Book*, Section 1.1).

So although in late OE times the West Saxon dialect had become a standard for writing, and therefore did not reflect differences of pronunciation, scribes sometimes 'mis-spelt' because changes in pronunciation were not matched by changes in the spelling. This is, however, important evidence for us about the changes that were taking place in OE.

2.8 The Norman Conquest

In 1066, Duke William of Normandy defeated King Harold at Hastings and became King William I of England. This event had the most profound effects on the country and on the language (see Chapter 3), and when we read English texts from the twelfth century onwards, we notice changes at every level of language – spelling and vocabulary, word form and grammar.

To end this chapter, here are two further extracts from the *Anglo-Saxon Chronicle*, one very short and the other much longer, describing the events of 1066. If you are able to study the longer Text 19 from the *Peterborough Chronicle*, you will understand a little of how historians have to interpret original sources when writing history. The annal is written in the simple narrative style of the chronicle, with each event prefaced by *and*. Reference to individuals as *he* or *him* is sometimes rather confusing. Here is an outline of the events told in the chronicle.

King Edward the Confessor died on 28 December 1065, and was buried on 6 January 1066. He was succeeded by King Harold, but Duke William of Normandy also claimed the English throne, and prepared a force to attack southern England. But before this, King Harold, with Earls Edwin and Morcar, had to fend off attacks on the north of England by the Norwegian Harald Hardrada. Harold defeated the Norwegian at Stamford Bridge near York. Tostig, the Earl of Northumberland, was King Harold's brother, but he had defected to the Norwegian Harald. King Harold made a forced march southwards immediately after the battle at Stamford Bridge, but his army was defeated by William at the Battle of Hastings. Duke William was crowned William I soon after.

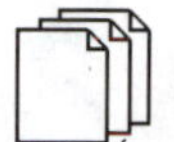

■ Activity 2.12

Rewrite the following texts in MnE and comment on the language.

TEXT 18 – Chronicle for 1066

m.lxvi. Her forðferde eaduuard king. ⁊ harold eorl feng to ðam rice. ⁊ heold hit .xl. wucena. ⁊ ænne dæg. ⁊ her com Willelm ⁊ gewann ænglaland.
(*Parker Chronicle*)

wucena. ⁊ ænne dæg. ⁊ her
T. lxvi her forðferde eaduuard king. ⁊ harold eorl feng to ðam rice. ⁊ heold hit .xl.
cō willelm ⁊ gewann ængla land.

1066. Here died edward king. & harold earl seized the kingdom. & held it 40 of-weeks. & one day. & here came william & conquered england.

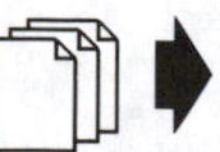

TEXT 19 – Chronicle for 1066

M.1xvi. On þissū geare man halgode þet
mynster æt westmynstre on cilda mæsse dæg. ⁊ se cyng
eadward forðferde on twelfta mæsse æfen. ⁊ hine mann
bebyrgede on twelftan mæsse dæg. innan þære niwa
halgodre circean on westmynstre. ⁊ harold eorl feng
to englalandes cynerice. swa swa se cyng hit him geuðe.
⁊ eac men hine þærto gecuron. ⁊ wæs gebletsod to cynge on twelftan mæsse dæg. ⁊ þy'ilcan geare þe he cyng
wæs. he for ut mid sciphere togeanes Willme. ⁊ þa hwile cō tostig eorl into humbran mid .lx. scipu. Eadwine eorl cō landfyrde. ⁊ draf hine ut. ⁊ þa butsecarlas
hine forsocan. ⁊ he for to scotlande mid .xii. snaccū. ⁊ hine gemette harold se norrena cyng mid .ccc. scipū ⁊
tostig hī to beah. ⁊ hi bægen foran into humbran oð þet
hi coman to eoferwic. ⁊ heō wið feaht morkere eorl. ⁊
eadwine eorl. ⁊ se norrena cyng alne siges geweald. ⁊ man
cydde haro(l)de cyng hu hit wæs þær gedon ⁊ geworden.
⁊ he cō mid mycclū here engliscra manna. ⁊ gemette hine
æt stængfordes brycge. ⁊ hine ofsloh. ⁊ þone eorl tostig.
⁊ eallne þone here ahtlice ofercō. ⁊ þa hwile cō willm eorl
upp æt hestingan on scē michaeles mæsse dæg. ⁊ harold
cō norþan ⁊ hī wið feahte ear þan þe his here come eall. ⁊
þær he feoll. ⁊ his twægen gebroðra Gyrð ⁊ leofwine. and
Willelm þis land ge eode. ⁊ cō to westmynstre. ⁊ ealdred
arceb̄ hine to cynge gehalgode. ⁊ menn guldon him gyld.
⁊ gislas sealdon. ⁊ syððan heora land bohtan.

(*Peterborough Chronicle*: the lines of the text correspond to those of the manuscript, and the textual abbreviations have also been reproduced)

1066. In this year one consecrated the
minster at westminster on children's mass day* & the king
edward died on twelfth mass eve* & him one
buried on twelfth mass day*. in the new
consecrated church at westminster. & harold earl succeeded
to england's kingdom. as the king it to-him granted.
& as men him thereto chose. & was blessed (= *consecrated*) as king
on twelfth mass day. & the same year that he king
was. he went out with ship-force against William. & meanwhile
came tostig earl into humber with 60 ships. Ed-
win earl came (with) land-army. & drove him out. & the shipmen
him forsook. & he went to Scotland with 12 vessels. & him
met harold the norwegian king with 300 ships. &
tostig him to submitted. & they both went into humber until
they came to york. & them against fought morcar earl. &
edwin earl. & the norwegian king all victory gained. & one
told harold king how it was there done & happened.
& he came with great army of-english men. & met him
at stamford bridge. & him slew. & the earl tostig.
& all the host manfully overcame. & meanwhile came william earl
up at hastings on st michael's mass day*. & harold
came from-north & him against fought before his army came all. &
there he fell. & his two brothers Gurth & leofwine. and
William this land conquered. & came to westminster. & ealdred
archbishop him to king consecrated. & men paid him tribute.
& hostages gave. & then their lands bought-back.

cont ...

On þissū geare man halgode þet
mynster æt ƿestmynstre on cilda mæsse dæg · ⁊ se cyng
eadƿard forðferde on tƿelfta mæsse æfen · ⁊ hine mann
bebyrgede on tƿelftan mæsse dæg · innan þære niƿa
halgodre circean on ƿestmynstre · ⁊ harold eorl feng
to englalandes cynerice · sƿa sƿa se cyng hit him geude ·
⁊ eac men hine þær to gecuron · ⁊ ƿæs gebletsod to cyn
ge on tƿelftan mæsse dæg · ⁊ þy ilcan geare þe he cyng
ƿæs · he for ut mid sciphere to geanes Willme · ⁊ þa hƿile cō tostig eorl into humbran mid · lx · scipū · ead
ƿine eorl cō land fyrde · ⁊ draf hine ut · ⁊ þa butsecarlas
hine forsocan · ⁊ he for to scotlande mid · xii · snaccū · ⁊ hi
ne gemette harold se norrena cyng mid · ccc · scipū · ⁊
tostig hī to beah · ⁊ hi bægen foran into humbran oð þet
hi coman to eoferƿic · ⁊ heō ƿið feaht morkere eorl · ⁊
eadƿine eorl · ⁊ se norrena cyng ahte siges geƿeald · ⁊ man
cydde harode cyng hu hit ƿæs þær gedon ⁊ geƿorden ·
⁊ he cō mid mycclū here englisca manna · ⁊ gemette hine
æt stængfordes brycge · ⁊ hine ofsloh · ⁊ þone eorl tostig ·
⁊ eallne þone here ahtlice ofercō · ⁊ þa hƿile cō ƿillm eorl
upp æt hestingan on scē michaeles mæsse dæg · ⁊ harold
cō norðan ⁊ hī ƿið feaht ear þan þe his here come eall · ⁊
þær he feoll · ⁊ his tƿægen gebroðra Gyrð ⁊ leofƿine · and
Willelm þis land geeode · ⁊ cō to ƿestmynstre · ⁊ ealdred
arceb hine to cynge gehalgode · ⁊ menn guldon him gyld ·
⁊ gislas sealdon · ⁊ syððan heora land bohtan ·

* children's mass day = Holy Innocent's Day, 28 December
*twelfth mass eve = Eve of Epiphany, 5 January
*twelfth mass day = Twelfth Night, Epiphany, 6 January
* St michael's mass day = St Michael's Day, 29 September

2.9 The pronunciation of OE

A more detailed description of the pronunciation of OE is provided in Commentary 1 of the *Text Commentary Book.* Changes of pronunciation that take place over a long period of time have important effects on word structure and grammar, and so cannot properly be separated from those aspects of language if you want to understand some of the reasons for language change.

2.10 The inflections of OE

A description of the inflections of nouns, adjectives and verbs is set out in Commentary 2 of the *Text Commentary Book*, but for fuller details you should consult a grammar book of OE (see the Bibliography).

3. From Old English to Middle English

3.1 The evidence for linguistic change

The ways in which we have identified and described features of the language in the OE texts of Chapters 1 and 2 are those that we can systematically apply to any text of English. To remind you once more, we look at any one or more of the following 'levels' of language and observe:

- changes in spelling conventions, letter forms and the alphabet used – these are only a guide in OE and ME texts to the pronunciation of the language;
- changes in pronunciation, inferred from the written words;
- changes in word structure, suffixes (inflections) and prefixes;
- changes in the grammar and word order;
- changes in the vocabulary – new words appear, old ones are no longer used.

We call the language from about 1150 to 1450 **Middle English** (ME), because from our point of view in time it comes between the periods of Old and Modern English. The evidence for change and development in ME, before the first printing press was set up by William Caxton in 1476, lies in written manuscripts, just as for OE. Every copy of a book, letter, will or charter had to be written out by hand, but only a few of the existing manuscripts in ME are originals, in the hand of their author. Many copies of popular books, like Chaucer's *The Canterbury Tales*, for example, have survived, although Chaucer's original manuscripts have been lost. On the other hand, other works are known through a single surviving copy only.

As a result of the social and political upheaval caused by the Norman Conquest (see Section 3.2), the West Saxon standard system of spelling and punctuation was in time no longer used. Writers used spellings that tended to match the pronunciation of their spoken dialect, and scribes sometimes changed the spelling of words they were copying to match their own dialectal pronunciation. After several copies, therefore, the writing might contain a mixture of different dialectal forms. But for students of language today, the loss of the OE standard system of writing means that there is plenty of evidence for the different dialects of ME.

Today, we are used to reading printed books and papers in Standard English which all use a spelling and punctuation system that has been almost unchanged for over 200 years. We are taught to use Standard English and standard spelling when we learn to write. MnE spelling is neutral to pronunciation, and written texts can be read in any regional accent. Misspelled words and non-standard forms look 'wrong'.

The writings of most authors from the late fifteenth century onwards, including the plays of Shakespeare and the King James Bible of 1611, are prepared for printing in modern editions by editors who almost always convert the original spelling and punctuation into modern standard forms. For example, an early edition of Shakespeare's *Henry IV Part 1* printed in 1598 contains these words spoken by Falstaff:

> If I be not ashamed of my soldiours, I am a souct gurnet, I haue misused the kinges presse damnablie. No eye hath seene such skarcrowes. Ile not march through Couentry with them, thats flat.

It contains several unfamiliar features of spelling and punctuation which would be marked wrong if you used them. There is also the problem of interpreting the meaning of *souct* for certain – probably *soused*. At a glance, it doesn't look like 'good English'.

The policy of modernising the spelling and punctuation of old texts from the fifteenth century onwards leaves us unaware of the *gradual* development of modern spelling and punctuation. We read Chaucer's original 1390s spelling, but not Shakespeare's of the 1590s. The examples of historical English texts in this book are reproduced with their original spelling, because this is part of the development of written English.

All printed versions of old texts must compromise in reproducing the originals – only facsimiles are completely authentic, but it needs experience to be able to decipher handwriting styles of the past.

3.2 The Norman Conquest and the English language

In Chapters 1 and 2, we looked at OE in the West Saxon dialect, which had become the standard form for writing by the first half of the eleventh century in all dialectal areas. A standard orthography (spelling system) means that changes in pronunciation tend not to be recorded. On the other hand, any inconsistencies in spelling that do occur are a clue to changes that were taking place in pronunciation and word form (see Section 2.7.4 of this book and Commentary 1 of the *Text Commentary Book*, Section 1.1).

After the conquest of England by William I in 1066, Norman French, not English, became the language of the ruling classes and their servants, because almost all of the former English nobility were dispossessed of their lands. The chronicler Robert Mannyng, writing in the NE Midlands dialect in 1338, refers to this.

To Frankis & Normanz for þare grete laboure
To Flemmynges & Pikardes þat were with him in stoure (= *in battle*)
He gaf londes bityme of whilk þer successoure
Hold ȝit þe seyseyne (= *possession of land*) with fulle grete honoure.

Here is another short account of the Conquest in an anonymous chronicle, written in the fourteenth century, which still showed hostility to the Norman domination of England.

TEXT 20 – Anonymous short metrical chronicle

SW Midlands dialect

Suþþe regnede a goude gome	After reigned a good man
Harold Godwynes sone	Harold Godwin's son
He was icluped Harefot	He was called Harefoot
For he was renner goud	For he was runner good
Bote he ne regnede here	But he ne-reigned here
Bot .ix. monþes of a ȝere	But 9 months of a year
Willam bastard of Normandye	William bastard of Normandy
Hym cant þat was a vilanye	Him deposed that was a villainy
Harold liþ at Waltham	Harold lies at Waltham
& Willam bastard þat þis lond wan	& William bastard that this land won
He regnede here	He reigned here
On & tuenti ȝere	One & twenty years
Suþþe he deide at þe hame	Then he died at (the) home
At Normandye at Came	In Normany at Caen

(*An Anonymous Short Metrical Chronicle*, E. Zettl (ed.), EETS 196)

Activity 3.1

Rewrite Robert Mannyng's text and Text 20 in MnE.

William's policy of dispossessing the Anglo-Saxon nobility held in the Church also. French-speaking bishops and abbots were in time appointed to the principal offices, and many French monks entered the monasteries. Latin remained the principal language of both Church and State for official writing in documents, while French became the 'prestige language' of communication. We can compare the status of French in England from 1066 onwards with that of English in the British Empire in the nineteenth and early twentieth centuries. The situation that developed is described by another verse chronicler, known as Robert of Gloucester, writing about 1300. His attitude towards Harold and William I is different from that of the anonymous chronicler of Text 20.

TEXT 21 – Robert of Gloucester's chronicle

Southern dialect

þus lo þe englisse folc. vor noȝt to grounde com.
vor a fals king þat nadde no riȝt. to þe kinedom.
& come to a nywe louerd. þat more in riȝte was.
ac hor noþer as me may ise. in pur riȝte was.
& þus was in normannes hond. þat lond ibroȝt iwis ...

þus com lo engelond. in to normandies hond.
& þe normans ne couþe speke þo. bote hor owe speche.
& speke french as hii dude at om. & hor children dude also teche.
so þat heiemen of þis lond. þat of hor blod come.
holdeþ alle þulk speche. þat hii of hom nome.
vor bote a man conne frenss. me telþ of him lute.
ac lowe men holdeþ to engliss. & to hor owe speche ȝute.
ich wene þer ne beþ in al þe world. contreyes none.
þat ne holdeþ to hor owe speche. bote engelond one.
ac wel me wot uor to conne. boþe wel it is.
vor þe more þat a mon can. þe more wurþe he is.
þis noble duc willam. him let crouny king.
at londone amidwinter day. nobliche þoru alle þing.
of þe erchebissop of euerwik. aldred was is name.
þer nas prince in al þe world. of so noble fame.

(*Rerum Britannicarum Medii Aevi Scriptores – Rolls Series* No. 86)

thus lo the English folk. for nought to ground came (= *were beaten*).
for a false king that ne-had no right. to the kingdom.
& came to a new lord. that more in right was.
but their neither (= *neither of them*) as one may see. in pure right was.
& thus was in norman's hand. that land brought certainly ...

thus came lo England. into Normandy's hand.
& the Normans ne-could speak then. but their own speech.
& spoke French as they did at home. & their children did also teach.
so that high-men of this land. that of their blood come.
hold all the-same speech. that they from them took.
for but a man knows French. one counts of him little.
but low men hold to English. & to their own speech yet.
i believe there ne-are in all the world. countries none.

cont ...

that ne-hold to their own speech. but England alone.
but well one knows for to know. both well it is.
for the more that a man knows. the more worthy he is.
this noble duke William. him(self) caused to crown king.
at London on mid-winter's day. nobly through all things.
by the archbishop of york. aldred was his name.
there ne-was prince in all the world. of so noble fame.

Activity 3.2

Rewrite Robert of Gloucester's chronicle in MnE.

3.3 The earliest surviving ME text

The manuscript of the *Anglo-Saxon Chronicle* which was written in the abbey at Peterborough is of special interest for two reasons, one historical and the other linguistic. Firstly, it is the only copy of the chronicle that describes events up to the middle of the twelfth century, nearly 100 years after the Norman Conquest. Secondly, it gives us the first direct evidence of the changes in the language that had taken place by the 1150s.

We know that a disastrous fire at Peterborough destroyed most of the monastery's library in 1116, including its copy of the chronicle. Later, another chronicle was borrowed and copied. This rewritten copy has survived and is the one known as the *Peterborough Chronicle*. The entries for the years up to 1121 are all in the same hand, and copied in the 'classical' West Saxon OE orthography. But there are two 'continuations' of the annals, probably written down by two scribes, one recording events from 1122 to 1131, and the other from 1132 to 1154, where the chronicle ends.

The importance of the continuations is that the language is not the classical West Saxon OE of the older chronicle to 1121, but is markedly different. It is good evidence of current English usage of that area in the first half of the twelfth century. The monks of Peterborough were probably local men, so spoke the East Midlands dialect of English. Peterborough was within the Danelaw, so some influence of ON might be expected too. The tradition of writing in classical OE spelling was by now lost, and as the continuations of the annals were probably written from dictation, the scribes would tend to spell English as they heard and spoke it. Scribes were also now trained in the writing of French as well as Latin, and some conventions of writing French would influence their spelling of words.

Activity 3.3

Text 22 is part of the annal for 1140 in the second continuation of the *Peterborough Chronicle*.

(i) Read through the text to see whether you can understand the gist of it without referring to the translation.
(ii) Use the literal translation to write a version in MnE.
(iii) List any differences between the language of the text and that of the chronicle annals in Texts 1–19 which you immediately notice.
(iv) Comment on the words of French derivation in the text: *uuerre*, *castel*, *prisun*.

TEXT 22 – Chronicle for 1140

mc.xl. On þis gær wolde þe king Stephne tæcen Rodbert eorl
of gloucestre þe kinges sune Henries. ac he ne myhte for he
wart it war. þer efter in þe lengten þestrede þe sunne 7 te
dæi. abuton nontid dæies. þa men eten. ð me lihtede candles
to æten bi ... wæron men suythe of wundred ...

þer efter wæx suythe micel uuerre betuyx þe king 7 Randolf
eorl of cæstre noht for þi ð he ne iaf him al ð he cuthe axen
him. alse he dide all othre. oc æfre þe mare he iaf heom. þe
wærse hi wæron him. þe eorl heold lincol agænes þe king 7
benam him al ð he ahte to hauen. 7 te king for þider 7
besætte him 7 his brother Willelm de Romare in þe castel. 7
te æorl stæl ut 7 ferde efter Rodbert eorl of gloucestre. 7
brohte him þider mid micel ferd. 7 fuhten suythe on
Candelmasse dæi agenes heore lauerd. 7 namen him for his men
him suyken 7 flugæn. 7 læd him to Bristowe 7 diden þar in
prisun 7 in feteres. þa was al engleland styred mar þan ær
wæs. 7 al yuel wæs in lande ...

þa ferde Eustace þe kinges sune to france 7 nam þe kinges
suster of france to wife. wende to bigæton normandi þærþurh.
oc he spedde litel 7 be gode rihte for he was an yuel man.
for ware se he com he dide mar yuel þanne god. he reuede þe
landes 7 læide micele geldes on. He brohte his wif to
engleland. 7 dide hire in þe castel in cantebyri. God wimman
scæ wæs. oc scæ hedde litel blisse mid him. 7 Crist ne wolde
ð he sculde lange rixan. 7 wærd ded 7 his moder beien ...

WW

1140. In this year wished the king Stephen take Robert earl
of Gloucester the king's son Henry's. but he ne was-able for he
became it aware. there after in the lent darkened the sun & the
day. about noontide day's. when men eat. that one lighted candles
to eat by ... were men very amazed ...

thereafter waxed violently much war between the king & Randolph
earl of chester not because he ne gave him all that he could demand
from-him. as he did all others. but ever the more he gave to-them. the
worse they were to-him. the earl held lincoln against the king &
took from-him all that he ought to have. & the king fared thither &
beseiged him & his brother William de Romare in the castle. &
the earl stole out & went after Robert earl of gloucester. &
brought him thither with great army. & fought violently on
Candlemass day against their lord. & captured him for his men
him betrayed & fled. & led him to Bristol & put there in
prison & in fetters. then was all England disturbed more than before
was. & all evil was in land ...

then went Eustace the king's son to france & took the king's
sister of france to wife. hoped to obtain normandy there-through.
but he sped little & by good right for he was an evil man.
for where so he came he did more evil than good. he robbed the
lands & laid great taxes on. He brought his wife to
england. & put her in the castle in canterbury. Good woman
she was. but she had little bliss with him. & Christ ne wished
that he should long reign. & became dead & his mother both ...

(For a detailed commentary on the language of Text 22, and the evidence of marked change in the language, see Commentary 4 of the *Text Commentary Book*.)

There are three words in Text 22 adopted from Anglo-Norman, the form of Old Northern French spoken by the Normans in England: *castel*, *prisun*, *uuerre*.

Other words adopted into English about this time are:

abbat (= *abbot*)	cuntesse (= *countess*)	market
capelein (= *chaplain*)	curt (= *court*)	prior
cancelere (= *chancellor*)	duc (= *duke*)	rent
cardinal	iustise (= *justice*)	serfise (= *service*)
clerc (= *clerk*)	legat (= *legate*)	tresor (= *treasure*)

Activity 3.4

Is there any significance in the meanings of the earliest French words in the chronicle and those in the foregoing list?

An analysis of a short text like this shows how much information a close examination can yield. The scribe of the chronicle does not appear to be familiar with the former OE West Saxon spelling, and he tends to write according to the pronunciation of the words. It provides clear evidence of changes which are only hinted at in late OE texts.

The most important change is the beginning of the loss of most of the inflections of OE, mainly by their reduction in sound. This leads to a greater reliance on word order, and the more frequent use of prepositions to show the meanings that formerly might have been signalled by inflections. Consequently, the chronicle text reads much more like MnE to us than the OE texts, even though there is still some way to go.

The next extract is followed by a version in West Saxon OE, so that you can see the extent of the changes in the language.

TEXT 23 – Chronicle for 1137, c.1154

I ne can ne i ne mai tellen alle þe
wunder ne alle þe pines ð hi diden wreccemen on þis land. 7 ð laste-
de þa .xix. wintre wile Stephne was king 7 æure it was uuerse 7
uuerse.

þa was corn dære. 7 flec 7 cæse 7 butere. for nan ne wæs o þe land.
Wreccemen sturuen of hungær.

war sæ me tilede. þe erthe ne bar nan corn. for þe land was al
fordon. mid suilce dædes. 7 hi sæden openlice ð crist slep 7 his halechen. Suilc 7 mare þanne we cunnen sæin. we þolenden .xix. wintre
for ure sinnes.

(From facsimile edition of the *Peterborough Chronicle*, Dorothy Whitelock (ed.), Copenhagen: Rosenkilde & Bagger, 1954)

Version in the former OE standard written form

ic ne cann ne ic ne mæg tellan ealle þa
wundor ne ealle þa pinas þe hie dydon wreccum mannum on þissum lande. 7 þæt læste-
de þa .xix. wintra þa hwile þe Stephne cyning wæs 7 æfre hit wæs wyrsa 7
wyrsa.

þa wæs corn deore. 7 flesc 7 cese 7 butere. for nan ne wæs on þæm lande.
wrecce menn sturfon of hungre.

swa hwær swa man tilode. seo eorþe ne bær nan corn. for þæt land wæs eall
fordon. mid swilcum dædum. 7 hie sædon openlice þæt crist slep 7 his ha-
lgan. swilc 7 mare þanne we cunnon secgan. we þolodon .xix. wintra
for ure synna.

WW I ne can ne I ne may tell all the horrors ne all the pains that they caused wretched-men in this land. & that lasted the 19 winters while Stephen was king & ever it was worse & worse.

then was corn dear. & flesh & cheese & butter. for none ne was in the land. Wretched-men died of hunger.

where so one tilled. the earth ne bore no corn. for the land was all ruined. with such deeds. & they said openly that christ slept & his saints. Such & more than we can say. we suffered 19 winters for our sins.

I ne canne i ne mai tellen alle þe ƿunder ne alle þe pineſ ð hi diden ƿreccemen on þiſ land. ⁊ ð laſtede þa .xix. ƿintre ƿile Stephne ƿaſ king ⁊ æure it ƿaſ uuerſe ⁊ uuerſe.

Þa ƿaſ corn dære. ⁊ flec ⁊ cæſe ⁊ butere. for nan ne ƿæſ o þe land. Ƿreccemen ſturuen of hungær.

Ƿar ſæ me tilede. þe erthe ne bar nan corn. for þe land ƿaſ al for don. mid ſuilce dædeſ. ⁊ hi ſæden openlice ð xpiſt ſlep. ⁊ his halechen. Suilc ⁊ mare þanne ƿe cunnen ſæin. ƿe þolenden .xix. ƿintre for ure ſinnes.

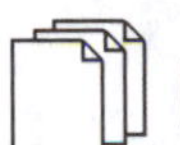

Activity 3.5

(i) Write a version of Text 23 in MnE.

(ii) Use the OE version or the word list in the accompanying *Word Book* to make a study of the changes that you can observe in the language. Look particularly at the following words or phrases:

OE NPs and PrepPs	Chronicle	OE Verbs	Chronicle
ic	I	ic ne mæg tellan	I ne mai tellen
hit	it	hie dydon	hi diden
we	we	þæt læstede	ðat lastede
hi/hie	hi	Stephne wæs	Stephne was
man	me	hit wæs	it was
nan	nan	corn wæs	corn was
nan corn	nan corn	nan ne wæs	nan ne wæs
ealle þa wundor	alle þe wunder	menn sturfon	men sturuen
ealle þa pinas	alle þe pines	man tilode	me tilede
on þæm lande	o þe land	seo eorþe ne bær	þe erþe ne bar
seo eorþe	þe erþe	þæt land wæs fordon	þe land was fordon

OE NPs and PrepPs	Chronicle	OE Verbs	Chronicle
þæt land	þe land		
þa xix wintra	þa xix wintre	hie sædon	hi sæden
on þissum lande	on þis land	Crist slep	Crist slep
his halgan	his halechen	we cunnon secgan	we cunnen sæin
for ure synna	for ure sinnes	we þolodon	we þolede
wreccum mannum	wrecce men		
wrecce menn	wrecce men		
mid swilcum dædum	mid suilce dædes		
xix wintra	xix wintre		
cyning	king		
corn (deore)	corn (dære)		
flæsc/flesc	flec		
cyse/cese	cæse		
butere	butere		
Crist	Crist		
of hungre	of hunger		

3.4 The book called *Ormulum*

Another early text dating from the late twelfth century is an important source of information about the state of the language. It was written by a monk called Orm (a Danish name, as we have seen in Section 2.5.1). Text 24 consists of an extract from the opening of the book, where Orm explains why he has written it.

TEXT 24 – *Ormulum*, late twelfth century (i)

þiss boc iss nemmned Orrmulum. Forrþi þatt Orrm itt wrohhte.	this book is called Ormulum. Because Orm it wrought (= *made*).
Icc hafe wennd inntill Ennglissh. Goddspelles hallʒhe lare. Affterr þatt little witt þatt me. Min Drihhtin hafeþþ lenedd.	I have turned into English. (*The*) gospel's holy lore. After that little wit that me. My Lord has lent (= *granted*).
Annd wha-se wilenn shall þiss boc. Efft oþerr siþe writenn. Himm bidde icc þat he't write rihht. Swa-summ þiss boc himm tæcheþþ. All þwerrt-ut affterr þatt itt iss. Uppo þiss firrste bisne. Wiþþall swillc rime alls her iss sett. Wiþþall þe fele wordess. Annd tatt he loke wel þatt he. An bocstaff write twiʒʒess. Eʒʒwhær þær itt uppo þiss boc. Iss writenn o þatt wise. Loke he wel þatt he't wrote swa. Forr he ne maʒʒ nohht elless. Onn Ennglissh writenn rihht te word. þatt wite he wel to soþe.	And whoever intend shall this book. Again another time write. Him ask I that he it copy right. In the same way (*that*) this book him teaches. Entirely after (*the way*) that it is. According to this first example. With all such rhyme as here is set (*down*). With all the many words. And (*I ask*) that he look well that he. A letter writes twice. Everywhere it in this book. Is written in that way. (*Let him*) Look well that he it wrote so. For he must not else (= *otherwise*). In English write correctly the word. That (*should*) know he well for sure.

Activity 3.6

(i) Read Orm's text aloud, pronouncing every final <-e> with the vowel /ə/, unless it comes before a word beginning with another vowel or <h>, when it is not pronounced.
(ii) How many syllables are there between each 'full-stop'?
(iii) What do the 'full-stops' mark?

3.4.1 Commentary on Text 24

There are fifteen syllables to every line, without exception, so the text is in verse and the metre is absolutely regular. Single unstressed and stressed syllables (or off-beats and beats) alternate, always with an initial and final unstressed syllable:

x / x / x / x / x / x / x / x
þiss boc iss nemmned Orrmulum. Forrþi þatt Orrm itt wrohhte.

and the stops in the text mark the end of each half-line and line.

Activity 3.7

(i) Write out a version of Orm's text in MnE.
(ii) Check the sources of the vocabulary (see the word list in the *Word Book*).

Here is the text set out in metrical form:

þiss /**boc** iss /**nemm**-ned /**Orr**-mu/**lum**. Forr/**þi** þatt /**Orrm** itt /**wrohh**-te.

Icc /**ha**-fe /**wennd** inn/**till** Enng/**lissh**. Godd/**spell**-es /**hall**-ʒhe /**la**-re.
Aff/**terr** þatt /**litt**-le /**witt** þatt /**me**. Min /**Drihh**-tin /**ha**-feþþ /**le**-nedd.

Annd /**wha**-se /**wil**-enn /**shall** þiss /**boc**. Efft /**o**-þerr /**si**-þe /**wri**-tenn.
Himm /**bidd**(e) icc /**þat** he't /**wri**-te /**rihht**. Swa-/**summ** þiss /**boc** himm /**tæ**-cheþþ.
All /**þwerrt**-ut /**aff**-terr /**þatt** itt /**iss**. Upp/**o** þiss /**firr**-ste /**bis**-ne.
Wiþþ/**all** swillc /**rim**(e) alls /**her** iss /**sett**. Wiþþ/**all** þe /**fe**-le /**wor**-dess.
Annd /**tatt** he /**lo**-ke /**wel** þatt /**he**. An /**boc**-staff /**wri**-te /**twi**-ʒʒess.
Eʒʒ/**whær** þær /**itt** upp/**o** þiss /**boc**. Iss /**wri**-tenn /**o** þatt /**wi**-se.
Lok(e) /**he** wel /**þatt** he't /**wro**-te /**swa**. Forr /**he** ne /**maʒʒ** nohht /**ell**-ess.
Onn /**Enng**-lissh /**wri**-tenn /**rihht** te /**word**. þatt /**wit**(e) he /**wel** to /**so**-þe.

3.4.2 A note on Orm's spelling

There are two important things to remember about Orm's spelling: firstly, it is consistent; secondly, it is an attempt to reform the system and relate each sound to a symbol. For example, he introduced three symbols for <g>, to differentiate between the three sounds that it had come to represent (see Commentary 1 of the *Text Commentary Book*, Section 2.7 iiid). In the texts, you will notice his use of <wh> for OE <hw>, for example, *wha-se*, *whas* for *hwa swa*, *hwæs* (MnE *whoso*, *whose*), and <sh> for <sc>, for example, *shall*, *Ennglissh* for *sceal*, *Englisc*, both of which are familiar in MnE.

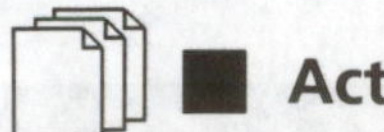

Activity 3.8

Read the following extract from *Ormulum* and write a version in MnE.

TEXT 25 – The Shepherds at the Manger, *Ormulum* (ii)

An enngell comm off heffness ærd. inn aness weress hewe.
Till hirdess þær þær þeȝȝ þatt nihht. biwokenn þeȝȝre faldess.
Þatt enngell comm annd stod hemm bi. wiþþ heffness lihht annd leme.
Annd forrþrihht summ þeȝȝ sæȝhenn himm. þeȝȝ wurrdenn swiðe offdredde.
Annd Godess enngell hemm bigann. to frofrenn annd to beldenn.
Annd seȝȝde hemm þuss o Godess hallf. wiþþ swiþe milde spæche.
Ne be ȝe nohht forrdredde off me. acc be ȝe swiþe bliþe ...
Forr ȝuw iss borenn nu todaȝȝ. hælennde off ȝure sinness.
An wennchell þatt iss Iesu Crist. þatt wite ȝe to soþe ...
ȝe shulenn findenn ænne child. I winnde-clutess wundenn.
Annd itt iss inn a cribbe leȝȝd. annd tær ȝe't muȝhenn findenn.

Annd sone anan ðeȝȝ ȝedenn forþ. till Beþþleæmess chesstre.
Annd fundenn Sannte Marȝe þær. annd Iosæp hire macche.
Annd ec þeȝȝ fundenn þær þe child. þær itt wass leȝȝd i cribbe ...
Annd sone anan þeȝȝ kiddenn forþ. amang Iudisskenn þede.
All þatt teȝȝ haffdenn herrd off Crist. annd seȝhenn wel wiþþ eȝhne.

Annd ure laffdiȝ Marȝe toc. all þatt ȝho sahh annd herrde ...
Annd leȝȝde itt all to-samenn aȝȝ. I swiþe þohhtfull herrte.
All þatt ȝho sahh annd herrde off Crist. whas moderr ȝho ȝwass wurrþenn.

WW

An angel came from heaven's land. in a man's form.
To shepherds there where they that night. watched their folds.
The angel came and stood them by. with heaven's light and brightness.
And immediately as they saw him. they became very afraid.
And God's angel them began. to comfort and to encourage.
And said them thus on God's behalf. with very mild speech.
Ne be ye not afraid of me. but be ye very blithe ...
For to-you is born now today. saviour of our sins.
A child that is Jesus Christ. that know ye for truth ...
Ye shall find a child. in swaddling-clothes wound.
And it is in a crib laid. and there ye it may find.

And soon at once they went forth. to Bethlehem's city.
And found Saint Mary there. and Joseph her husband.
And also they found there the child. where it was laid in crib ...
And soon at once they made-known forth. among Jewish nation.
All that they had heard of Christ. and saw well with eyes.

And our lady Mary took. all that she saw and heard ...
And laid it all together always. in very thoughtful heart.
All that she saw and heard of Christ. whose mother she was become.

3.4.3 Orm's writing as evidence of language change in early ME

Orm's 20 000 odd lines of verse are important evidence for some of the changes that had taken place in the language by the late twelfth century in his part of the country, just over 100 years after the Norman Conquest. His lines are, however, monotonous to read, since they are absolutely regular in metre. Students of literature do not place Orm high on their list, but for students of language his writing is very valuable.

Because Orm probably lived in northern Lincolnshire (now South Humberside), he wrote in an East Midlands dialect of English, like the *Peterborough Chronicle* continuations. His object was to teach the Christian faith in English, and the verses were to be read aloud. So he devised his own system of spelling, to help a reader to pronounce the words properly. What is especially noticeable is the number of **double consonant letters.**

(The relationship of Orm's spelling to the pronunciation of his East Midlands dialect is explained in Commentary 5 of the *Text Commentary Book.*)

3.5 The origins of present-day Standard English in ME

Standard English today is the form of the language normally used in writing. It is also the spoken form for some people. It is not a regional variety of English. It may be spoken in a regional accent, or in the accent known as Received Pronunciation (RP), which developed during the nineteenth century and is not a regional accent. You cannot tell where someone speaking Standard English in RP today comes from.

All present-day dialects of English, including Standard English, can be traced back to the dialects of the ME period (c.1150–1450) in their pronunciation, vocabulary and grammar. There was no standard form of the language then, and the spelling, pronunciation, vocabulary and grammar varied from one part of the country to another. Differences of spelling, vocabulary and grammar in the manuscripts are first-hand evidence of differences of usage and pronunciation, and of the changes that took place over the ME period.

We shall now look at some of the evidence for change and development in the dialects of ME, remembering that this helps us to explain many of the differences between the dialects of MnE today.

3.6 Evidence of changes in pronunciation

If you examine any ME text, you can compare the form of a word with its original form in OE, ON or OF and see whether the evidence of the spelling suggests that it has changed in pronunciation. When this is done systematically, knowledge of the probable dialectal area in which a text was written can be deduced.

Demonstrating this in accurate detail is the work of ME scholars, and beyond the scope of an introductory textbook, but we can learn a little by taking two contrasting short texts, one in a Southern dialect and the other in a Northern dialect, and seeing what we can find out about changes in the language since the OE period.

3.6.1 *The Fox and the Wolf*

Here is the opening of a poem called *The Fox and the Wolf*, which is a southern text dating from the early thirteenth century.

TEXT 26 – *The Fox and the Wolf*, early thirteenth century

Southern dialect

A vox gon out of þe wode go
Afingret so þat him wes wo
He nes neuere in none wise
Afingret erour half so swiþe.
He ne hoeld nouþer wey ne strete
For him wes loþ men to mete.
Him were leuere meten one hen
Þen half an oundred wimmen.
He strok swiþe oueral
So þat he ofsei ane wal.
Wiþinne þe walle wes on hous.
The wox wes þider swiþe wous
For he þohute his hounger aquenche
Oþer mid mete oþer mid drunche.

A fox went out of the wood (*gon ... go = went*)
Hungered so that to-him was woe
He ne-was never in no way
Hungered before half so greatly.
He ne held neither way nor street
For to-him (it) was loathsome men to meet.
To-him (it) were more-pleasing meet one hen
Than half a hundred women.
He went quickly all-the-way
Until he saw a wall.
Within the wall was a house.
The fox was thither very eager (to go)
For he intended his hunger quench
Either with food or with drink.

Activity 3.9

(i) Use the WW translation to write a version in MnE.
(ii) Use the word list in the *Word Book* to compare the forms of the ME words and their OE sources, and discuss the possible reason for the following:
- (a) The use of the letters <v>, <w> and <u> in the words *vox*, *wox*, *neuere*, *leuere*, *oueral* and *wous*.
- (b) The use of letter <e> for the main vowel in *neuere*, *wes*, *nes*, *erour*, *strete* and *þen*.
- (c) The spelling <ou> for the vowel in *out*, *oundred*, *hous*, *wous* and *hounger*.
- (d) The spellings <qu> and <ch> in *aquenche*.
- (e) The spelling <o> for the long vowels of *go*, *wo*, *none*, *so*, *nouþer*, *loþ*, *one* and *strok*.
- (f) The spelling and possible pronunciations of *drunche* (it is a rhyming word with *aquenche*).
- (g) The spelling of the vowels of *half*, *oueral*, *wal/walle* and *leuere*.

The observations that we make about changes in the language in this short text cannot be conclusive – there is far too little evidence. If we studied the whole of *The Fox and the Wolf*, we would find inconsistencies in spelling and word forms. There is only one copy of the poem, and it is not the original. It must have been written and copied in the South of England, but it cannot be identified more closely with a particular dialectal area. Here are two comments by ME scholars:

> It appears to be in a Western dialect, but rhymes indicate that it was originally composed in some district in which south-eastern and Midland forms could be used.
>
> (*Early Middle English Texts*, Bruce Dickins and R. M. Wilson, 1951)
>
> Probably Southern; the text does not yield evidence for any more specific localization.
>
> (*Early Middle English Verse & Prose*, J. A. W. Bennett and G. V. Smithers, 1968)

But even in these few lines we find clear indications of some of the changes discussed earlier in the chapter (for a detailed description see Commentary 5 of the *Text Commentary Book*).

The evidence, especially the shifting or 'rounding' of OE /ɑː/ to /ɔː/, in words like *go*, *wo* and *loþ*, which had developed from OE *gan*, *wa* and *laþ*, points to its southern dialectal form. The vowel had not changed in northern dialects (see Section 3.6.2). There are also scarcely any words of ON derivation, which is further proof that it was written outside the boundaries of the former Danelaw.

3.6.2 *Cursor Mundi*

Cursor Mundi was written in the North of England in the last quarter of the thirteenth century. It consists of 30 000 lines of verse, retelling Christian legends and the stories of the Bible (*cursor* is Latin for *runner* or *messenger*; *mundi* for *of the world*).

The following couplet is one indicator of its Northern origins:

Þe **wrang** to here o right is **lath**
And pride wyt buxsumnes is **wrath**.

Wrong-doing is loth to hear of justice
And pride is angry with humility.

because the words *wrang* (OE *wrang*), *lath* (OE *lāþ*) and *wrath* (OE *wrāþ*) still retain the long back vowel /ɑː/. In Southern and Midlands dialects, they became *wrong*, *loth* and *wroth*.

Activity 3.10

Examine the following extract from *Cursor Mundi* for evidence of change, or lack of change, in the language of the text.

(i) Use the word list in the *Word Book* to compare the ME words with their OE sources, group them into sets of similar features and try to explain any differences.
(ii) Examine the pairs of rhyming words for any further proof of change.
(iii) Rewrite the text in MnE.

TEXT 27 – *Cursor Mundi*, c.1300

Northern dialect

Adam had pasid nine hundret yere	Adam had passed nine hundred years
Nai selcut þof he wex unfere	No wonder though he waxed infirm
Forwroght wit his hak and spad	Exhausted with his hoe and spade
Of himself he wex al sad.	Of himself he waxed all weary.
He lened him þan apon his hak	He leaned him then upon his hoe
Wit Seth his sun þusgat he spak	With Seth his son this-way he spoke
Sun, he said, þou most now ga	Son, he said, thou must now go
To Paradis þat I com fra	To Paradise that I came from
Til Cherubin þat þe yate ward.	To Cherubim that the gate guards.
Yai sir, wist I wyderward	Yes sir, knew I whitherwards

cont ...

Þat tat vncuth contre ware
Þou wat þat I was neuer þare.
Þus he said I sal þe sai
Howgate þou sal tak þe wai.
Toward þe est end of þis dale
Find a grene gate þou sale.

That that unknown country were
Thou knowest that I was never there.
Thus he said I shall to-thee say
How thou shalt take the way.
Toward the east end of this dale
Find a green path thou shalt.

(A description of the language can be found in Commentary 6 of the *Text Commentary Book*.)

3.6.3 Other features of *The Fox and the Wolf* and *Cursor Mundi*

So far, we have discussed some of the evidence of changes in pronunciation which can be deduced from the patterns of spelling in the manuscripts. One important development, the reduction of many unstressed suffixes to <e>, pronounced /ə/, was not simply a sound change. The loss of inflections leads to, and is a part of, a change in the grammar. Other features of ME grammar can be seen in these two texts.

Grammatical changes

The following three examples of a construction that is found in OE, but which is no longer seen in MnE, occur in *The Fox and the Wolf.* A literal translation is also given:

him wes wo	to-him was woe
him wes loþ	to-him was hateful
him were leuere	to-him were more pleasing

There is no subject to the verb. In MnE, we have to supply one, the 'dummy subject' *it*, as in *it was hateful/pleasing to him*. The ME *him* is the old dative case, so in MnE we have to add the preposition *to* to give the same meaning. This is called an **impersonal** construction.

As in OE and most MnE dialects today, the **double** or **multiple negative** was used:

He **nes neuere** in **none** wise ...
He **ne** hoeld **nouþer** wey **ne** strete ...

This text also shows the development of the indefinite article *a/an* from the OE numeral *an*, which at first meant *one* only. Examples of both uses occur, with variant spellings:

Him were leuere meten **one** hen ...	**one** hen
half **an** oundred wimmen ...	half **a** hundred women
he ofsei **ane** wal ...	he saw **a** wall
Wiþinne þe walle wes **on** hous ...	**a** house

Vocabulary

All the vocabulary of *The Fox and the Wolf* is derived from OE. However, there are changes of meaning in apparently familiar words which sometimes cause difficulty in reading if we are unaware of the change. For example, *mete* in both OE and ME meant *food* in general. This meaning survives in the MnE collocation *meat and drink.*

The vocabulary of the northern text from *Cursor Mundi* contains a number of words derived from ON and OF: *fra*, *gate*, *tak*, *til* and *þof* from ON because it was written in the area of the Danish settlements, where OE and ON were gradually assimilated together, and *contre*, *pasid* and *sir* from OF probably because it is a later text than *The Fox and the Wolf* and so there had been more time for French words to be assimilated into the language and to be used in writing.

One important example of 'borrowing' from ON does not occur in Text 27, but can be seen in the following lines from the same poem.

Bot þou sal tak þis pepins thre
Þat I toke o þat appel-tre,
And do **þam** vnder his tong-rote.
Þai sal til mani man be bote:
Þai sal be cedre, siprese, and pine –
O **þam** sal man haue medicen.

But thou shalt take these pippins three
That I took from that apple-tree,
And put **them** under his tongue-root.
They shall to many men be remedy:
They shall be cedar, cypress and pine –
From **them** shall men have medicine.

We are unlikely to notice the use of *þai* (*they*) and *þam* (*them*) unless we are aware of the fact that the OE plural pronouns were *hi* (nominative and accusative), *hira* (genitive) and *him* (dative). This 'borrowing' from ON of distinctive forms of the plural pronouns, *they*, *them* and *their*, all beginning with <th>, began early on in the Northern dialect of ME. It also spread southwards, but was not completely assimilated into the Southern dialect even at the beginning of the fifteenth century. Chaucer, writing in the 1390s in the London dialect, used the new form for the subject pronoun, as in:

And thus **they** been accorded and ysworn

but the older forms for the object and possessive, as in:

And many a louely look on **hem** he caste
Men sholde wedden after **hir** estaat

3.7 The *Bestiary* – the eagle

Here is one further example of early ME from the thirteenth century, in the East Midlands dialect. It is part of the description of the eagle from the only surviving manuscript of a medieval *Bestiary*, or *Book of Beasts*. It was believed that the animal and plant world was symbolic of religious truths – 'the creatures of this sensible world signify the invisible things of God'. Later scientific knowledge shows that some of the descriptions are not true; some of the animals in the bestiaries, like the unicorn, phoenix and basilisk, are imaginary, like the following description of the eagle's flight.

TEXT 28 – The Eagle, *Bestiary*

Kiþen I wille þe ernes kinde
Also Ic o boke rede:
Wu he neweþ his guþhede
Hu he cumeþ ut of elde
Siþen hise limes arn unwelde
Siþen his bec is alto wrong
Siþen his fligt is al unstrong
And his egen dimme.
Hereþ wu he neweþ him:
A welle he sekeþ þat springeþ ai
Boþe bi nigt and bi dai
Þerouer he flegeþ and up he teþ
Til þat he þe heuene seþ
Þurg skies sexe and seuene
Til he cumeþ to heuene.
So rigt so he cunne
He houeþ in þe sunne.

Show I wish the eagle's nature
As I it in book read:
How he renews his youth
How he comes out of old age
When his limbs are weak
When his beak is completely twisted
When his flight is all weak
And his eyes dim.
Hear how he renews himself:
A spring he seeks that flows always
Both by night and by day
Thereover he flies and up he goes
Till that he the heaven sees
Through clouds six and seven
Till he comes to heaven.
As directly as he can
He hovers in the sun.

cont ...

Đe sunne swideþ al his fligt	The sun scorches all his wings
And oc it makeþ his egen brigt.	And also it makes his eyes bright.
His feþres fallen for þe hete	His feathers fall because of the heat
And he dun mide to þe wete.	And he down then to the water.
Falleþ in þat welle grund	Falls in the well bottom
Đer he wurdeþ heil and sund	Where he becomes hale and sound
And cumeþ ut al newe ...	And comes out all new ...

3.8 A note on ME spelling

When listing OE or ME words, only one representative spelling is usually given, but for many words there were many spellings, according to the time and the dialectal area in which the manuscript was copied. Examples can easily be found by looking in the *OED*. For example, the *OED* lists these spellings for *shield*, from OE to MnE:

scild – scyld – sceld
seld – sseld – sheld – cheld
scheld – sceild – scheeld – cheeld – schuld
scelde – schulde – schylde – shilde
schelde – sheeld
schield – childe – scheild – shild – shylde – sheelde
schielde – sheild – shield

4. Middle English I – Southern and Kentish dialects

4.1 The dialectal areas of ME

In OE, the evidence of the writings suggests that there were four main dialectal areas: West Saxon, Kentish, Mercian and Northumbrian. In ME, they remained roughly the same, except that the Mercian Midlands of England showed enough differences between the eastern and western parts for there to be two distinct dialects. So the five principal dialects of ME were: Southern, Kentish (the SE of England), East Midlands, West Midlands and Northern (see Map 4). The dialects of Northern English spoken in southern Scotland were known as *Inglis* until about 1500, when writers began to call it *Scottis*, present-day *Scots*.

Map 4. Middle English dialectal areas

In the ME period, there was no single dialect or variety of the language whose spelling, vocabulary and grammar were used for writing throughout the country – in other words, there was no Standard English. After the Norman Conquest, the language of the Norman ruling class was Northern French. The language of the English court in the twelfth century was Parisian French, which carried more prestige than Anglo-Norman and other varieties – remember Chaucer's ironical comment in the 1390s on the Prioress's French, learned in a nunnery in east London:

And Frenssh she spak ful faire and fetisly
After the scole of Stratford-at-the-Bowe ...

The language of instruction in English schools was French until the second half of the fourteenth century. John of Trevisa wrote in 1385:

For Iohan Cornwal, a mayster of gramere, chayngede þe lore in gramerscole and construccion of Freynsch into Englysch, so þat now, in al the gramerscoles of Engelond childern leueþ Frensch, and construeþ and lurneþ an Englysch ...

After 1362, English was used in the law courts and Parliament was opened in English, instead of French.

By the end of the fourteenth century, the educated language of London was beginning to become the standard form of writing throughout the country, although the establishment of a recognised Standard English was not completed for several centuries. In ME, there were only dialects, and writers or copyists used the forms of speech of their own region. Chaucer implied the lack of a standard and the diversity of forms of English at the end of his poem *Troilus and Criseyde*, written about 1385:

Go, litel bok, go, litel myn tragedye ...

And for ther is so gret diversite
In Englissh and in writyng of oure tonge,
So prey I God that non myswrite the,
Ne the mysmetre for defaute of tonge.

as did John of Trevisa, also in the same year: 'þer buþ also of so meny people longages and tonges' (see Text 29).

The following sections give some other examples of the 'diversity of tongues', taken from writings from different parts of the country in the ME period. They show some of the variations of spelling and form in the same words. Notice how there is inconsistency within a dialectal area, and even within the same manuscript sometimes. It is difficult to know whether some of the differences are simply variations in the spelling, or in the form and pronunciation of a word. As always, spelling tended to remain the same even though the pronunciation of a word had altered.

(WW translations follow each text. References are to text and line numbers in *Early Middle English Verse & Prose*, Bennett and Smithers, 1968.)

4.1.1 1st person singular pronoun (MnE *I*)

Also **Ic** it o boke rede (EMidl) XII.2
As **I** it in book read

Forr **Icc** amm sennd off heffness ærd (Orm, EMidl) XIII.81
For **I** am sent from heaven's land

Weste **Hic** hit miȝtte ben forholen (EMidl) VI.237
Knew **I** it might be hidden (= *If I knew* ...)

Gode þonk nou hit is þus
Þat **Ihc** am to Criste vend. (S) V.159
God thank now it is thus
That **I** am to Christ gone

'Darie,' he saide, '**Ich** worht ded
But **Ich** haue of þe help and red.'
'Leue child, ful wel **I** se
þat þou wilt to deþe te.' (EMidl) III.75
'Darie,' he said, '**I** were dead (= *shall die*)
Unless **I** have of thee help and advice.'
'Dear child, full well **I** see
That thou wilt to death draw.' (= *you will die*)

Certes for þi luf ham **Hi** spilt. (N) XV.22
Certainly for thy love am **I** spilt. (= *ruined*)

4.1.2 3rd person singular feminine pronoun (MnE *she*)

First group

For þan heom þuhte þat **heo** hadde
þe houle ouercome ... (SE late twelfth century) I.619
Therefore to-them (it) seemed that **she** had
The owl overcome ...

Ho was þe gladur uor þe rise (SE late twelfth century) I.19
She was the gladder for the branch

And in eche manere to alle guodnesse **heo** drouȝ (SW thirteenth century) VII.12
And in every way to all goodness **she** drew

He song so lude an so scharpe ... (SE late twelfth century) I.97
She sang so loud and so sharp ...

He wente him to þen inne
þer **hoe** wonede inne (EMidl) VI.19
He went (him) to the inn
Where **she** dwelled (in)

God wolde **hue** were myn! (WMidl) VIII.K.28
God grant **she** were mine!

... **ha** mei don wið Godd al þet **ha** eauer wule (WMidl) XVIII.74
... **she** may do with God all that **she** ever wishes

Nu ne dorste **hi** namore sigge, ure Lauedi; hac **hye** spac
to þo serganz þet seruede of þo wyne ... (Kentish thirteenth century) XVII.94
Now ne-dared **she** no more say, our Lady; but **she** spoke
to the servants that served (of) the wine ...

Second group

þo he seghȝ hit nas nowth ȝ**he** ... (EMidl thirteenth century) III.197
When he saw it ne-was not **she** ...

Leiȝande **sche** saide to Blaunchflour ... (EMidl thirteenth century) III.241
Laughing **she** said to Blaunchflour ...

She is my quene, Ich hire chalenge (SE early fourteenth century) II.61
She is my queen, I her claim

And te Lundenissce folc hire wolde tæcen and **scæ** fleh (*Peterborough Chronicle*, EMidl twelfth century) XVI.262
And the London(ish) folk her wished (to) take and **she** fled

Fro hir schalt þou or **scho** fro þe ... (N c.1300) XIV.60
From her shalt thou or **she** from thee ...

Hir luue **sco** haldes lele ilike (N c.1300) XIV.75
Hir love **she** holds true constantly

Yo hat mayden Malkyn Y wene (N) XV.47
She is called maiden Malkin I believe

Annd tær ȝ**ho** barr Allmahhtiȝ Godd (Orm, EMidl late twelfth century) XIII.49
And there **she** bore Almighty God

The variant spellings for *she* are evidence of a different evolution in different areas. Both the initial consonant and the vowel varied, and the development from OE *heo* might have been influenced by OE *seo* (feminine *the*, *that*).

Some early ME dialects, as a result of certain sound changes, had come to use the word *he* for three different pronouns, MnE *he*, *she* and *they* (OE *he*, *heo* and *hi*/*hie*), which seems very confusing and ambiguous to us. For example:

He ne shulde nouȝth þe kyng ysee ... (SE)
He was not allowed to see the king ...

He schal ben chosen quen wiȝ honur (EMidl)
She will be chosen queen with honour

Þanne **he** com þenne **he** were bliþe
For hom he brouhte fele siþe ... (EMidl)
When **he** came then **they** were glad
For to-them he brought many times ...

The borrowing of the ON plural pronouns beginning with <th> has already been discussed in Section 3.6.3. Where there was a large Scandinavian population, in the North, all three forms *they*, *them* and *their* replaced the older OE pronouns beginning with <h>. In the South, the OE forms remained for much longer. In the Midlands, *they* was used, but still with the object and possessive pronouns *hem* and *hire*.

The forms for *she* and *they* are therefore two of the clues which help to determine the dialect of a manuscript. The following section gives some examples of the variant forms for *they* and *them* in the dialects of ME.

4.1.3 3rd person plural pronouns (MnE *they, them*)

Hi holde plaiding suþe stronge ... (SE) I.12
They held debate very strongly ...

An alle **ho** þe driueþ honne ... (SE) I.66
And **they** all thee drive hence ...

Þat þi dweole-song **heo** ne forlere. (SE) I.558
That thy deceitful-song **they** (should) shun.

(*All three forms* ***hi***, ***ho*** *and* ***heo*** *in one manuscript*)

And **hie** answerden and seyde (Kentish) XVII.185
And **they** answered and said

Alle **he** arn off one mode (EMidl) XII.112
All **they** are of one mind

Nuste Ich under Criste whar **heo** bicumen weoren (WMidl) X.33
Ne-knew I under Christ where **they** come were
(= *I didn't know where they had gone on earth*)

Þo þat hit com to þe time
Þat **hoe** shulden arisen ine ... (S) V.263
When that it came to the time
That **they** should rise in ...

And bispeken hou **huy** miȝten best don þe luþere dede (SW) VII.38
And plotted how **they** might best do the wicked deed

... for na lickre ne beoþ **ha** (WMidl) XVIII.66
... for no more-like ne-are **they**

And þilke þat beþ maidenes clene
Þai mai **hem** wassche of þe rene. (EMidl) III.53
And the-same that be maidens pure
They may **them**(selves) wash in the stream.

For many god wymman haf **þai** don scam (N) XV.29
For (to) many good women have **they** done shame

A red **þei** taken hem bitwene (EMidl) IV.260
A plan **they** made them between

So **hem** charged þat wroþ þai were (EMidl) III.178
So **them** burdened that angry they were

And slæn **heom** alle clane ... (WMidl) X.64
And slain **them** all completely ...

Hii sende to Sir Maci þat he þun castel ȝolde
To **hom** and to þe baronie (SW) XI.27
They sent to Sir Maci that he the castle (should) yield
To **them** and to the barons

Godd walde o sum wise schawin **ham** to men (WMidl) XVIII.64
God wished in some way (to) show **them** to men

Þe pipins war don vnder his tung
Þar ras o **þam** thre wandes yong (N) XIV.281
The seeds were put under his tongue
There rose from **them** three young shoots

4.2 How to describe dialect differences

Dialects are varieties of a single language which are 'mutually comprehensible'; that is, speakers of different dialects can talk to and understand each other. An unfamiliar dialect may be difficult to understand at first because of its pronunciation or the use of unknown dialect words, but with familiarity, these difficulties disappear. This is not the case with a foreign language.

Dialects have most of their vocabulary and grammar in common; therefore, we can make a fairly short list of features to look for when describing the differences between dialects. Today, dialects are usually compared with Standard English. The story of the emergence of a standard language – a prestige dialect – which derived from the educated dialect of the London area, begins in the fifteenth century, and is described in later chapters. In medieval times, as we have seen, there was no national standard form of English, only local standards.

The texts that have been described in some detail so far suggest that the main linguistic features that mark ME dialectal differences are:

Spelling: The alphabetical symbols used and their relation to the contrasting sounds of the dialectal accent. We have to be careful not to assume that there is a one-to-one relation between sound and letter. Some differences of spelling in ME texts do not reflect differences of pronunciation, e.g., <i> <y>; <u> <v>; <ȝ> <gh>; <ss> <sch> <sh>; <þ> <th>; <hw> <wh> <qu> etc. Remember that spelling tends to be conservative and does not necessarily keep up with changed pronunciation.

Pronunciation (inferred from the spelling): Differences from OE and between dialects; for example:

(a) Has the OE long vowel /ɑ:/ shifted to /ɔ:/ or not? (See Commentary 3 of the *Text Commentary Book*, Section 3.1.)
(b) What vowel is used for the OE front rounded vowel /y/? For example, is MnE *hill* (from OE *hyll*) spelt *hill*, *hell* or *hull*? (See Commentary 3 of the *Text Commentary Book*, Section 3.5.4.)
(c) What vowels have developed from OE <eo>, <ea> and <æ>? (See Commentary 3 of the *Text Commentary Book*, Sections 3.5.2 and 3.5.3.)

Word forms – pronouns: What are the forms of personal pronouns? Have the ON 3rd person plural forms beginning with <th> been adopted? What is the feminine singular pronoun?

Word forms – inflections:
(a) On nouns: What suffixes are used to mark the plural?
(b) On verbs: What are the present tense suffixes, and the forms of past tense (strong or weak), past and present participles, and infinitive?
(c) What are the forms of the common verb *be*?

Grammar:
(a) Examine word order within the phrase and the clause.
(b) How are negatives and questions formed?
(c) Find constructions that are no longer used in MnE.

Vocabulary: Is the source of the words OE, ON, OF or another language, and in what proportion?

We can now use this list, or parts of it, to examine some ME texts which provide examples of the different dialects.

4.3 An example of a fourteenth century SW dialect

The following text, written in the 1380s by John of Trevisa, describes one man's view of the linguistic situation at that time. The complete work is a translation, with Trevisa's own additions, of a history called *Polychronicon*, written in Latin earlier in the century. John of Trevisa was vicar of Berkeley near Gloucester when he translated *Polychronicon*.

This work is a reminder to us of the historical origins of English and its dialects. Trevisa's attitude is not unlike that of some people today in his talk of the *apeyring* or *deterioration* of the language, but the reasons he gives are different. He blames it on the fashion for speaking French. He is writing in the SW dialect of ME, although his use of the dialect is said to be 'impure'. (*moreyn* is a reference to the Black Death of the 1340s.)

TEXT 29 – John of Trevisa on the English language in 1385 (i)

As hyt ys y-knowe houȝ meny maner people buþ in þis ylond þer buþ also of so meny people longages and tonges. Noþeles walschmen and scottes þat buþ noȝt ymelled wiþ oþer nacions holdeþ wel nyȝ here furste longage and speche ...

Also englischmen þeyȝ hy hadde fram þe bygynnyng þre maner speche souþeron norþeron and myddel speche in þe myddel of þe lond, as hy come of þre maner people of Germania, noþeles by commyxstion and mellyng furst wiþ danes and afterward wiþ normans in menye þe contray longage ys apeyred and some vseþ strange wlaffyng chyteryng harryng and garryng, grisbittyng.

> This apeyring of þe burþ tonge ys bycause of twey þinges – on ys for chyldern in scole aȝenes þe vsage and manere of al oþer nacions buþ compelled for to leue here oune longage and for to construe here lessons and here þinges a freynsch, and habbeþ suþthe þe normans come furst into engelond.
>
> Also gentil men children buþ ytauȝt for to speke freynsch fram tyme þat a buþ yrokked in here cradel and conneþ speke and playe wiþ a child hys brouch. And oplondysch men wol lykne hamsylf to gentil men and fondeþ wiþ gret bysynes for to speke freynsch for to be more ytold of ...
>
> Þys manere was moche y-used tofore þe furste moreyn and ys seþthe somdel y-chaunged ... now, þe ȝer of oure Lord a þousond þre hondred foure score and fyve, in al the gramerscoles of Engelond childern leueþ Frensch, and construeþ and lurneþ an Englysch ...
>
> Also gentil men habbeþ now moche yleft for to teche here childern frensch. Hyt semeþ a gret wondur houȝ englysch, þat ys þe burþ-tonge of englyschmen and here oune longage and tonge ys so dyvers of soun in þis ylond, and þe longage of normandy ys comlyng of anoþer lond and haþ on maner soun among al men þat spekeþ hyt aryȝt in engelond.

(*Fourteenth Century Verse & Prose*, Kenneth Sisam (ed.), OUP, 1921 – manuscript written c.1400. A version from another manuscript is given in Text 61, which illustrates the kinds of variation to be found in a different copy of a text.)

(The language of Text 29 is described in Commentary 7 of the *Text Commentary Book*.)

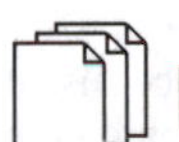

Activity 4.1

Rewrite Text 29 in MnE and identify some of the differences between this fourteenth century dialect and the earlier English that we have seen so far. (For vocabulary and derivation of words, use the word list in the *Word Book* or a dictionary.)

(i) Spelling: List some of the new combinations of letters and sounds.
(ii) Inflections: Do any suffixes remain from OE?
(iii) Grammar: Which constructions mark the text as ME and not MnE?
(iv) Vocabulary: What kinds of word have been taken into Trevisa's SW dialect of ME from other languages?

4.4 Grammar

Many of the contrasts between older and present-day English are matters of style rather than significant grammatical differences. We can read Trevisa's text without much difficulty, but it does not transcribe word for word into colloquial MnE. For example, the phrases *meny maner people* and *þre maner speche* today require the preposition *of*, hence *three varieties of speech*. In OE, the words for *people* and *speche* would have been in the genitive case, and the ME form has a similar construction (see Section 2.7.3).

The phrase *a child hys broche*, *a child's toy*, is a new construction for the possessive, which survived for some time but has now been lost. It does not derive from OE.

Infinitives that complement a main verb are marked by *for to*, as in *compelled* **for to leue** *... and* **for to construe** and *fondeþ wiþ gret bysynes* **for to speke** *frensch* **for to be** *more* **ytold of**. This construction is still used in some MnE dialects, but is now non-standard. Notice also that the last quotation is an example of a 'preposition at the end of a sentence', centuries before prescriptive grammarians ruled that the construction was ungrammatical.

Activity 4.2

Rewrite Text 30, which is a continuation of Trevisa's writing, in MnE and make a similar study of its linguistic features.

TEXT 30 – John of Trevisa on the English language in 1385 (ii)

... also of þe forseyde saxon tonge þat is deled a þre and ys abyde scarslych wiþ feaw vplondyschmen and ys gret wondur, for men of þe est wiþ men of þe west, as hyt were vnder þe same party of heuene, acordeþ more in sounyng of speche þan men of þe norþ wiþ men of þe souþ.

Þerfore hyt ys þat mercii, þat buþ men of myddel engelond, as hyt were parteners of þe endes, vndurstondeþ betre þe syde longages, norþeron and souþeron, þan norþeron and souþeron vndurstondeþ eyþer oþer.

Al þe longage of þe norþumbres and specialych at ȝork ys so scharp slyttyng and frotyng and vnschape þat we souþeron men may þat longage vnneþe vndurstonde. Y trowe þat þat ys bycause þat a buþ nyȝ to strange men and aliens þat spekeþ strangelych ...

4.5 A SE, or Kentish, dialect

The single manuscript of a book called *Ayenbite of Inwyt*, 'the remorse of conscience', is of great interest to students of language for two reasons. Firstly, its author and exact date are both written on the manuscript:

> Þis boc is Dan Michelis of Northgate, ywrite an English of his oȝene (= *own*) hand, þet hatte (= *is called*) Ayenbite of Inwyt; and is of the boc-house of Saynt Austines of Canterberi.
>
> Þis boc is uolueld (= *fulfilled, completed*) ine þe eue of þe holy apostles Symon an Iudas (= October 27) of ane broþer of the cloystre of Sauynt Austin of Canterberi, in the yeare of oure Lhordes beringe (= *birth*) 1340.

That is, Michael of Northgate, a monk of St Augustine's, Canterbury, finished the book, a translation from a French original, on October 27, 1340.

The second reason is that the book is spelled consistently, and so provides good evidence for the dialect of Kent at that time, as illustrated in the following extract.

Kentish dialect

Nou ich wille þet ye ywyte
Hou it is ywent
Þet þis boc is ywrite
Mid Englis of Kent.
Þis boc is ymad uor lewede men
Hem uor to berȝe uram alle
manyere zen

Now I wish that you know
How it is went
That this book is written
With English of Kent.
This book is made for lewd men
Them for to protect from all
manner sin

Now I want you to know
How it has come about
That this book has been written
In the English of Kent.
This book is made for common folk
To protect them from all
kinds of sin

Ayenbite of Inwyt is therefore unique in providing an example of a ME dialect in an original copy whose date, author and place of writing are exactly known. It is as close to a 'pure' dialect that we can get, remembering that the written form of language can never provide a really accurate account of how a dialect was spoken.

We finish this chapter with some short exemplary tales which illustrate the virtue of showing mercy and generosity.

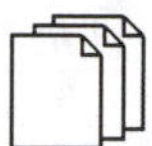

Activity 4.3

(i) Rewrite Text 31 in MnE.
(ii) Before reading the commentary on Text 31, examine the language under the headings provided in Section 4.2. Here are some questions to consider:
  (a) How far has the Kentish dialect of 1340 lost or changed the inflections of OE?
  (b) Which vowel seems to be more frequent in Kentish than in other ME dialects?
  (c) What can you say about the pronunciation of Kentish from the evidence of the spellings *uram*, *uor*, *þeruore*, *bevil*, *uol*, *zuo* and *mezeyse*?

TEXT 31 – *Ayenbite of Inwyt*, 1340 (i)

Kentish dialect

Efterward Saint Gregori telþ þet Saint Boniface uram þet he wes child he wes zuo
piteuous þet he yaf ofte his kertel and his sserte to þe poure uor God, þaȝ his
moder him byete ofte þeruore. Þanne bevil þet þet child yseȝ manie poure þet hedden
mezeyse. He aspide þet his moder nes naȝt þer. An haste he yarn to þe gerniere,
and al þet his moder hedde ygadered uor to pasi þet yer he hit yaf to þe poure. And
þo his moder com and wyste þe ilke dede, hy wes al out of hare wytte. Þet
child bed oure Lhorde, and þet gernier wes an haste al uol.

Afterward Saint Gregory tells that Saint Boniface from that he was child he was so piteous that he gave often his coat and his shirt to the poor for God, though his mother him beat often therefore. Then befell that the child saw many poor that had suffering. He espied that his mother ne-was not there. In haste he ran to the granary, and all that his mother had gathered for to last the year he it gave to the poor. And when his mother came and learned the same deed, she was all out of her wit. The child prayed our Lord, and the granary was in haste all full.

4.5.1 Commentary on Text 31

Grammar

The common basic structures of MnE were present in OE, so it is not surprising that the grammar of ME causes us few problems in conveying meaning. However, as we read older English, we come across phrases and combinations of words that are definitely 'old-fashioned', and which we would not use today. Sometimes the order of words is no longer acceptable; sometimes words appear to be missing, or to be superfluous when compared with English today; sometimes particular combinations of words are no longer used. In addition, as Michael of Northgate was translating from French, it is possible that some constructions are not genuine ME, so we can observe differences, but not draw any firm conclusions from them. The following examples illustrate these points.

uram þet he wes child — from that he was child

MnE requires *from when* or *from the time that*, and the addition of a determiner in the NP, e.g., *a child*.

he yaf ofte his kertel	he gave often his coat

The adverb *often* in MnE either precedes the verb, *he often gave*, or follows the object, *he gave his coat often*.

his moder him byete ofte	his mother him beat often
he hit yaf to þe poure	he it gave to the poor

The direct object, *him* or *it*, now follows the verb in MnE: *his mother beat him often* and *he gave it to the poor*.

þanne bevil þet	then befell that

A MnE clause must contain a subject; here the 'dummy subject' *it* would be used, hence *then it befell that*.

þet hedden mezeyse	that had suffering

This is perhaps not ungrammatical in MnE, but it is a phrase that would sound strange.

his moder nes naȝt þer	his mother ne was not there

The OE negative *ne* preceded the verb, as in *ne wæs*, *was not*. The emphatic *noȝt, naȝt* came to be used to reinforce the negative (it did not make it positive). In ME, the multiple negative form with *ne* before and *noȝt*, or another negative word like *never*, after the verb was commonly used. In time, the older *ne* was dropped, particularly in Standard English when it developed later, although the use of the multiple negative is still very common in most spoken dialects of English today.

for to pasi þet yer	(in order) to last the year

The phrase *for to* in a structure like *I want for to go* is found in all ME texts, but is no longer Standard English, although it is still used in some dialects (see Section 4.4).

Word structure

A short text may not contain a sufficient variety of word forms to enable us to come to any conclusions about the range of inflections. For example, there are no plural nouns in this text, so we cannot observe whether the *-es* or *-en* plurals were used. But the NP *þet gernier* shows the use of the older neuter OE pronoun *þæt* for MnE *the*, while the PrepP *to þe gerniere* has a dative case inflection *-e* on the noun but the common form *þe* for the determiner. The NP *oure Lhorde* also has the inflection *-e* on the noun to mark the dative case after *to*, *to our Lord*.

There are no adjectives apart from possessive pronouns like *his* and *oure*, so there is no evidence here of the survival of inflections on adjectives.

There is only one example of a present tense verb, *telþ*, with the 3rd person singular inflection *-(e)þ*. The past participle *ygadered* retains the prefix *y-*, from the OE *ge-*.

The newer pronouns *she*, *they*, *them* and *their* are not used.

Even these limited observations suggest that Kentish was a conservative dialect; that is, when compared to other dialects it has retained more features of the OE system of inflections, even though greatly reduced. These features are very similar to those of South Western texts, and can be compared with John of Trevisa's. This fact is not surprising when we consider the geographical position of Kent, relatively cut off and distant from the Midlands and the North of England, but accessible to the rest of the South.

Pronunciation and spelling

The vowel <e> is much in evidence in Kentish texts, partly from the pronunciation of the vowel in words derived from OE words with /æ/, like *þet* (*þæt*), *wes* (*wæs*), *hedden* (*hæfdon*), *þer* (*þær*), *dede* (*dæde*) and *bed* (*bæd*), and partly from the shift of OE /y/ to /e/ (see Commentary 3 of the *Text Commentary Book*, Section 3.5.4), like *kertel*, *sserte* from OE *cyrtel*, *scyrte*.

The following spellings:

Kentish:	uram	uor	þeruore	bevil	uol	zuo	mezeyse
MnE:	from	for	therefore	befell	full	so	misease

suggest that the consonants pronounced /f/ and /s/ in other dialects were 'voiced' at the beginning of a word or root syllable in Kentish, and pronounced /v/ and /z/. This **initial voicing** of **fricative consonants** is still a feature of SW dialects in Devon, Somerset, Dorset, Somerset, Wiltshire and Hampshire, although no longer in Kent (see *A Structural Atlas of the English Dialects*, P. M. Anderson, 1987, pp. 141–3). This is probably also the case for the consonant /θ/, both in Kentish and ME, but it has never been recorded in spelling, because the letters <þ> or <th> are used for both the voiced and voiceless forms of the consonant, as in *thin* and *then*.

Activity 4.4

(i) Write a version of Text 32 in MnE.

(ii) Using the word list in the *Word Book* or a dictionary, write a commentary on the evidence for changes in pronunciation, word form and grammar from OE, and of any special characteristics of the Kentish dialect in the fourteenth century.

TEXT 32 – *Ayenbyte of Inwyt*, 1340 (ii)

Kentish dialect

Efterward þer wes a poure man, ase me zayþ, þet hedde ane cou; and yherde zigge of his preste ine his prechinge þet God zede ine his spelle þet God wolde yelde an hondreduald al þet me yeaue uor him. Þe guode man, mid þe rede of his wyue, yeaf his cou to his preste, þet wes riche. Þe prest his nom bleþeliche, and hise zente to þe oþren þet he hedde. Þo hit com to euen, þe guode mannes cou com hom to his house ase hi wes ywoned, and ledde mid hare alle þe prestes ken, al to an hondred. Þo þe guode man ysez þet, he þoȝte þet þet wes þet word of þe Godspelle þet he hedde yyolde; and him hi weren yloked beuore his bissoppe aye þane prest. Þise uorbisne ssseweþ wel þet merci is guod chapuare, uor hi deþ wexe þe timliche guodes.

Afterward there was a poor man, as one says, that had a cow; and heard say from his priest in his preaching that God said in his gospel that God would yield a hundredfold all that one gave for him. The good man, with the advice of his wife, gave his cow to his priest, that was rich. The priest her took blithely, and her sent to the others that he had. When it came to evening, the good man's cow came home to his house as she was accustomed, and led with her all the priest's kine, all to a hundred. When the good man saw that, he thought that that was the word of the Gospel that to-him* had restored (them); and to-him they were adjudged before his bishop against the priest. These examples show well that mercy is good trading, for it does increase the temporal goods.

* The obscure English is the result of a mis-translation of the French original.

(The French original of the text can be found in *Fourteenth Century Verse & Prose*, Kenneth Sisam (ed.), 1921, p. 213)

Activity 4.5

Text 21 by Robert of Gloucester was written about 1300. Use the text and the word list in the *Word Book* or a dictionary to see whether you can find evidence for any of the following features of the Southern dialect of ME:

(i) The rounding of OE /ɑ:/ to /ɔ:/; that is, OE words spelt with <a> now spelt with <o>.
(ii) OE <y> now spelt with <u>, although retaining the same sound.
(iii) OE <eo> now spelt <o>; the diphthong has 'smoothed' and become a single vowel.
(iv) Verb forms:
  (a) Present tense plural and 3rd person singular: <-eþ>
  (b) Present participle: <-inde>.
  (c) Past participle begins with <i-> and has lost its final <-n>.
  (d) Infinitive has lost its final <-n>.
(v) /f/ at the beginning of a syllable is voiced /v/.
(vi) 3rd person pronoun forms still begin with <h->.

The Kentish dialect, although similar in its features to other Southern dialects, was distinctive because two other OE vowels happened to fall together with the vowel spelt <e>. The OE vowels were <eo> and <y> (see Commentary 3 of the *Text Commentary Book*, Sections 3.4.3 and 3.4.4). This made the vowel <e> much more frequent in Kentish than in other dialects.

5. Middle English II – Northern dialects

The Northern dialects of ME came from the Northumbrian dialects of OE. The present-day dialects of Scotland and the North of England are still markedly distinct from Standard English and other dialects in features of the grammar and vocabulary, and from RP and Southern accents in pronunciation.

John of Trevisa's comments in the fourteenth century on the Northumbrian dialect at York (see Text 30) as 'scharp slyttyng and frotyng and unschape' can no doubt also be heard today (although in different words that convey the same meaning) in the South, say, where people are unfamiliar with accents like Geordie, Glaswegian or rural North Yorkshire. Equally, Northern speakers may make similar disparaging remarks about Southern speech. Our reaction to other dialects and accents is, of course, dependent upon our familiarity with them. One person's 'thick accent' is another's familiar speech, and beauty is in the ear of the listener rather than in any objective standard.

But as we cannot reproduce the actual sound of the dialects of the past, we cannot follow up this aspect of language study. The only evidence we have of the language at that time is in the form of manuscripts, so we have to speculate about pronunciation in the abstract, recognising some of the main changes but not properly hearing them. Most of our attention therefore has to be on vocabulary and grammar.

5.1 A fourteenth century Scots English dialect

The *Bruce* is a verse chronicle of the life and heroic deeds of Robert Bruce (1274–1329), written by John Barbour in about 1375 – *The Actes and Life of the Most Victorious Conqueror, Robert Bruce King of Scotland*. Barbour was Archdeacon of Aberdeen and had studied and taught at Oxford and Paris. The following extract comes from Book I.

TEXT 33 – John Barbour on freedom, *Bruce*, c.1375 (i)

Northern (Scots) dialect

A fredome is a noble thing
Fredome mays man to haiff liking
Fredome all solace to man giffis
He levys at es yat frely levys
A noble hart may haiff nane es
Na ellys nocht yat may him ples

cont ...

Gyff fredome failʒhe, for fre liking
Is ʒharnyt our all oyer thing.
Na he yat ay has levyt fre
May nacht knaw weill the propyrte
Ye angyr na ye wrechyt dome
Yat is cowplyt to foule thyrldome
Bot gyff he had assayit it.

(*Scottish Text Soc*, Vol. II, M. P. McDiarmid and J. A. C. Stevenson (eds), 1980, Book I, ff. 225)

Once you have deciphered some unusual spellings, you will find that this Northern Scots dialect is much closer to MnE than Southern dialects of England. That is, the loss of the inflections of OE is almost complete, and has gone as far as it will go. We can rewrite the text in present-day standard spelling, and it reads more or less like MnE.

Ah freedom is a noble thing
Freedom makes man to have liking (= *free choice*)
Freedom all solace to man gives
He lives at ease that freely lives
A noble heart may have no ease
Nor else nought that may him please
If freedom fails, for free liking
Is yearned over all other thing.
Nor he that aye has lived free
May not know well the property
The anger nor the wretched doom
That is coupled to foul thraldom
But if (= *unless*) he had assayed it.

5.1.1 Commentary on Text 33

The text is too short to illustrate more than a few features of this dialect, but it is at an 'advanced' stage in its loss of the inflectional system of OE.

Vocabulary

The derivation of the vocabulary can be found in the word list in the *Word Book* for this text. In a Northern dialect, we would expect to find words derived from ON, but the text contains only two, *angyr* and *ay*, as against seven from OF. Barbour was a scholar writing a literary romance, so it is not surprising that he used words like *propyrte* and *solace*.

Spelling and pronunciation

The metre of the verse is regular: an eight-syllable line rhyming in couplets. If you compare some of Chaucer's contemporary verses, you will notice that many of Chaucer's words end in a final <e>, some of which have to be pronounced to fit the metre of the verse, and some not. Perhaps this is what Chaucer was referring to when he hoped that no one would 'mysmetre' his verse (see Section 4.1). For example, the final <e> is pronounced in these lines from *The Book of the Duchess* as indicated:

For /nature /wold-**e** /nat suf/fys-**e**
/To noon /erthly /crea/ture
Nat /long-**e** /tym-**e** /to en/dure
Wi/thout-**e** /slep and /be in /sorw-**e**.

But as already indicated it is not always pronounced, and it is always elided when it precedes a word beginning with a vowel, so that none of the final <e> spellings are pronounced in the following lines:

/Purely /for de/faut(**e**) of /slep
That /by my /trouth(**e**) I /tak(**e**) no /kep ...

/Pass(**e**) we /over /untill /eft;
That /wil not /be mot /ned(**e**) be /left.

The pronunciation of the final <e> was all that was left of many of the former OE suffix inflections, and the fact that Chaucer could choose whether or not to pronounce them suggests that there was still variation between speakers.

In Barbour's verse, there is scarcely any evidence even of this remnant of the OE inflectional system (see also Text 34).

<ei> <ai> – Scots writers had adopted the convention of using <i> as a diacritic letter to mark a long vowel. In *haiff*, the <ai> represents /a:/; in *weill*, the <ei> is /e:/. Not all uses of <i> following a vowel mark this feature, however. In *failȝhe*, <ai> marks the diphthong derived from OF *faillir*; similarly, the pronoun *thai*.

<ȝh> – is written for <ȝ>, representing the consonant /j/, as in *failȝhe*, /faɪljə/, and *ȝharnyt*, /jarnɪt/.

<ch> – is written for <ȝ> or <gh> used in other dialectal areas for the sound /x/, as in *nocht*, as well as for the /tʃ/ in *wrechyt*.

<ff> – these doubled letters probably indicate unvoiced final consonants in *haiff* and *gyff*.

<y> – is used for <th> (from OE <þ>) in some function words like *the* and *that*, as well as an alternative for <i>.

Word forms and inflections

Nouns

None of the nouns is plural, but evidence of the plural inflection can be found in Text 34. The *-ing* suffix on *liking* marks a noun which derives from a verb, sometimes called a **gerund**.

Verbs

The infinitive has no inflection, as in *haiff*, *knaw* and *pless*. Present tense: the 3rd person singular inflection is spelt <is> or <ys>, as in *giffis* and *levys*. Other verbs have only /s/, as in *has* and *mays*. Past participle: this is spelt <yt>, as in *ȝharnyt*, *levyt* and *cowplyt*, and the OE prefix *ge-* has been lost.

Grammar

The word order of verse is often more marked and less normal than that of prose, as in *Fredome all solace to man giffis*, in which the direct object *all solace* and adverbial *to man* precede the verb, and so cannot be good evidence of normal spoken usage.

The relative pronoun is *that*, as in MnE, but spelt *yat*.

Activity 5.1

(i) Write a version of Text 34 in MnE.
(ii) See if any of the following linguistic features of the Northern dialect of ME are to be found in the text:
 (a) Vocabulary: comment on the OE, ON and OF words.
 (b) Words retaining the OE long vowel /ɑ:/.
 (c) Spelling words with <i> as a diacritic for a long vowel.
 (d) Spelling <s> for /ʃ/.
 (e) Spelling <quh> for OE <hw>.
 (f) Present participle inflection of verbs <-and>.
 (g) Past tense 3rd person singular/plural inflection of weak verbs <-it>.
 (h) Past participle inflection of verbs <-it> (or <-yt>).
 (i) Plural inflection of nouns <-is> or <-ys>.
 (j) ON form of 3rd person plural pronouns beginning with <th->.

TEXT 34 – John Barbour on the siege of Berwick, *Bruce*, c.1375 (ii)

Northern (Scots) dialect

Engynys alsua for to cast
Yai ordanyt & maid redy fast
And set ilk man syne till his ward.
And schyr Walter ye gud steward
With armyt men suld rid about
And se quhar yat yar war mast dout
And succour yar with his menȝe.
And quhen yai in sic degre
Had maid yaim for defending
On ye Rud Ewyn in ye dawing
Ye Inglis ost blew till assail.
Yan mycht men with ser apparaill
Se yat gret ost cum sturdely
Ye toun enweround yai in hy
And assailyt with sua gret will
For all yar mycht yai set yartill
Yat thaim pressyt fast on ye toun.
Bot yai yat gan yaim abandoun
To dede or yan to woundis sar
Sa weill has yaim defendit yar
Yat leddrys to ye ground yai slang
And with stanys sa fast yai dan
Yar fayis yat fele yar left liand
Sum dede sum hurt and sum swonand.

WW

Machines also for to throw
They ordained (= *set up*) & made ready fast
And set each man next to his post.
And Sir Walter the good Stewart
With armed men should (= *had to*) ride about
And see where that there was most doubt
And succour (= *bring help*) there with his company.
And when they in such state
Had made them (= *themselves*) for defending
On the Rood Even (= *Eve of the Feast of the Exaltation of the Cross,* September 13) in the daybreak
The English host blew to attack.
Then might men with various gear
See that great host come resolutely
The town surrounded they in haste
And attacked with so great will
For all their might they set thereto
Yet them advanced fast on the town.
But they that had them resigned
To death or else to wounds sore
So well them (= *themselves*) defended there
That ladders to the ground they slung
And with stones so fast they struck
Their foes that many there stayed lying
Some dead some hurt and some swooning.

(*Scottish Text Soc*, Vol. II, M. P. McDiarmid and J. A. C. Stevenson (eds), 1980, Book XVII, ff. 625)

5.2 Another Northern dialect – York

The York 'mystery plays' consist of a cycle of 50 short episodes which tell the story of the world according to medieval Christian tradition, from the Fall of the Angels and the Creation to the Last Judgement. Each trade gild of the city was responsible for the costs and production of a play, which was performed in procession on a pageant-wagon in the streets of York. Some of the plays were obviously assigned to a gild whose occupation was reflected in the story. For example, the bakers played The Last Supper, the shipwrights The Building of the Ark, the fishers and mariners The Flood, and the vintners The Marriage at Cana.

The cycle was produced each year at the feast of Corpus Christi, from the late fourteenth century into the early sixteenth century. Twelve 'stations' were set up in the streets and each pageant-wagon moved in procession from one station to another to perform its play. The procession of wagons began at 4.30 am and the last play was probably finished after midnight. Banners were set up to mark the positions of the stations and a proclamation was made.

TEXT 35 – The York proclamation for the Corpus Christi plays, 1415

Oiez &c. We comand of þe kynges behalue and þe mair & þe shirefs of þis Citee þat no man go armed in þis Citee with swerdes, ne with carlill axes, ne none othir defences in distourbaunce of þe kynges pees & þe play, or hynderyng of þe processioun of Corpore Christi; and þat þai leue þare hernas in þare ines, saufand knyghtes and squwyers of wirship þat awe haue swerdes borne aftir þame, of payne of forfaiture of þaire wapen & inprisonment of þaire bodys. And þat men þat brynges furth pacentes, þat þai play at the places þat is assigned þerfore, and nowere elles, of the payne of forfaiture to be raysed þat is ordayned þerfore, þat is to say xl s ... And þat all maner of craftmen þat bryngeth furthe ther pageantez in order & course be good players, well arayed & openly spekyng, vpon payn of lesing of c s., to be paid to the chambre withoute any pardon. And that euery player that shall play be redy in his pagiaunt at convenyant tyme, that is to say at the mydhowre betwix iiijth & vth of the cloke in the mornyng, & then all oþer pageantes fast folowyng ilkon after oþer as þer course is, without tarieing ...

(*The York Plays*, Richard Beadle (ed.), Edward Arnold, 1982)

Activity 5.2

(i) Write a version of the proclamation in MnE.
(ii) Discuss the language and style of the proclamation:
  (a) The different functions of the word *þat*.
  (b) Verb inflections.
  (c) Noun inflections.
  (d) Forms of personal pronoun.
  (e) The sources of the vocabulary – OE, ON or OF (see the word list in the *Word Book* or use a dictionary).
  (f) Spelling.

The only copy of *The York Plays* to survive was written about 1470, and this was originally the property of the corporation of the city. It was probably compiled from the various prompt copies belonging to each gild that performed a play, and so the language may therefore be that of the earlier part of the fifteenth century.

The dialect is Northern, but the scribes introduced a lot of modifications from the East Midlands dialect, the evidence for which is in the variations of spelling of the same words. The use of some East Midlands forms is evidence of the beginning of a standardised system of spelling.

The plays are written in a variety of verse stanza patterns, with both rhyme and alliteration, so that they cannot be read as natural everyday speech, in spite of the liveliness of the dialogue. The following extract is from the potters' 'Pentecost Play', which retells the story of the coming of the Holy Spirit at Pentecost, or Whitsuntide, after the Ascension of Christ. It fills out the story in the Acts of the Apostles, Chapter 2. The play does not attempt to portray the actual coming of the Spirit as it is told in the Bible.

> While the day of Pentecost was running its course they were all together in one place, when suddenly there came from the sky a noise like that of a strong driving wind, which filled the whole house where they were sitting. And there appeared to them tongues like flames of fire, dispersed among them and resting on each one. And they were all filled with the Holy Spirit and began to talk in other tongues, as the Spirit gave them the power of utterance.
>
> (*The New English Bible*, 1961)

The following four stanzas of the play span the coming of the Spirit, which is represented by the singing of the ancient hymn *Veni Creator Spiritus* (*Come Creator Spirit*). Two 'doctors' speak contemptuously of the claim of the apostles that Jesus was alive again. After the hymn, Mary and Peter celebrate the coming of the Holy Spirit.

TEXT 36 – The York potters' 'Pentecost Play', c.1470

I doctor

Harke maistir for mahoundes peyne
Howe þat þes mobbardis maddis nowe
Þer maistir þat oure men haue slayne
Hase garte þame on his trifullis trowe

II doctor

Þe lurdayne sais he leffis agayne
Þat mater may þei neuere avowe
For as þei herde his prechyng pleyne
He was away þai wiste noȝt howe

I doctor

They wiste noght whenne he wente
Þerfore fully þei faile
And sais þam schall be sente
Grete helpe thurgh his counsaille

II doctor

He myghte nowdir sende clothe nor clowte
He was neuere but a wrecche alway
But samme oure men and make a schowte
So schall we beste yone foolis flaye

I doctor

Nay nay þan will þei dye for doute
I rede we make noȝt mekill dray
But warly wayte when þai come oute
And marre þame þanne if þat we may

II doctor

Now certis I assente þer tille
Yitt wolde I noght þei wiste
Ȝone carles þan schall we kill
But þei liffe als vs liste

Angelus tunc cantare veni creator spiritus
Angel then to sing Come Creator Spirit

Honnoure and blisse be euer nowe — Maria
With worschippe in þis worlde alwaye
To my souerayne sone Ihu (Jesu)
Oure lorde allone þat laste schall ay
Nowe may we triste his talis ar trewe

cont ...

ius Doctor

Harke maistir for mahoundes peyne
Howe þat þes mobbardis maddis nowe
þer maistir þat oure men haue slayne
Hase started þame on his trifullis trowe

ijus Doctor

þe lurdayne sais he leffis agayne
þat water may þei neuer avowe
For as þei herde his prechyng pleyne
He was away þei wiste nozt howe

ius Doctor

They wiste nozt whenne he wente
þerfore fully þei faile
And sais þam shall he sente
Grete helpe thurgh his counsaille

ijus Doctor

He myzthe nowdir sende clothe nor clowte
He was neuer but a wrecche alway
But samme oure men and make a schowte
So shall we beste yone foolis flaye

ius Doctor

Nay nay þan will þei dye for doute
I rede we make nozt mekill dray
But warly wayte when þei come oute
And marre þame þanne if þat we may

ijus Doctor

Now certis I assente þer tille
Yitt wolde I nozt þei wiste
Yone carles þan shall we kill
But þei liffe als vs liste

Angelus tunc cantare

Honnoure and blisse be euer nowe
With worschippe in þis worlde alwaye
To my souerayne sone and þe
Oure lorde allone þat laste shall ay
Nowe may we triste his talis ar trewe

cont ...

Be dedis þat here is done þis day
Als lange as ȝe his pase pursue
Þe fende ne (= *he*) fendis yow for to flay
For his high hali gaste
He lattis here on ȝou lende
Mirthis and trewthe to taste
And all misse to amende

____________________________________Petrus

All mys to mende nowe haue we myght
Þis is the mirthe oure maistir of mente
I myght noȝt loke, so was it light
A loued be þat lorde þat itt vs lente
Nowe hase he holden þat he vs highte
His holy goste here haue we hente
Like to þe sonne itt semed in sight
And sodenly þanne was itt sente

____________________________________II Apostolus

Hitt was sente for oure sele
Hitt giffis vs happe and hele
Me thynke slike forse I fele
I myght felle folke full feel

(*The York Plays*, Leeds Medieval Drama Facsimiles)

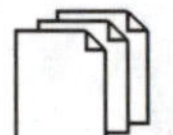

Activity 5.3

(i) Use the word list in the *Word Book* to write a MnE version of the text.
(ii) Examine and explain the metre, the rhyme scheme and the alliteration.
(iii) Make a study of the language of the text in comparison with MnE, with reference to:
  (a) Spelling and probable pronunciation.
  (b) Word forms and inflections of nouns and verbs.
  (c) Sources of vocabulary.
  (d) Grammar.
(iv) Examine the forms of personal pronoun. Why are they evidence of the Northern dialect?
(v) Are the final <e> spellings still pronounced as inflections? Use your reading of the poetic metre of the text as evidence.

5.3 Northern and Midlands dialects compared

John de Thoresby became Archbishop of York in 1352. He found many of his parish priests ignorant and neglectful of their duties, and as one remedy for this he wrote a 'Catechism' in Latin, setting out the basic doctrines of the faith. It was translated into English by a monk of St Mary's Abbey in York in 1357. This version is called *The Lay Folk's Catechism*. An extended version was written a little later by John Wyclif. He had been born in the North Riding of Yorkshire, but because he had lived and worked for a long time in Oxford and Leicestershire, his writings were in a variety of the Midlands dialect. By comparing the two versions of Archbishop Thoresby's 'Catechism', we can therefore clearly see some of the differences between the dialects of the North and the Midlands.

The dedis þat here is done þis day
Als saunȝe as ȝe þis pase present
þe fende ne fendis ȝow for to flay
ffor his hyght halynyste
He lattis here on ȝon lende
Mirthis and trewthe to triste
And all misse to amende

Petrus.

All mys to mende nowe haue we myght
þis is þe mirthe oure maistir of mente
Myght ne noȝt loke, so was it light
A loued be þat lorde þat itt vs lente
Now hase he holden þat he vs highte
His holy goste here haue we hente
Like to þe sonne itt semed in sight
And sodenly þanne was itt sente

i apostolus.

Hitt was sente for oure sele
Hitt giffis vs happe and hele
Me thynke slike forse I fele
I myght felle folke full feele

Activity 5.4

(i) Compare the following short extracts from *The Lay Folk's Catechism* and list the differences that mark them as different dialects.

(ii) Which of them is closer to MnE in its word forms? (For typical markers of ME Northern dialects see Activity 5.1. The verbs *are* and *ware* from the verb *be* are derived from ON.)

TEXT 37 – *The Lay Folks' Catechism*, 1357

This er the sex thinges that I have spoken of,
That the lawe of halikirk lies mast in
That ye er al halden to knawe and to kun (= *to learn*),
If ye sal knawe god almighten and cum un to his blisse:
And for to gif yhou better will for to kun tham,
Our fadir the ercebisshop grauntes of his grace
Fourti daies of pardon til al that kunnes tham,
Or dos their gode diligence for to kun tham ...
For if ye kunnandly (= *clearly*) knaw this ilk sex thinges
Thurgh thaim sal ye kun knawe god almighten,
Wham, als saint Iohn saies in his godspel,
Conandly for to knawe swilk (= *such*) als he is,
It is endles life and lastand bliss,
To whilk (= *which*) blisse he bring us that bought us. amen

TEXT 38 – John Wyclif's version of *The Lay Folks' Catechism*, c.1360

These be þe sexe thyngys þat y haue spokyn of
þat þe law of holy chirche lys most yn.
þat þey be holde to know and to kunne;
yf þey schal knowe god almyȝty and come to þe blysse of heuyn.
And for to ȝeue ȝow þe better wyl for to cunne ham.
Our Fadyr þe archiepischop grauntys of hys grace.
Forty dayes of Pardoun. to alle þat cunne hem and rehercys hem ...
For yf ȝe cunnyngly knowe þese sexe thyngys;
þorwȝ hem ȝe schull knowe god almyȝty.
And as seynt Ion seyþ in hys gospel.
Kunnyngly to know god almyȝty
ys endles lyf. and lastynge blysse.
He bryngge vs þerto. þat bowȝt vs
With hys herte blod on þe cros Crist Iesu. Amen.

(*The Lay Folks' Catechism*, T. F. Simmons and H. E. Nolloth (eds), EETS OS 118, 1901)

5.4 Chaucer and the Northern dialect

Chaucer's *The Reeve's Tale* features two undergraduate characters, 'yonge poure scolers':

Iohn highte that oon and Aleyn highte that oother
Of oon town were they born that highte Strother
Fer in the north, I kan noght telle where.

Chaucer makes their northern origins clear by marking their speech with some of the features that his readers would recognise. He wrote in the educated London dialect (see Chapter 7), which differed from the Northern dialect in its grammar and pronunciation. Here is an extract from the tale. The northern words are printed in bold type. Aleyn and Iohn have come to a mill and greet Symkyn, the miller. They intend to supervise the grinding of their corn, as millers were notorious for cheating their customers.

TEXT 39 – Chaucer's *The Reeve's Tale*

Aleyn spak first: Al hayl Symkyn in faith
How **fares** thy faire doghter and thy wyf?
Aleyn welcome, quod Symkyn, by my lyf
And Iohn also. How now what do ye here?
By god, quod Iohn, Symond, nede has **na** peere.
Hym **bihoues** serue hymself that has **na** swayn
Or ellis he is a fool, as clerkes sayn.
Oure maunciple, I **hope** he wol be deed,
Swa werkes ay the **wanges** in his heed.
And therfore **is** I come and eek Alayn
To grynde oure corn and carie it **heem** agayn ...

It **sal** be doon, quod Symkyn, by my fay.
What wol ye doon whil that it is in hande? ...

By god, right by the hopper wol I stande,
Quod Iohn, and se how the corn **gas** in.
Yet saw I neuere by my fader kyn
How that the hoper **wagges til** and **fra** ...

Aleyn answerde: Iohn, wiltow **swa**?
Thanne wil I be byneth by my crown
And se how that the mele **falles** down
Into the trogh. That **sal** be my desport.
For, Iohn, in faith I may been of youre sort,
I **is** as **ille** a millere as **ar** ye.

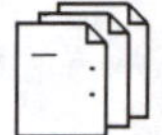

Activity 5.5

Refer to the list of northern features in Activity 5.1 and identify them in Text 39. Some are marked for pronunciation and some for different inflections. There are also some dialectal differences of meaning, as listed in the following table.

Text 39	Source	MnE
ar	OE Northern arun	are
falles	OE feallan	falls
fares	OE faran	fares
fra	ON fra	fro
gas	OE gan	goes
heem	OE ham	home
hope	OE hopian	hope = believe
hym bihoues	OE behofian	him behoves = he must
ille	ON illr	ill = bad
is	OE is	is
na	OE nan	no
sal	OE sceal	shall
swa	OE swa	so
swayn	ON sveinn	swain = servant
til	ON til	till = to
wagges	OE wagian	wags
werkes	OE wyrcan	works = aches
wanges	OE wang	wangs = back teeth

This is only part of the dialogue between the miller and the two 'clerkes'. Other words that give away their dialect are:

alswa	OE alswa	also
banes	OE ban	bones
bathe	ON baþir	both
fonne	?	fon = fool
ga/gane	OE gan	go/gone
il-hail	ON illr ON heill	ill health = bad luck
lang	OE lang ON langr	long
naan	OE nan (ne + an)	none
ra	OE ra ON ra	roe (deer)
sang	OE sang	song
saule	OE sawol	soul
waat	OE wat *fr.* witan	wist = knows
wha	OE hwa	who

6. Middle English III – West Midlands dialects

In the Anglo-Saxon invasion and settlement of Britain, the Angles occupied the Midlands, the North of England and what is now southern Scotland. The general term Anglian is used to describe their dialect of OE, but its northern and southern varieties were different enough for two dialects to be recognised: Northumbrian (north of the river Humber) and Mercian (south of the Humber).

During the ME period, the Mercian (Midlands) dialect developed in different ways. The East Midlands was part of the Danelaw (see Section 2.3), but the West Midlands was not, so the language of the East Midlands changed partly under the influence of the Danish Old Norse speakers who settled there. As a result, OE Mercian became two ME dialects: East Midlands and West Midlands.

Within what we call a dialect, there are always other variations, so that the more closely we examine the speech or writing of a dialectal area, the more differences we observe, until we arrive at the concept of an individual person's own variety of language, an **idiolect**.

The two texts that have been chosen to illustrate the West Midlands dialect are sufficiently similar to be called the 'same dialect'; however, they show differences which have led scholars to place one in the north and the other in the south of the West Midlands.

6.1 A NW Midlands dialect

Sir Gawayn and þe Grene Knyȝt is a romance in alliterative verse which tells a story of the legendary court of King Arthur. The one surviving manuscript was probably written towards the end of the fourteenth century, and scholars are agreed that the dialect is that of Cheshire or south Lancashire. The author's name is not known.

6.1.1 A note on the use of the letter <ȝ> in the poem

We think of MnE spelling as being irregular and inconsistent in the relationship of letters to sounds. This, however, began long before modern times, and the manuscript of *Sir Gawayn and þe Grene Knyȝt* provides a good example of the use of a single letter to represent several different sounds.

The letter <ȝ> was used in this poem to represent several sounds because it had developed from two sources; firstly, from the OE letter <ȝ> (see Section 2.2.4) and, secondly, as a form of letter <z>. It was therefore used for all the following sounds (the words are from Texts 40 and 41).

/j/ – for example, yȝe-lyddeȝ, *eye-lids*; ȝederly, *promptly*; ȝolden, *yielded*; ȝeres, *years*; ȝet, *yet*. We use <y> in MnE.

/ç/ – similar to the sound in German *ich*, /iç/, and usually followed by /t/ in <ȝt>: for example, knyȝt, *knight*; hyȝt, *height*; lyȝtly, *lightly*; lyȝt, *light*. We use <gh> in MnE, although the sound has now been lost in these words.

/x/ – similar to Scots *loch* /lox/ or German *bach* /bax/ after /a/, /o/ or /u/: for example, þurȝ, *through*; raȝt, *reached*; laȝt, *laughed*; boȝeȝ, *boughs*; flaȝe, *fled*; laȝe, *laugh*. Again, <gh> is used in MnE, and the sound has either changed to /f/ or has been lost.

/w/ – a developing sound change from OE /ɣ/: for example, þaȝ, *though* (also, elsewhere: arȝe, *arrow*; saȝe, *saw*; broȝeȝ, *brows*). Letter <w> is also used in the poem for this sound, as in *blowe* and *lawe*.

/s/ – <ȝ> and <tȝ> were both used for letter <z> – letters <z> and <tz> had been used in OF for the sound /ts/, which changed to /s/ and later to /z/. This French convention was used in the poem for the sound /s/: for example, hedleȝ, *headless*; resounȝ, *reasons*; hatȝ, *has*.

/z/ – <ȝ> represented the voiced sound /z/ in <-es> noun and verb suffixes: for example, discouereȝ, lokkeȝ, renkkeȝ, boȝeȝ, cachcheȝ, steppeȝ, strydeȝ, haldeȝ, etc. However, letter <s> is also used in the text, as in houes, *hooves*; bones, schonkes, *shanks*, etc.

The poem is written in 101 stanzas which have a varying number of unrhymed alliterative lines followed by five short rhymed lines. Like all OE and ME verse, it was written to be read aloud to an audience. Although it was contemporary with Chaucer's writing, you will find it more difficult to read than a comparable passage of Chaucer's, partly because some of the vocabulary is from a stock of words reserved for use in poetry, and partly because many words of the West Midlands dialect came down into MnE spoken dialects, but not into written Standard English.

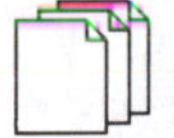

Activity 6.1

The story so far: during the New Year celebrations at King Arthur's court, a Green Knight rides in, carrying a battle-axe, and challenges any knight to strike him a blow with the axe, provided that he can give a return blow a year and a day later. Gawain takes up the challenge.

(i) Read the stanza (Text 40) and see what you can understand without looking up the words.
(ii) Translate the stanza using the word list in the *Word Book*, and note the number of words that have not survived into MnE and their source.

Before you read the commentary which follows:

(iii) Describe the patterns of alliteration and rhyme.
(iv) Describe some of the dialectal features and differences from MnE under the headings set out in Section 4.2.

TEXT 40 – *Sir Gawayn and þe Grene Knyȝt*, late fourteenth century (i)

The grene knyȝt vpon grounde grayþely hym dresses
A littel lut with þe hede, þe lere he discouereȝ
His longe louelych lokkeȝ he layd ouer his croun
Let the naked nec to þe note schewe.
Gauan gripped to his ax & gederes hit on hyȝt
Þe kay fot on þe fold he before sette
Let hit doun lyȝtly lyȝt on þe naked
Þat þe scharp of þe schalk schyndered þe bones
& schrank þurȝ þe schyire grece & scade hit in twynne.
Þat þe bit of þe broun stel bot on þe grounde.

cont ...

Þe fayre hede fro þe halce hit to þe erþe
Þat fele hit foyned wyth her fete þere hit forth roled.
Þe blod brayd fro þe body þat blykked on þe grene
& nawþer faltered ne fel þe freke neuer þe helder
Bot styþly he start forth vpon styf schonkes
& runyschly he raȝt out, þere as renkkeȝ stoden,
Laȝt to his lufly hed & lyft hit vp sone
& syþen boȝeȝ to his blonk, þe brydel he cachcheȝ,
Steppeȝ into stelbawe & strydeȝ alofte
& his hede by þe here in his honde haldeȝ
& as sadly þe segge hym in his sadel sette
As non vnhap had hym ayled, þaȝ hedleȝ he were
in stedde.
He brayde his bluk aboute
Þat vgly bodi þat bledde
Moni on of hym had doute
Bi þat his resounȝ were redde.

(A detailed commentary on the spelling and pronunciation of Text 40 is given in Commentary 9 of the *Text Commentary Book*.)

6.1.2 Alliteration and rhyme

The poem is evidence that the oral traditions of OE alliterative verse were unbroken (see Section 2.4). Each line divides into two, with a short break, or **cesura**, in the middle. There are usually four stresses in a line, two in the first half and two in the second, three of which alliterate together, but this could vary; for example:

/**G**auan /**g**ripped to his /ax & /**g**ederes hit on /hyȝt
þe kay /**f**ot on þe /**f**old he be/**f**ore /sette
/**L**et hit doun /**l**yȝtly /**l**yȝt on þe /naked
Þat þe /**sch**arp of þe /**sch**alk /**sch**yndered þe /bones
& /**sch**rank þurȝ þe /**sch**yire grece & /**sc**ade hit in /twynne,
Þat þe /**b**it of þe /**b**roun stel /**b**ot on þe /grounde.

Each stanza ends with a group of rhyming lines. The first short line was called the 'bob', which rhymed with two alternate lines of the following four, called the 'wheel' – ababa:

in **stedde**.
He brayde his bluk **aboute**
Þat vgly bodi þat **bledde**
Moni on of hym had **doute**
Bi þat his resounȝ were **redde**.

6.1.3 Grammar

Pronoun forms

One stanza of the poem will obviously not include all the pronouns. Text 40 gives us:

3rd person sg: he/hym/his/hit
3rd person pl: her (= their)
rel. pronoun: þat

From Text 41, we can add:

1st person sg: I/me
2nd person sg: þou/þe
3rd person sg: his (= its)
pl: þay

That is, from two stanzas; we have:

	Singular			**Plural**
1st person subject	I			
object	me			
genitive				
2nd person subject	þou			
object	þe			
genitive				
	Masculine	**Feminine**	**Neuter**	
3rd person subject	he		hit	þay
object	hym		hit	
genitive	his		his	her
Relative pronoun	þat			

Activity 6.2

Complete the chart above by identifying the remaining pronouns from the following lines of the poem (all the pronouns are in bold type).

Scho (= *she*) made hym so gret chere
Þat watȝ so fayr of face ...

Ho (= *she*) commes to þe cortyn & at þe knȝt totes (= *peeps*).
Sir Gawyn **her** welcumed worþy on fyrst
And **ho hym** ȝeldeȝ (= *replies*) aȝayn ful ȝerne (= *eager*) of **hir** wordeȝ,
Setteȝ **hir** sofly by **his** syde & swyþely (= *very much*) **ho** laȝeȝ (= *laughs*) ...

He sayde, **ȝe** ar welcum to welde (= *use*) as **yow** lykeȝ;
Þat here is (= *that which is here*), al is **yowre** awen to haue at **yowre** wylle & welde ...

Where is now **your** sourquydrye (= *pride*) & **your** conquestes?

Where schuld **I** wale (= *find*) **þe**, quoþ Gauan, where is **þy** place? ...

Bot **ȝe** schal be in **yowre** bed, burne (= *knight*), at **þyn** ese ...

I schal gif **hym** of **my** gyft þys giserne (= *battle-axe*) ryche (= *splendid*) ...

To wone (= *remain*) any quyle in þis won (= *place*), **hit** watȝ not **myn** ernde (= *errand*) ...

And **we** ar in þis valay verayly **oure** one (= *on our own*);
Here ar no renkes (= *men*) **vs** to rydde, rele as **vus** likeȝ ([*it*] *pleases us*).

A comloker knyȝt neuer Kryst made **hem** þoȝt ([*it*] *seemed to them*).

And syþen (= *afterwards*) on a stif stange (= *pole*) stoutly **hem** hanges ...

As fortune wolde fulsun (= *help*) **hom** (= *them*) ...

How ledes (= *knights*) for **her** lele luf (= *their true love*) **hor** lyueȝ (= *lives*) han auntered (= *have risked*) ...

Noun inflections

Plural nouns in the text are:

lokkeʒ bones fete schonkes renkkeʒ resounʒ

With the exception of *fete*, which still retains its OE vowel change to mark plural, these nouns are marked by the <s/ʒ> or <es/eʒ> suffix. This derives from the former OE strong masculine <-as> plural (see Commentary 2 of the *Text Commentary Book*, Section 2.1), and is now the regular MnE plural suffix.

It is probable that a final <-e> no longer marks a suffix such as the former dative case inflection of OE (see Section 2.7.3).

Verb inflections

Refer to Commentary 2 of the *Text Commentary Book*, Sections 2.4.4 and 2.4.5, or to an OE grammar book to see the range of inflections on OE weak and strong verbs. We know that a principal feature of ME is the progressive change and eventual loss of many OE inflections, and also that one marker of ME dialects is the variety of verb inflections. Text 40 provides some information about verb inflections in the NW Midlands dialect, as listed below. Where it does not, other words from the poem are listed in brackets.

Present tense		
1st person sg:	I	(bere, craue, telle, ask)
2nd person sg:	þou	(redeʒ, hattes, hopes, deles)
3rd person sg:	he/ho/hit	dresses, gederes
		discouereʒ, boʒeʒ, cachcheʒ, steppeʒ, strydeʒ, haldeʒ
plural:	we/ʒe/þay	(fallen; helden = *turn*; ʒelden)
Past tense		
1st person sg:	I	(lakked; seʒ = *saw*; cheued = *got*)
2nd person sg:	þou	(gef = *gave*; fayled; kyssedes = *kissed*)
3rd person sg:	he/ho/hit	**Strong verbs:**
		bot, fel, let, schrank, start
		Weak verbs:
		blykked, faltered, foyned, gripped, roled, schyndered
		bledde, brayde/brayd, hit, layd, laʒt, lyft, raʒt, scade, sette
plural:	we/ʒe/þay	stoden (maden)
Infinitive		schewe (tak, gif, prayse)
Imperative		(gif = *give*; kysse; lepe; lach = *seize*)
Present participle		(sykande = *sighing*; wreʒande = *denouncing*)
Past participle		lut (ayled, payed, hunted, slayn)

Several of these inflections are familiar to us in MnE, and it is clear that in this dialect the loss of OE inflections has gone further than in others.

Inflections in ME

The loss of most of the OE inflections is called **levelling**, and the reduction in the variety of the remaining inflections is called **regularisation**. Both developments took place more quickly in the North of England, as well as in those Midlands dialects that were closer to the North than others. The effect of the Viking settlement in the Danelaw was not only an influx of Scandinavian words, but also the kinds of simplification that are known to take place when people speaking similar languages communicate together, or when a pidgin language begins to be spoken.

Because Northern and North Midlands dialects were more 'advanced' in their loss of grammatical inflections, they tend to resemble MnE more closely in their grammar. The barrier to the easy reading of *Sir Gawayn and þe Grene knyʒt* is due to its vocabulary, with its large number of ON, OF and dialect words that have not survived in Standard English, and not its grammar.

Activity 6.3

Text 41 is the next stanza of the poem and tells what happened when Gawain took up the Green Knight's challenge to strike a blow with the axe. Rewrite it in MnE and make some analysis of its language.

TEXT 41 – *Sir Gawayn and þe Grene Knyȝt* (ii)

For þe hede in his honde he haldeȝ vp euen
Toward þe derrest on þe dece he dresseȝ þe face
& hit lyfte vp þe yȝe-lyddeȝ & loked ful brode
& meled þus much with his muthe, as ȝe may now here:
Loke, Gawan, þou be grayþe to go as þou hetteȝ
& layte as lelly til þou me, lude, fynde,
As þou hatȝ hette in þis halle, herande þise knyȝtes.
To þe grene chapel þou chose, I charge þe, to fotte
Such a dunt as þou hatȝ dalt – disserued þou habbeȝ –
To be ȝederly ȝolden on Nw ȝeres morn.
Þe knyȝt of þe grene chapel men knowen me mony;
Forþi me for to fynde if þou fraysteȝ, fayleȝ þou neuer.
Þerfore com, oþer recreaunt be calde þe behoues.
With a runisch rout þe rayneȝ he torneȝ,
Halled out at þe hal dor, his hed in his hande,
Þat þe fyr of þe flynt flaȝe fro fole houes.
To quat kyth he becom knwe non þere,
Neuer more þen þay wyste fram queþen he watȝ wonnen.
What þenne?
Þe kyng & Gawen þare
At þat grene þay laȝe & grenne
ȝet breued watȝ hit ful bare
A meruayl among þo menne.

6.2 A SW Midlands dialect

Piers Plowman is one of the most famous poems in ME. It must have been a very popular work because over 50 manuscripts have survived. The poem is an allegory of the Christian life, and of the corruption of the contemporary Church and society, written in the form of a series of dreams or 'visions':

Ac on a May mornyng on Maluerne hulles (= *hills*)
Me biful for to slepe ...
And merueylousliche me mette (= *dreamed*), as y may telle.

(*C-text* Prologue, lines 6–7, 9)

Piers Plowman, a humble poor labourer, stands for the ideal life of honest work and obedience to the Church.

The author was William Langland, but almost nothing is known about him except what can be inferred from the poem; however, we must remember that the 'dreamer' of the visions is a character in the story, and may not always be identified with the author. For example, his name, is Will, as indicated in the following extracts:

A louely lady of lere (= *face*) in lynnene yclothed
Cam doun fro þe castel and calde me by name
And sayde '*Wille*, slepestou?' ...

(*C-text* I, lines 4–6)

Ryht with þat ran Repentaunce and rehersede (= *spoke*) his teme (= *text*)
And made *Will* to wepe water with his eyes.

(*C-text* VI, lines 1–2)

or William *Langland*:

I haue lyued in *londe*, quod Y, my name is *Longe Wille* ...

(*B-text* XV, lines 152–3)

If his nickname is Long Will', he must have been a tall man, and unfit for hard physical work:

Y am to wayke (= *too weak*) to worche with sykel or with sythe
And to long (= *too tall*), lef me, lowe to stoupe (= *to stoop low*)
To wurche as a werkeman eny while to duyren (= *to last, endure*)

(*C-text* V, lines 23–5)

He lived in London, in Cornhill, with Kit and Calote (perhaps his wife and daughter, although there is no other evidence), and in the country:

Thus y awakede, woet god (= *God knows*), whan y wonede (= *lived*) in Cornehull
Kytte and y in a cote (= *cottage*) ...

(*C-text* V, lines 1–2)

And so y leue yn London and opelond (= *in the country*) bothe.

(*C-text* V, line 44)

... and riht with þat y wakede
And calde Kitte my wyf and Calote my douhter.

(*C-text* XX, lines 471–2)

He was sent to university (*scole*):

When y ȝong was, many ȝer hennes (= *many years ago*)
My fader and my frendes foende (= *provided for*) me to scole ...

(*C-text* V, line 36)

There are three versions of the poem, today called the A, B and C texts, which show that Langland continually revised and extended the poem from the 1360s until the 1380s, when the *C-text* was probably completed. It is a fine fourteenth century example of the tradition of alliterative verse in English. The dialect is SW Midlands 'but rather mixed'. There are many variant spellings in the 50 different manuscripts, quite apart from the successive versions of the text itself. As a result, the editors of modern versions have to make choices from the alternatives available.

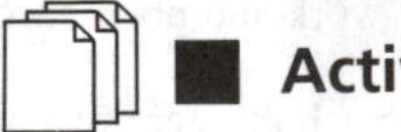

Activity 6.4

Rewrite Text 42 in MnE. This is from the Prologue of *Piers Plowman*, in which the writer dreams of a 'fair field full of folk', the world of contemporary society.

TEXT 42 – *Piers Plowman*, c.1370 (i)

In a somur sesoun whan softe was þe sonne
Y shope me into shroudes as y a shep were
In abite as an heremite vnholy of werkes,
Wente forth in þe world wondres to here
And say many sellies and selkouthe thynges.
Ac on a May mornyng on Maluerne hulles
Me biful for to slepe, for werynesse of-walked
And in a launde as y lay, lened y and slepte
And merueylousliche me mette, as y may telle.
Al þe welthe of the world and þe wo bothe
Wynkyng, as hit were, witterliche y sigh hit;
Of treuthe and tricherye, tresoun and gyle,
Al y say slepynge, as y shal telle.
Estward y beheld aftir þe sonne
And say a tour – as y trowed, Treuthe was there-ynne.
Westward y waytede in a while aftir
And seigh a depe dale – Deth, as y leue,
Woned in tho wones, and wikked spiritus.
A fair feld ful of folk fond y þer bytwene
Of alle manere men, þe mene and þe pore,
Worchyng and wandryng as þis world ascuth ...

(*C-text*, Derek Pearsall (ed.), Edward Arnold, 1978)

Activity 6.5

Describe some of the linguistic features of this ME dialect from the evidence provided in Text 42 under the following headings:

(i) Spelling conventions.
(ii) Evidence of pronunciation changes from OE.
(iii) Pronoun forms.
(iv) Noun and verb inflections.
(v) Grammatical structures and word order.
(vi) Sources of vocabulary.

The printed text is *edited*; that is, it is based on one of the *C-text* manuscripts but uses other manuscript readings or makes changes where the manuscript does not make good sense. Abbreviations are also filled out and modern punctuation added. We are therefore not reading exactly what is in a manuscript.

Remember also that the manuscripts used by the editor are copies, not the original. Consequently, any observations we make about either Langland's dialect or the SW Midlands dialect in general would need to be verified from other evidence. Refer to Section 4.2 on how to describe dialect differences, and use the data in the *Word Book* which groups the words of Text 42 (a) according to their pronunciation in OE and (b) by word class and source. (A more detailed description of the language of Text 42 can be found in Commentary 10 of the *Text Commentary Book*.)

6.2.1 Commentary on Text 42

Vocabulary

There are relatively few words of French origin, and even fewer from ON. The south and west of England had not been settled by Danes and Norwegians, so the scarcity of ON words is understandable. The proportion of French words in one short text cannot, of course, be used to come to any useful conclusions. We need a lot more evidence to be able to comment, but the text does perhaps demonstrate the solid core of OE vocabulary which is the basis of our language.

Wrath and Patience

Of the ME manuscripts that have come down to us, a large proportion are in the form of sermons or homilies which set out the ideals of the Church and the Christian life. A typical example is contained in 'The Parson's Tale' in Chaucer's *The Canterbury Tales*, in which the first prominent theme is sin and repentance for sin, or penitence:

> Seint Ambrose seith that penitence is the plenynge of man for the gilt that he hath doon and namoore to doon any thyng for which hym oghte to pleyne.

The second theme is the Seven Deadly Sins, those sins which were thought to be the most offensive and serious:

> Now is it behouely thing to telle whiche ben dedly synnes, that is to seyn chieftaynes of synnes ... Now ben they clepid chieftaynes for as muche as they ben chief and sprynge of alle othere synnes.

The Seven Deadly Sins were pride, envy, wrath, sloth, covetousness, gluttony and lust. Chaucer's Parson defines wrath (anger, or ire) as:

> This synne of ire, after the discryuyng of seint Augustyn, is wikked wil to ben auenged by word or by ded.

In *Piers Plowman*, the dreamer vividly personifies each of the Seven Deadly Sins as men or women seeking repentance. In Text 43, Wrath appears.

TEXT 43 – *Piers Plowman*, c.1370 (ii)

Now awakeþ Wraþe wiþ two white eiȝen
And neuelynge wiþ þe nose and his nekke hangyng
I am Wraþe quod he. I was som tyme a frere
And the couentes gardyner for to graffen impes.
On lymitours and listres lesynges I ymped
Til þei beere leues of lowe speche lordes to plese
And siþen þei blosmede abrood in boure to here shriftes.
And now is fallen þerof a fruyt – þat folk han wel leuere
Shewen hire shriftes to hem þan shryue hem to hir persons.
And now persons han parceyued þat freres parte wiþ hem
Thise possessioners preche and depraue freres
And freres fyndeþ hem in defaute as folk bereþ witnesse
That whan þei preche þe peple in many places aboute
I Wraþe walke wiþ hem and wisse hem of my bokes.
Þus þei speken of spiritualte, þat eiþer despiseþ ooþer
Til þei be boþe beggers and by my spiritualte libben
Or ellis al riche and ryden aboute; I Wraþe reste neuere
That I ne moste folwe þis folk, for swich is my grace.

(*B-text*, G. Kane and E.T. Donaldson (eds), Athlone Press, 1975, Vol.1, Passus V, pp. 135–50)

Activity 6.6

Translate Text 43 into MnE, using the word list in the *Word Book*.

Activity 6.7

(i) Rewrite Text 44 (which is a continuation of Text 43) in MnE using the word list in the *Word Book*.
(ii) Make an analysis of Texts 43 and 44 in the style of the commentaries on preceding texts.

TEXT 44 – *Piers Plowman*, c.1370 (iii)

I haue an aunte to nonne and an abbesse boþe.
Hir were leuere swowe or swelte þan suffre any peyne.
I haue be cook in hir kichene and the couent serued
Manye monþes wiþ hem and wiþ monkes boþe.
I was þe prioresse potager and oþer pouere ladies
And maad hem joutes of janglyng – þat dame Johane was a bastard
And Dame Clarice a knyȝtes douȝter – ac a cokewold was hir sire
And Dame Pernele a preestes fyle – prioresse worþ she neuere
For she hadde child in chirie tyme, al oure chapitre it wiste.
Of wikked wordes I Wraþe hire wortes made
Til 'þou lixt!' and 'þou lixt!' lopen out at ones
And eiþer hitte ooþer under þe cheke.
Hadde þei had knyues by Crist hir eiþer hadde kild ooþer.

Here is a facsimile of an extract from one of the *C-text* manuscripts, part of which is transcribed. In the first line, a question is put to Patience by Activa Vita (Active Life). They are allegorical characters in the poem. Piers Plowman is seeking how to live a good life, and the next Passus (section) goes on to describe the life of Dowel – that is, how to do well. The text is from Passus XV, beginning at line 274.

TEXT 45 – *Piers Plowman*, c.1370 (iv)

Transcription

What is parfit pacience • quod Actiua uita. (*Question*)

Mekenesse and mylde speche • and men of on wil (*Answer*)
Þe whiche wile loue lede • to oure lordes place
And þat is charite chaumpion • chef of all vertues -------
And þat is pore pacience • alle pereles to suffre

wheþer pouerte and pacience • plece more god al myȝti (*Question*)
Þan so rithful richesse • and resonableli to spende --------

Ȝe quis est ille quod concience • quik laudabimus eum (*Answer*)
Þalk men reden of richesse • rith to þe worldes ende
And whan he drou him to þe deth • that he ne drat hym sarre
Þan eny pore pacient • and þat i preue bi reson ----------

(*Cotton MS Vespasian* B XVI f. 64v)

The printed modern edition containing the same extract is conflated from several *C-text* manuscripts. Modern punctuation has been added, as is usual.

TEXT 46 – Edited version of Text 45

'What is parfit pacience?' quod Actiua Vita.

'Meeknesse and mylde speche and men of o will,
The whiche wil loue lat to our lordes place,
And þat is charite, chaumpion, chief of all vertues;
And þat is pore pacient, alle perelles to soffre.'

Where (= *whether*) pouerte and pacience plese more god almyhty
Then rihtfullyche rychesse and resonableyche to spene?'

Ȝe, quis est ille?' (= *who is he*) quod Pacience, 'quik laudamus eum (= *let us praise him*)'
Thogh men rede of rychesse rihte to the worldes ende
I wiste neuere renke þat riche was, þat whan he rekene sholde
Then when he drow to þe deth, that he ne dradd hym sarrore
Then eny pore pacient, and þat preue y be resoun.

(*C-text*, Derek Pearsall (ed.), Edward Arnold, 1978)

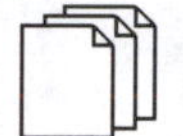

Activity 6.8

(i) Write out some lines from the manuscript of Text 45 that are not transcribed here.
(ii) Compare the transcription with the edited version printed as Text 46. Comment on the differences and the choices that the editor made in producing this text.
(iii) Does the text need modern punctuation?

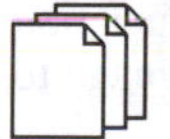

Activity 6.9

Examine one or more of the texts in this chapter for evidence that they are written in the West Midlands dialects. Typical markers of ME West Midlands dialects include:

(i) OE long vowel /ɑ:/ has shifted and is now spelt <o>.
(ii) OE vowel /y/ remains but is spelt <u>, as in *hull* for MnE *hill*.
(iii) Suffix <-ed> sometimes 'devoiced' and spelt <-et>.
(iv) Pronouns:
3rd person feminine *ha* or *heo*.
3rd person plural possessive *hare*.
(v) Verbs:
3rd person plural present tense suffix <-eþ>.
Present participle suffix <-ende>.

7. Middle English IV – East Midlands and London dialects

7.1 The origins of present-day Standard English

One of the reasons for learning about the development of the English language is to understand the relationship between the dialects and Standard English in present-day English. In the conglomeration of different dialects that we call 'Middle English', there is no one recognised standard form. If we were to study the political, social and economic history of England in relation to the language, we would observe that the conditions for a standard language were beginning to emerge by the late fifteenth century. From the sixteenth century onwards, there is evidence that people were actively discussing the need for a standard in spelling, pronunciation and grammar. This naturally raised the question of which dialect or variety of the language to use for the standard.

One definition of a standard language, in modern sociological terms, is,

> The Standard is that speech variety of a language community which is legitimised as the obligatory norm for social intercourse on the strength of the interests of dominant forces in that society.
>
> (*Sociolinguistics*, Norbert Dittmar, 1976)

that is, the choice is made by people imitating those with prestige or power in their society, while the latter tend to prescribe their variety of the language as the 'correct' one to use. A standard language is not superior in itself as a language for communication – all dialects are regular and 'rule-governed' – but in its adoption and development it is the language of those with social and political influence, although advocates of a standard will often claim an intrinsic superiority for it.

In 1589, the poet George Puttenham published a book called *The Arte of English Poesie*. In it, he gave advice to poets on their choice of language.

> It must be that of educated, not common people, neither shall he follow the speach of a craftes man, or other of the inferiour sort, though he be inhabitant or bred in the best towne and citie in this Realme. But he shall follow generally the better brought vp sort, ... ciuill and graciously behauoured and bred;

The recommended dialect was therefore Southern, not Northern or Western:

> ...the usuall speach of the Court, and that of London and the shires lying about London within lx. myles, and not much aboue.

(A longer extract from Puttenham's book is given in Text 81.)

This defines the literary language already in use in the sixteenth century, and clearly describes it as the prestigious language of the educated classes of London and the South-East. London was the centre of government, trade and commerce, and so the language of the 'dominant forces' in society would carry prestige, and others would seek to copy it. This is a simplified explanation of a complex state of affairs, but it helps to explain why the educated London dialect formed the basis of the standard language as it developed. If the centre of government and commerce had been York, no doubt the Northern dialect would have formed the basis for Standard English today.

The London dialect in the late fourteenth century derived from a mixture of ME dialects, but was strongly influenced by the East Midlands dialect in particular. London naturally attracted large numbers of men and women and their families from other areas of the country to find work, bringing their own dialectal speech with them. Historians have identified a considerable migration of people from the East Midlands to London from the late thirteenth century to the mid-fourteenth century, some of whom must have become the 'dominant social class' whose language carried prestige and was imitated by others. But because people from other parts of the country also migrated to London, there are also features of Southern and Kentish in the London dialect.

So present-day Standard English derives in its origins from the East Midlands dialect of ME, and this explains why it is comparatively easy to read Chaucer's English of the late fourteenth century, as well as other East Midlands texts. It will not be necessary therefore to examine the texts in this chapter in the detail given to those already described. You can apply the same principles of analysis to them, if you wish.

7.2 A SE Midlands dialect

The Travels of Sir John Mandeville was one of the most popular books written in the fourteenth century, with over 300 manuscripts having survived, but its title is misleading. The original book was written in French in the 1350s by a doctor of Liège called Jehan de Bourgogne. He probably never travelled outside France and based the stories on other men's travel writings, filling them out from his own imagination. It is believed that he adopted the name Sir John Mandeville and wrote a preface claiming to be an Englishman born in St Albans, although the facts are not known for sure. The text in English is a translation from the French by an unknown English writer using a SE Midlands dialect. It cannot be a translation by the French author, because it is sometimes an inaccurate rendering.

Another version was written in verse form. The verse was originally in a NE Midlands dialect, but the only surviving manuscript is in a 'modernised version' of the fifteenth century. It gives us some idea of the standard literary language that had evolved at that time, and the style that writers were beginning to use. Unfortunately, part of the manuscript that corresponds to Text 47 is missing, but enough remains for comparison.

TEXT 47 – *The Travels of Sir John Mandeville* (i)

SE Midlands dialect

Now schall I seye ȝou sewyngly (= *in what follows*) of contrees and yles
þat ben beȝonde the contrees þat I haue spoken of. Wherfore I seye ȝou,
in passynge be the lond of Cathaye toward the high Ynde, and toward Bacharye,
men passen be a kyngdom þat men clepen Caldilhe, þat is a full fair contre.
And þere groweth a maner of fruyt, as þough it weren gowrdes; and whan
þei ben rype, men kutten hem ato, and men fynden withinne a lytyll best,
in flesch, in bon, and blode as þough it were a lytill lomb, withouten wolle.
And men eten bothe the frut and the best: and þat is a gret mervueylle.
Of þat frute I haue eten, allþough it were wondirfull: but þat I knowe wel,
þat god is merueyllous in his werkes.

TEXT 48 – *The Boke of Mawndevile*

... That bereth applis grete plente
And who þat cleueth an appul atwyn (= *apart*, *in two*)
A litille beest he fyndith thereyn.
To a litille lombe liche it ys
Of bloode and bone and eke of flessh
And welle shapen atte folle (= *at full*, *in every detail*)
In al thinge saufe (= *save*, *except that*) it hath noo wolle
And men and women þere meest and leest (= *most and least*, *greatest and lowliest*)
Eten of þat frute so with þat beest.

(*The Metrical Version of Mandeville's Travels*, M. C. Seymour (ed.), EETS 269, 1973)

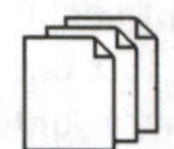

Activity 7.1

Rewrite Texts 47 and 48 in MnE and comment on their linguistic features.

Here is a page in facsimile from one of the Mandeville manuscripts, together with a transcription of the bottom part of the second column. Abbreviations in the original are filled out.

TEXT 49 – *The Travels of Sir John Mandeville* (ii)

Transcription

Nota de ter
ra egitti
Egipt is a strong contre
& manye perilous hauenys
ben therin for there lith
in eche heuene toun gret
ryches (= *rocks*) in the entre of the
hauene / Toward the est
is the rede se (= *Red Sea*) that rennyth
right to the cete of cos
tantyn (= *Constantine*) the Noble / The
contre of egipt is in
lenthe v iorneis but not
but iij in brede for desertys
that aryn there / Betwyn
egip & the lond that is
callyd Nundynea (= *Numidia*) arn
xii iourneis in desertis
The folk that wonyde
in that contre arn cris
tene (= *Christian*) men but thy aryn
blake of color[r] for the ouer
gret hete that is there

5 day's journeys = c.100 miles, 3 day's journeys = c.60 miles

(Bodley version of *Mandeville's Travels*, EETS OS 253, 1963 p. 33; facsimile from Bodleian MS E Musaeo 116 f. 15[rb])

cete that tyme But af
tyrwardys Cyrus & the kyg
of peres withdrow the
watyr & distroyede the
cete & al that contre ther
aboute for they departyn
the grete reuer of Eufra
tes & dedyn it renyn ccc
xl sundery weyes for he
hadde mad his grete oth
& swor his grete oth & so
grevously that be cause
that so manye noble
haddyn ben drenk ther
in that he shulde bryn
gyn it to swich astat that
women shulde wadyn
ther ovyr & not wetyn
here kneis & so he dede &
yit it standyth in that
degree ffor babyloyne
where that the soudo
dwellyth for to passe to
the grete babyloyne arn
xl iurneis thow desert
& it is not vndyr the sub
iection of the soudon but
wit inne the lordschepe
of the kyng of peres &
it is holdyn of the gre
te Came of tartarye the
whiche is a gret p[ar]le of
Cathay & of manye othe
re contreis & of a gret p[ar]

tye of Inde his lon is
nythebourgh & marchid wt
prester Jon is lond And
he hath so gret lordschep
that he wot neue wher
his lordschepe endyth
he is myghtiere wt outy
comparisoun than the soudon
of which gret stat & mages
te I thynke to speken of af
tyrward whan I haue
come therto & Iot de ter
ra egitti
Egypt is a strong contre
& manye p[er]lous havenys
ben therin for there lith
in eche havene ton gret
ryches in the entre of the
havene Toward the est
is the rede se that renyth
right to the cete of cos
tantyn the noble The
contre of egipt is in
lenthe v iorneis but not
but in brede for deserte
that aryn there Be twy
egipt & the lond that is
callyd Medyaca arn
xii iurneis in desertis
The folk that dwellyde
in that contre arn cris
tene men but thy arn
blake of colour for the on
gret hete that is there

Activity 7.2

Transcribe some of the first column of the facsimile.

7.3 The London dialect – Chaucer

7.3.1 Chaucer's prose writing

Geoffrey Chaucer was born in the 1340s and died in 1400. He was acknowledged in his own day as the greatest contemporary writer, not only in poetry but also in the arts of rhetoric and philosophy. The following tribute to Chaucer after his death is from a poem by Thomas Hoccleve:

Alas my worthy mayster honorable
Thys landes verray tresouur and rychesse
Deth by thy deth hath harme irriparable
Vnto vs don; hir vengeable duresse
Despoyled hath this land of the swetnesse
Of rethorik, for vnto Tullius
Was nere man so lyk amonges vs.

Also, who was hier in philosophy
To Aristotle in our tonge but thou?
The steppes of Virgile in poesie
Thow filwedist eek, men wot wel enow ...

Chaucer wrote in the London dialect of the ME of his time; that is, the literary form of the language based on the speech of the educated class. The dialect of the mass of ordinary people living in London must have been as different from Chaucer's, both in form and pronunciation, as present-day Cockney is from educated RP and Standard English.

The Canterbury Tales is Chaucer's best-known work, but some of the tales are much more widely read than others. Most of them are in verse, and it is unlikely that the two tales in prose will ever be popular, since their content and style are now out of fashion. The first prose tale is supposed to be told by Chaucer himself, after his comic satire on narrative romances, 'The Tale of Sir Thopas', has been interrupted by the Host:

Namoore of this for goddes dignytee ...

Chaucer agrees to tell 'The Tale of Melibeus':

I wol yow telle a litel thyng in prose
That oghte like yow as I suppose
Or ellis certes ye be to daungerous.
It is a moral tale vertuous ...

The tale is a translation from a French prose work which is itself based on a Latin original. Here are the opening paragraphs.

TEXT 50 – Chaucer's 'The Tale of Melibeus'

A yong man whilom called Melibeus myghty and riche bigat vp on his wif, þ^{t} called was Prudence a doghter, which þ^{t} called was Sophie | vpon a day bifel þ^{t} he for his desport is went into the feeldes hym to pleye | his wif & eek his doghter, hath he laft inwith his hous, of which the dores weren faste yshette | thre of his olde foos, han it espied, & setten laddres to the walles of his hous, and by wyndowes ben entred, & betten his wif, & wounded his doghter with fyue mortal woundes in fyue sondry places | this is to seyn, in hir feet, in hir handes, in hir erys, in hir nose, and in hir mouth, and leften hir for deed & wenten awey || Whan Melibeus retourned was in to his hous, & seigh al this meschief, he lyk a mad man rentynge his clothes, gan to wepe and crye | Prudence his wyf, as ferforth as she dorste, bisoughte hym of hys wepyng for to stynte | but nat for thy he gan to crye & wepen euere lenger the moore.

(Transcribed from a facsimile of the Hengwrt manuscript of *The Canterbury Tales*.)

Commentary on Text 50

(a) *whilom* meant *formerly*; it is used here rather like the formula *once upon a time*.
(b) *nat forthy* meant *nevertheless*.
(c) The verb *gan* in a clause like *he gan wepe* or *he gan to wepe* was used in ME as an auxiliary verb, to indicate past time, as in *he wept*.

The second prose tale has already been referred to in Chapter 6 – 'The Parson's Tale'. It is a translation of two treatises in Latin, the first on penitence and the second on the Seven Deadly Sins. The following text is the commentary on gluttony in the second treatise.

TEXT 51 – Chaucer's 'The Parson's Tale'

> After auarice comth glotonye which is expres eek agayn the comandement of god. Glotonye is vnmesurable appetit to ete or to drynke, or elles to doon ynogh to (= *to give way to, to go some way towards*) the vnmesurable appetit and desordeynee coueitise to eten or to drynke. This synne corrumped al this world as is wel shewed in the synne of Adam and of Eue. ... He that is vsaunt to this synne of glotonye, he ne may no synne withstonde. He moot been in seruage of alle vices, for it is the deueles hoord ther he hideth hym and resteth.
>
> This synne hath manye speces. The firste is dronkenesse that is the horrible sepulture of mannes resoun, and therfore whan a man is dronken he hath lost his resoun – and this is deedly synne. But soothly whan that a man is nat wont to strong drynke and parauenture ne knoweth nat the strengthe of the drynke or hath feblesse in his heed or hath trauailed thurgh which he drynketh the moore, al be he sodeynly caught with drynke, it is no deedly synne but venyal. The seconde spece of glotonye is that the spirit of a man wexeth al trouble, for dronkenesse bireueth hym the discrecioun of his wit. The thridde spece of glotonye is whan a man deuoureth his mete and hath no rightful manere of etynge. The fourthe is whan, thurgh the grete habundance of his mete, the humours in his body been destempred. The fifthe is foryetelnesse by to muchel drynkynge, for which somtyme a man foryeteth er the morwe what he dide at euen or on the nyght biforn ...
>
> Thise been the fyue fyngres of the deueles hand by whiche he draweth folk to synne.

(*The Canterbury Tales*, N. F. Blake (ed.), Edward Arnold, 1980 pp. 642–3)

■ Activity 7.3

(i) Examine Texts 50 and 51 for evidence of those features of Chaucer's London dialect that mark it as different from other ME dialects (see Section 4.2).
(ii) Use the following checklist to describe some of the differences in the word forms and grammatical structures of Chaucer's English which contrast with MnE.

Nouns

(a) What are the noun inflections for plural? Are all plural nouns inflected?
(b) What are the forms of the personal pronouns, 1st, 2nd and 3rd person, singular and plural?
(c) Is the use of the definite and indefinite articles the same as in MnE?
(d) What relative pronouns are used? Is the relative pronoun sometimes deleted?

Verbs

(a) Is the infinitive inflected?
(b) What are the inflections for present tense, 1st, 2nd and 3rd person, singular and plural?
(c) Examine forms of the past tense for evidence of strong and weak verbs and their MnE form.
(d) Distinguish verbs that use *have* from those that use *be* in forming the perfect tense.

(e) Are there any examples of passive voice?
(f) Look for any impersonal constructions using *me* or *him*.
(g) Look for *do* meaning *to cause to happen* – that is, its causative use – and *ginnen/gan* used as auxiliary verbs to form a past tense.

Prepositions

(a) Are any prepositions used after their noun phrase complements, rather than before, as is now normal?

Grammar

(a) Look for marked changes of normal word order in the clause – SPCA.
(b) Is the subject omitted? Or any other expected element of the clause?
(c) What is the usual form of the negative, single or multiple?
(d) Is *do* used in forming the interrogative?

(iii) Use the list of lexical words from Texts 50 and 51 in the *Word Book* to comment on the sources of the vocabulary and any changes of meaning that have since developed.

7.3.2 Chaucer's verse

Here is the transcription of the opening of the prologue to and the beginning of 'The Friar's Tale' about a summoner in Chaucer's *The Canterbury Tales*. It is accompanied by another version of the text from another manuscript.

TEXT 52 – Chaucer's 'The Friar's Tale'

Transcription

This worthy lymytour þis noble ffrere
he made alway a louryinge cheere
upon the sompnor. but for honeste
No vileyns worde. ȝit to him spak he
But atte last he sayd unto þe wyf
Dame quod he. god ȝiue ȝow good lyf
ȝe han her touchid also mot I the
In scole matter gret difficulte
ȝe han sayd mochel þing right wel I say
But dame right as we ryden by þe way
Us needeþ nouȝt but for to speke of game
And lete auctorites in goddes name
To preching and to scoles of clergie
But if it like to þis companye
I wil ȝow of a sompnour telle a game

(*English Literary Manuscripts*, H. Kelliher and S. Brown, The British Library, 1986)

Alternative version

This worthy lymytour / this noble frere
He made alwey / a manere louryng cheere
Vp on the Somnour / but for honestee
No vileyns word / as yet to hym spak he
But atte laste / he seyde vn to the wyf
Dame quod he / god yeue yow right good lyf
Ye han heer touched / al so mote I thee
In scole matere / greet difficultee
Ye han seyd muche thyng / right wel I seye
But dame / here as we ryden by the weye
Vs nedeth nat / to speken / but of game
And lete Auctoritees / on goddes name
To prechyng / and to scole of clergye
But if it like / to this compaignye
I wol yow / of a Somnour telle a game

(*The Canterbury Tales: A Facsimile and Transcription of the Hengwrt MS*, Paul G. Ruggiers (ed.), 1979)

Activity 7.4

Compare the two versions of the text and discuss the differences and any difficulties which an editor of the texts would have to resolve.

7.3.3 Using Chaucer's rhymes as evidence of change in pronunciation

Changes and variations in the pronunciation of a language are inevitable, but they are much more difficult to study than changes in vocabulary and spelling, for example. Until the invention of sound recording, the evidence for change in pronunciation has been indirect, through written texts. One useful source of evidence is rhyme in verse.

If two words rhyme, we presume that they contain the same sounds. We can then look up the derivations of the words and compare the spellings and probable pronunciations. There are three possibilities:

(i) The words (OE, ON or OF) from which the rhyming pair derive also rhymed, and their pronunciation has not changed significantly; for example, *wyght/knyght* from OE *wiht/cniht*.
(ii) The words (OE, ON or OF) from which the rhyming pair derive also rhymed, but the pronunciation of both words has changed; therefore, an identical sound change has taken place, as in *breeth/heeth* from OE *bræþ/hæþ*.
(iii) The words (OE, ON or OF) from which the rhyming pair derive did not rhyme; therefore one or more sound changes have taken place to cause the words to 'fall together' and rhyme in Chaucer's English, as in *brist/list* from OE *breost/hlystan*.

The comparison of Chaucer's rhyming pairs with their MnE reflexes (if any) will produce, in many of them, evidence of continuing sound change. As an example, we can list the rhymes of the opening 162 lines of Chaucer's prologue to *The Canterbury Tales*, compare them with their OE, ON or OF derivations, and see what changes in pronunciation we can discover in the ME and MnE pairs. (Note that we have to select a reasonable number of pairs in order to produce a sufficient variety of words.)

The principal changes are in the vowels, but you will find some consonant developments too. There are also some interesting changes in the stress pattern of some words from ME to MnE, so that identical words no longer rhyme in present-day English. The loss of inflections will affect the contrast between some OE words and their ME reflexes.

Activity 7.5

List the rhyming words in the opening lines of Chaucer's prologue to *The Canterbury Tales*.

Either:

(i) Select some of the pairs that show evidence of change and describe the differences.

Or (for a more systematic description):

(ii) Group the pairs into sets according to the rhyming vowel and see if you can discover any patterns of change in pronunciation or stress.

(The list of rhyming words, with their etymologies and MnE reflexes, and a full descriptive commentary, is given in Commentary 11 of the *Text Commentary Book*.)

7.4 The London dialect – Thomas Usk

From the late fourteenth century onwards, we begin to find many more examples of everyday language surviving in letters and public documents than we do for earlier English. Literary language draws on the ordinary language of its time, but in a special way, and we cannot be sure that the literature of a period tells us how people actually spoke.

In Chaucer's day, London was, from time to time, the scene of violence and demonstration in the streets, and the following text describes one such series of incidents in the 1380s. Thomas Usk was involved with what turned out to be the wrong side in the political factions of his day, for he was unsuccessful in the appeal from which Texts 53 and 54 are taken, and was later executed.

The appeal is 'an example of the London English of a fairly well-educated man'. The original spelling is retained, but the punctuation is modern.

TEXT 53 – Thomas Usk's appeal, 1384 (i)

I Thomas Vsk ... knowleched thes wordes & wrote hem with myn owne honde ...

... Also, that day that Sir Nichol Brembre was chose mair, a non after mete kom John Northampton to John Mores hows, & thider kom Richard Norbury & William Essex, & ther it was accorded that the mair, John Northampton, sholde sende after the persones that thilk tyme wer in the comun conseil of craftes, and after the wardeyns of craftes, so that thei sholde kome to the goldsmithes halle on the morwe after, & ther the mair sholde speke with hem, to loke & ordeigne how thilk eleccion of Sir Nichol Brembre myght be letted; &, nad it be for drede of our lord the kyng, I wot wel eueri man sholde haue be in others top. And than sente he Richard Norbury, Robert Rysby, & me, Thomas Vsk, to the Neyte, to the duk of lancastre, to enforme hym in thys wyse: 'Sir, to day, ther we wolden haue go to the eleccion of the mair in goddes peas & the kynges, ther kom jn an orrible companye of criers, no man not whiche, & ther, with oute any vsage but be strength, chosen Sir Nichol Brembre mair, a yein our maner of eleccion to forn thys vsed; wher fore we preye yow yf we myght haue the kynges writ to go to a Newe eleccion.' And the duk seide: 'Nay, certes, writ shul ye non haue, auise yow amonges yowr selue.' & her of I appele John Northampton, John More, Richard Norbury, & William Essex.

(*A Book of London English 1384–1425*, R. W. Chambers and Marjorie Daunt (eds), OUP, 1931, pp. 28–9)

Activity 7.6

(i) Use the word list in the *Word Book* to write a version of Text 53 in MnE.
(ii) List some of the lexical and grammatical features of Usk's language that mark its differences from MnE.

Activity 7.7

Repeat Activity 7.6 for Text 54.

TEXT 54 – Thomas Usk's appeal, 1384 (ii)

Also, atte Goldsmithes halle, when al the people was assembled, the mair, John Northampton, reherced as euel as he koude of the eleccion on the day to forn, & seyde that truly: 'Sirs, thus be ye shape for to be ouer ronne, & that,' quod he, 'I nel noght soeffre; lat vs rather al be ded atones than soeffre such a vylenye.' & than the comunes, vpon these wordes, wer stered, & seiden truly they wolde go to a nother eleccion, & noght soeffre thys wrong, to be ded al ther for attones in on tyme; and than be the mair, John Northampton, was euery man boden gon hom, & kome fast a yein strong in to Chepe with al her craftes, & I wene ther wer a boute a xxx craftes, & in Chepe they sholden haue sembled to go to a newe eleccion, &, truly, had noght the aldermen kome to trete, & maked that John Northampton bad the poeple gon hoom, they wolde haue go to a Newe eleccion, & in that hete haue slayn hym that wolde haue letted it, yf they had myght; and ther of I appele John Northampton.

Activity 7.8

Examine one or more of the texts in this chapter for evidence that they are written in the East Midlands or London dialect. Some of the features that mark the East Midlands and London ME dialects are:

(i) OE long /ɑ:/ has rounded to /ɔ:/ and is now spelt <o> or <oo>.
(ii) OE short /æ/ written <æ> is now /a/ and written <a>.
(iii) OE <eo> has smoothed and is now spelt <e>.
(iv) OE /y/ has unrounded to /i/, spelt <i>, but there are inconsistencies in the London dialect, and some words originally with OE /y/ use Kentish /e/ or Southern /u/.
(v) Pronouns:
3rd person plural: East Midlands *he*, *here* or *hem*; London *they*, *hir* or *hem*.
(vi) Verbs:
3rd person singular present tense suffix <-eþ>.
3rd person plural present tense suffix <-en>.
Past participle suffix <-en> is retained, but the prefix <y-> is lost in general in the East Midlands dialect; this is not consistent in the London dialect, which sometimes retains prefix <y-> and drops the suffix <-en>.
Infinitive suffix <-en> is generally retained (East Midlands) but may be dropped in London dialect (Southern dialect influence).

8. Early Modern English I – the fifteenth century

8.1 The beginnings of EMnE

You should have found the fourteenth century texts in Chapter 7 relatively easy to read without the help of a glossary – it is usually possible to make out the sense of late ME writings in the East Midlands and London dialects because they are the origins of Standard English today. The following fifteenth century was a period of transition to present-day English, and we talk of the **Early Modern English** (EMnE) period, from about 1450, in the development of the language. The date is, of course, arbitrary, as the normal development of a language is gradual and continuous.

8.2 Early fifteenth century East Midlands dialect

Margery Kempe (c.1373–c.1439) was a married woman from King's Lynn, Norfolk, who gave up married life as a result of her mystical experiences to devote herself to religion. She made many pilgrimages during her lifetime and later, in the 1420s, dictated a book describing her visions, temptations and journeys.

As the book was written down from Margery Kempe's own dictation, it is probably reliable evidence of ordinary speech in the early fifteenth century. The dialect is East Midlands, but we cannot tell how accurate the scribe's reproduction of Margery's speech was, or that of the only surviving manuscript, which was copied in the mid-fifteenth century.

Here she describes her early marriage. Throughout the book she refers to herself as 'this creature'.

TEXT 55 – *The Boke of Margery Kempe*, c.1420 (i)

East Midlands dialect

Whan þis creatur was xx ȝer of age or sumdele mor sche was maryed to a worschepful burgeys of Lyn and was wyth chylde wyth in schort tyme as kynde wolde. And aftyr þat sche had conceyued sche was labowrd wyth grett accessys tyl þe chyld was born & þan what for labowr sche had in chyldyng & for sekenesse goyng beforn sche dyspered of hyr lyf, wenyng sche mygth not leuyn.

When this creature was 20 years of age or something more she was married to a worshipful burgess of Lynn and was with child within short time as nature wills. And after (that) she had conceived she was in labour with great fevers till the child was born & then what for labour she had in childbirth & for sickness going before she despaired of her life, thinking she might not live.

(A description of the language of the Margery Kempe texts is given in Commentary 12 of the *Text Commentary Book*.)

Here she describes her first mystical vision.

TEXT 56 – *The Boke of Margery Kempe*, c.1420 (ii)

On a nygth as þis creatur lay in hir bedde wyth hir husbond sche herd a sownd of melodye so swet & delectable hir þowt as sche had ben in paradyse. And þerwyth sche styrt owt of hir bedde & seyd Alas þat euyr I dede synne, it is ful mery in hevyn. Thys melodye was so swete þat it passyd alle þe melodye þat euyr mygth be herd in þis world wyth owtyn ony comparyson, & caused þis creatur whan sche herd ony myrth or melodye aftyrward for to haue ful plentyuows & habundawnt teerys of hy deuocyon wyth greet sobbyngys & syhyngys aftyr þe blysse of heuen, not dredyng þe schamys & þe spytys of þe wretchyd world.

On a night as this creature lay in her bed with her husband she heard a sound of melody so sweet & delectable to-her (it) seemed as she had been in Paradise. And therewith she started out of her bed & said Alas that ever I did sin, it is full merry in heaven. This melody was so sweet that it passed all the melody that ever might be heard in this world without any comparison, & caused this creature when she heard any mirth or melody afterward for to have full plenteous and abundant tears of high devotion with great sobbings & sighings after the bliss of heaven, not dreading the shames and the spites of the wretched world.

Text 57 shows the opening of the book in facsimile. Abbreviations have been filled out in the transcription.

TEXT 57 – *The Boke of Margery Kempe*, c.1420 (iii)

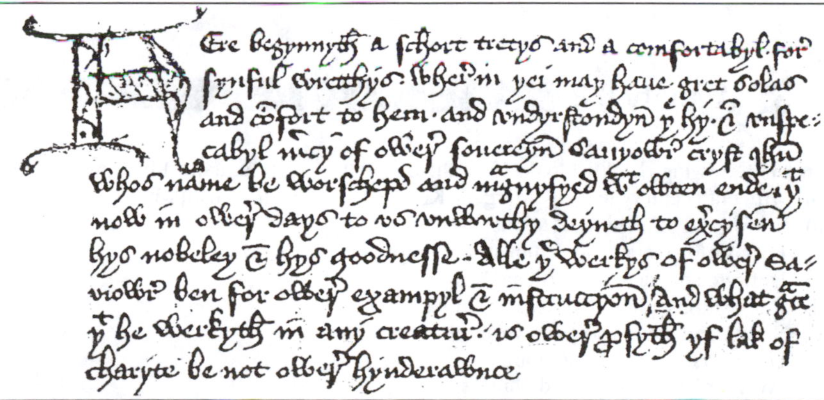

Here begynnyth a schort tretys and a comfortabyl for synful wrecchys. wher in þei may haue gret solas and comfort to hem. and vndyrstonyn þe hy & vnspe cabyl mercy of ower soueryn Sauyowr cryst Ihesu whos name be worschepd and magnyfyed wythowten ende. þat now in ower days to vs vnworthy deyneth to exercysen hys nobeley & hys goodnesse.

Activity 8.1

(i) Rewrite Text 57 in MnE.
(ii) Transcribe the rest of the facsimile

The next extract in transcription is typical of many descriptions of Margery Kempe's religious experiences, her tears of repentance and sense of sin and guilt.

TEXT 58 – *The Boke of Margery Kempe*, c.1420 (iv)

As þis creatur lay in contemplacyon sor wepyng in hir spiryt sche seyde to owyr lord Ihesu cryst. A lord maydenys dawnsyn now meryly in heuyn, xal not I don so. for be cawse I am no mayden, lak of may denhed is to me now gret sorwe. me thynkyth I wolde I had ben slayn whan I was takyn fro þe funt ston þat I xuld neuyr a dysplesyd þe. & þan xuldyst þu blyssed Lorde an had my maydenhed wyth owtyn ende. A der God I haue not lovyd þe alle þe days of my lyue & þat sor rewyth me. I haue ronnyn a wey fro þe, & þow hast ronnyn aftyr me. I wold fallyn in dyspeyr & þu woldyst not suffer me. A dowtor how oftyn tymes haue I teld þe þat thy synnes arn forȝoue þe & þat we ben onyd in loue to gedyr wyth owtyn ende / þu art to me a synguler lofe dowtyr. & þerfor I behote þe þu schalt haue a synguler grace in hevyn, dowtyr & I be hest þe þat I shal come to þin ende at þi deyng wyth my blyssed modyr & myn holy awngelys. & twelve apostelys. Seynt Katteryne. Seynt Margarete. Seynt Mary Mawdelyn. & many oþer seyntys þat ben in Hevyn. whech ȝevyn gret worshep to me. for þe grace þat I ȝeue to þe. thy God. þi lord Ihesu /

(*The Boke of Margery Kempe*, Sanford Brown Meech (ed.), EETS OS 212)

Activity 8.2

(i) Use the following checklist to describe the differences in grammatical features of these early fifteenth century texts by Margery Kempe which contrast with MnE.
  (a) Forms and inflections of nouns.
  (b) Forms of personal and demonstrative pronouns.
  (c) Definite and indefinite articles.
  (d) Prepositions, phrasal verbs and conjunctions.
  (e) Strong and weak verbs and verb inflections for tense.
  (f) Development of the verb phrase.
  (g) Word order in clauses and phrases.
(ii) Use the word list in the *Word Book* to examine and comment on the derivation of the vocabulary in these texts.
(iii) Describe the principal features of the spelling that contrast with present-day spelling.
(iv) Two forms of personal pronouns occur, *my/myn* and *þi/þin*, both used as determiners. What determines the choice of pronoun?

8.3 Later fifteenth century East Midlands dialect

The Pastons were a prosperous family who lived in Norfolk. A large collection of their letters written between the 1420s and 1500s has survived. The letters cover three generations of the family, and so are a valuable source of evidence for historians as well as students of language. Much of the period was troubled by the political upheavals of the Wars of the Roses, which is reflected in the Pastons' letters.

Two letters are printed here. Text 59 is to the first generation William Paston from his wife Agnes. This letter was dictated to a secretary but Agnes Paston signed it. It was probably written on 20 April, 1440. Text 60 is a Valentine letter from Margery Brews to the third generation John Paston, and was written in 1477. They were married later that year.

TEXT 59 – Paston letter, 1440

Dere housbond I recomaunde me to yow &c blyssyd be god I sende yow gode tydynggys of þe comyng and þe brynggyn hoom of þe gentylwomman þat ye wetyn of fro Redham þis same nyght ~~ae~~ acordyng to poyntmen þat ye made þer for yowre self and as for þe furste aqweyntaunce betwhen John Paston and þe seyde gentilwomman she made hym gentil chere in gyntyl wyse and seyde he was verrayly yowre son and so I hope þer shal nede no gret trete be twyxe hym | þe parson of Stocton toold me yif ye wolde byin here a goune here moder wolde yeue ther to a godely furre þe goune nedyth for to be had and of coloure it wolde be a godely blew or ellys a bryghte sanggueyn | I prey yow do byen for me ij pypys of gold | yowre stewes do weel | the Holy Trinite have yow in gouernaunce wretyn at Paston in hast þe Wednesday next after Deus qui errantibus for defaute of a good secretarye &c

Yowres
Agnes Paston

(*Paston Letters and Papers of the Fifteenth Century*, Norman Davis (ed.), OUP, 1971)

TEXT 60 – Paston letter, 1477

Vn to my ryght welbelouyd voluntyn John Paston squyer be þis bill
delyuered &c

Ryght reuerent and wurschypfull and my ryght welebeloued voluntyne I recommaunde me vn to yowe full hertely desyring to here of yowr welefare whech I beseche almyghty god long for to preserve vn to hys plesure and ȝowr hertys desyre | and yf it please ȝowe to here of my welefare I am not in good heele of body ner of herte nor schall be tyll I here from yowe

For þer wottys no creature what peyn þat I endure
And for to be deede I dare it not dyscure

And my lady my moder hath labored þe mater to my fadure full delygently but sche can no more gete þen ȝe knowe of for þe whech god knowyth I am full sorry | but yf that ȝe loffe me as I tryste verely that ȝe do ȝe will not leffe me þerfor. for if þat ȝe hade not halfe þe lyvelode þat ȝe hafe, for to do þe grettyst labure þat any woman on lyve myght I wold not forsake ȝowe

and yf ȝe commande me to kepe me true where euer I go
iwyse I will do all my myght ȝowe to love and neuer no mo
and yf my freendys say þat I do amys þei schal not me let so for to do
myn herte me byddys euer more to love ȝowe truly ouer all erthely thing
and yf þei be neuer so wroth I tryst it schall be bettur in tyme commyng

no more to yowe at this tyme but the holy trinite hafe yowe in kepyng and I besech ȝowe þat this bill be not seyn of non erthely creature safe only ȝour selfe &c and thys lettur was ȝndyte at Topcroft wyth full heuy herte &c

be ȝour own MB

Activity 8.3

(i) Rewrite the letters in modern spelling and add the appropriate punctuation.
(ii) Describe some of the regular features of the original spelling.
(iii) Comment on the punctuation of the original.
(iv) Describe the main differences between the grammar of the fifteenth century written Norfolk dialect and present-day English.

8.4 Late fifteenth century London English

William Caxton is known as the first English printer. The setting up of his printing press in London in 1476 was the beginning of a revolution in the production of books, which no longer had to be separately copied by hand. Copying did not, of course, die out immediately – the professional scriveners were able to earn a living for some time. Caxton was more than just a printer of other people's writing. He also translated into English and edited many of the books that he printed, and he provided a considerable number of prefaces and commentaries.

8.4.1 Caxton's revision of *Polychronicon*

In 1482, William Caxton printed a revised text of Trevisa's 1385 translation of Higden's *Polychronicon* (see Texts 29 and 30). This provides an excellent example of some of the changes that had taken place in the language within a hundred years. Caxton evidently found Trevisa's English old-fashioned and out of date, as he said in an epilogue:

> ... I William Caxton a symple persone have endeuoyred me to wryte fyrst overall the sayd book of *Proloconycon* and somwhat have chaunged the rude and old Englyssh, that is to wete certayn wordes which in these dayes be neither vsyd ne vnderstanden.

Caxton's fifteenth century modernised version of John of Trevisa's description of the languages of Britain is printed here alongside the fourteenth century text. This Trevisa text, which is taken from another manuscript and is slightly expanded, shows some interesting differences from Texts 29 and 30. It illustrates the lack of standardisation in ME and the way in which differences in the dialects of ME were reflected in writing. Some features of Caxton's punctuation, like his use of the virgule </>, are reproduced, but modern punctuation has been added.

TEXT 61 – John Trevisa, 1385

As it is i-knowe how meny manere peple
beeþ in þis ilond þere beeþ also so
many dyuers longages and tonges;
noþeles walsche men and scottes þat
beeþ nouȝt i-medled wiþ oþer naciouns
holdeþ wel nyh hir firste longage and
speche ...

Also englische men þey þei hadde from
þe bygynnynge þre maner speche
norþerne sowþerne and middel speche
in þe myddel of þe lond, as þey come
of þre manere peple of Germania,
noþeles by comyxtioun and mellynge

TEXT 62 – Caxton's version, 1482

As it is knowen how many maner peple
ben in this Ilond ther ben also many
langages and tonges. Netheles
walshmen and scottes that ben not
medled with other nacions kepe neygh
yet theyr first langage and
speche /

also englysshmen though they had fro
the begynnyng thre maner speches
Southern northern and myddel speche in
the middel of the londe as they come
of thre maner of people of Germania.
Netheles by commyxtion and medlyng

firste wiþ danes and afterward wiþ normans in meny þe contray longage is apayred and som vseþ straunge wlafferynge chiterynge harrynge and garrynge grisbitynge.

This apayrynge of þe burþe tonge is bycause of tweie þinges; oon is for children in scole aȝenst þe vsage and manere of alle oþere naciouns beeþ compelled for to leue hire owne langage and for to construe hir lessouns and here þynges a frensche, and so þey haueþ seþ þe normans come first in to engelond.

Also gentil men children beeþ i-tauȝt to speke frensche from þe tyme þat þey beeþ i-rokked in here cradel and kunneþ speke and playe wiþ a childes broche; and vplondisshe men wil likne hym self to gentil men and fondeþ wiþ greet besynesse for to speke frensce for to be i-tolde of ...

Þis manere was moche i-vsed to for firste deth and is siþþe sumdel i-chaunged. For Iohn Cornwaile, a maister of grammer, chaunged þe lore in gramer scole, and construccioun of frensche into englische; and Richard Pencriche lerned þe manere techynge of hym and oþere men of Pencrich; so þat now, þe ȝere of oure Lorde a þowsand þre hundred and foure score and fyue, in alle þe gramere scoles of engelond children leueþ frensche and construeþ and lerneþ an englische ...

Also gentil men haueþ now moche i-left for to teche here children frensche. Hit semeþ a greet wonder houȝ englische, þat is þe burþe tonge of englissh men and her owne langage and tonge, ys so dyuerse of sown in þis oon ilond, and þe langage of normandie is comlynge of anoþer londe and haþ oon manere soun among alle men þat spekeþ hit ariȝt in engelond.

... also of þe forsaide saxon tonge þat is i-deled a þre and is abide scarsliche wiþ fewe vplondisshe men is greet wonder; for men of þe est wiþ men of þe west, as it were vndir þe same partie of heuene, acordeþ more in sownynge of speche þan men of þe norþ wiþ men of þe souþ.

cont ...

first with danes and afterward with normans In many thynges the countreye langage is appayred / ffor somme use straunge wlaffyng / chytering harryng garryng and grisbytyng /

this appayryng of the langage cometh of two thynges / One is by cause that children that gon to scole lerne to speke first englysshe / & than ben compellid to constrewe her lessons in Frenssh and that have ben used syn the normans come in to Englond /

Also gentilmens childeren ben lerned and taught from theyr yongthe to speke frenssh. And uplondyssh men will counterfete and likene hem self to gentilmen and arn besy to speke frensshe for to be more sette by.

This maner was moche used to fore the grete deth. But syth it is somdele chaunged For sir Johan cornuayl a mayster of gramer chaunged the techyng in gramer scole and construction of Frenssh in to englysshe. and other Scoolmaysters use the same way now in the yere of oure lord / M.iij/C.lx.v. the /ix yere of kyng Rychard the secund and leve all frenssh in scoles and use al construction in englissh.

And also gentilmen have moche lefte to teche theyr children to speke frenssh Hit semeth a grete wonder that Englyssmen have so grete dyversyte in theyr owne langage in sowne and in spekyng of it / whiche is all in one ylond. And the langage of Normandye is comen oute of another lond / and hath one maner soune among al men that speketh it in englond ...

Also of the forsayd tong whiche is departed in thre is grete wonder / For men of the este with the men of the west acorde better in sownyng of theyr speche than men of the north with men of the south /

cont ...

Þerfore it is þat mercii, þat beeþ men of myddel engelond, as it were parteners of þe endes, vnderstondeþ bettre þe side langages, norþerne and souþerne, þan norþerne and souþerne vnderstondeþ eiþer oþer.	Therfor it is that men of mercij that ben of myddel englond as it were partyners with the endes understande better the side langages northern & sothern than northern & southern understande eyther other.
Al þe longage of þe norþumbres and specialliche at ȝork is so scharp slitting and frotynge and vnschape þat we souþerne men may þat longage vnneþe vnderstonde. I trowe þat þat is bycause þat þey beeþ nyh to straunge men and aliens þat spekeþ strongliche.	Alle the langages of the northumbres & specially at york is so sharp slytyng frotyng and unshape that we sothern men may unneth understande that langage I suppose the cause be that they be nygh to the alyens that speke straungely.

Activity 8.4

(i) Describe the changes that Caxton has made to 'the rude and old Englyssh' of the fourteenth century text.

(ii) Comment on the differences between the fourteenth century text in this version and in Texts 29 and 30. Do they suggest significant differences in the pronunciation or grammar of the language, or simply of spelling conventions?

8.4.2 Caxton on 'dyuersite & chaunge of langage'

A standard form of a language develops in a nation or society only at a particular time of its evolution, when the need becomes evident and pressing. We define the ME period partly by the fact that there was no one dialect that was accepted or used throughout the country as a standard in writing. The invention of printing was one factor, in the complex interaction of political and economic changes in England by the end of the fifteenth century, which led in time to the acceptance of the educated London dialect as the basis of Standard English.

One of Caxton's problems as printer and translator is clearly illustrated in a famous story that he tells in the preface to his translation of a French version of Virgil's Latin poem *The Aeneid*, called *Eneydos*. A revolution in communications was brought about by the printing of books. A book might be bought and read anywhere in the country, but which dialect of English should a printer use? For example, there were at least two words for *egg*, one derived from OE, the other from ON. The story is about the difficulty of asking for eggs for breakfast, but for Caxton it illustrates the problem of choosing a language in translation: 'Loo what sholde a man in thyse dayes now wryte, egges or eyren?' This is just one of the problems that had to be overcome in the establishment of an agreed standard literary form of English over the next 200 years.

TEXT 63 – Caxton on the diversity of English, 1490

(Caxton has decided to translate *Eneydes*)

And whan I sawe the fayr & straunge termes therin / I doubted that it sholde not please some gentylmen whiche late blamed me, sayeng that in my translacyons I had ouer curyous termes whiche coude not be vnderstande of comyn peple / and desired me to vse olde and homely termes in my translacyons. and fayn wolde I satisfye euery man / and so to doo, toke an olde boke and redde therin / and certaynly the englysshe was so rude and brood that I coude not wele vnderstande it. And also my lorde abbot of westmynster ded do shewe to me late, certayn euydences wryton on olde englysshe, for to reduce it in-to our englysshe now vsid / And certaynly it was

> wreton in suche wyse that it was more lyke to dutche than englysshe; I coude not reduce ne brynge it to be vnderstonden / And certaynly our langage now vsed varyeth ferre from that whiche was vsed and spoken whan I was borne / For we englysshe men / ben borne vnder the domynacyon of the mone, whiche is neuer stedfaste / but euer wauerynge / wexynge one season / and waneth & dyscreaseth another season / And that comyn englysshe that is spoken in one shyre varyeth from a nother. In so moche that in my dayes happened that certayn marchauntes were in a shippe in tamyse (= *the river Thames*), for to haue sayled ouer the see into zelande (= *Holland*) / and for lacke of wynde, thei taryed atte forlond (= *Foreland*), and wente to lande for to refreshe them; And one of theym named sheffelde (= *Sheffield*), a mercer, cam in-to an hows and exed for mete (= *food*); and specyally he axyd after eggys; And the goode wyf answerde, that she coude speke no frenshe. And the marchaunt was angry, for he also coude speke no frenshe, but wolde haue hadde egges / and she vnderstode hym not / And thenne at laste a nother sayd that he wolde haue eyren / then the good wyf sayd that she vnderstod hym wel / Loo, what sholde a man in thyse dayes now wryte, egges or eyren / certaynly it is harde to playse euery man / by cause of dyuersite & chaunge of langage ... but in my Iudgemente / the comyn termes that be dayli vsed, ben lyghter (= *easier*) to be vnderstonde than the olde and auncyent englysshe /

If you were to examine Caxton's language in detail, you would find that he did not devise a consistent and regular spelling system, and that many of his decisions about spelling and grammatical form were already old-fashioned for the language of the 1480s.

Here is a very short example of Caxton's printing. It is an advertisement, dating from about 1478, of Caxton's edition of the *Sarum Ordinal* (an ordinal is a book of church services; Sarum is the older name for Salisbury).

TEXT 64 – Caxton's advertisement, 1478

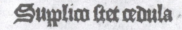

If it plese ony man spirituel or temporel to bye ony
pyes of two and thre comemoraciõs of salisburi vse
enpryntid after the forme of this presẽt lettre whiche
ben wel and truly correct, late hym come to westmo/
nester in to the almonesrye at the reed pale and he shal
haue them good chepe .·.

Supplico stet cedula

If it plese ony man spirituel or temporel to bye ony
pyes of two and thre comemoraciõs of salisburi use
enpryntid after the forme of this presẽt lettre whiche
ben wel and truly correct, late hym come to westmo
nester in to the almonesrye at the reed pale and he shal
haue them good chepe

Supplico stet cedula

Activity 8.5

(i) Examine Caxton's texts (Texts 63 and 64) for evidence of his inconsistency of choice in spelling and word form.
(ii) Rewrite Text 63 in MnE.
(iii) Describe those features of Caxton's English by which we would describe it as 'archaic' in comparison with MnE.
(iv) Comment on Caxton's style.

8.5 The medieval tales of King Arthur

In 1485, Caxton published a 'noble and joyous book entytled *Le Morte Darthur*'. He describes it in these words:

> ... a book of the noble hystoryes of the sayd Kynge Arthur and of certeyn of his knyghtes after a copye unto me delyvered. Whyche copye Syr Thomas Malorye dyd take oute of certeyn bookes of frensshe and reduced it into Englysshe.

We know that Sir Thomas Malory made his translations and adaptations from French while he was in prison. He wrote the following at the end of one of the books making up the collection.

> And I pray you all that redyth this tale to pray for hym that this wrote, that God sende hym good delyveraunce sone and hastely. Amen

Malory died in prison in 1471.

Caxton's printed book was the only known source of Malory's version of the legends of King Arthur until 1934, when a manuscript was found in the Fellows' Library of Winchester College. It is not Malory's own hand, but more authentic than Caxton's book, which has many alterations, emendations and omissions.

Here is the opening of the fourth story, 'The War with the Five Kings', in the first of the books, *The Tale of King Arthur*.

TEXT 65 – Sir Thomas Malory, c. 1460–70

So aftir thes questis of Syr Gawayne Syr
Tor and kynge **Pellynore** Than hit befelle that **Merly/**
on felle in dotage on the damesell that kynge **Pellynore**
brought to courte and she was / one of the damesels / of the Lady of the
laake that hyght **Nenyve** But **Merlion** wolde nat lette her have
no reste but / all wayes / he wolde be wyth. her And ever she made
M[erlion] good chere tylle sche had lerned of hym all maner of thyng
that sche desyred and he was assoted uppon hir that he
myght nat be from hir // So on a tyme he tolde to kynge
Arthure that he scholde nat endure longe but for all
his crafts he scholde be putte into the erthe quyk / and so
he tolde the kyng many thyngis that scholde be falle
but allwayes he warned the kyng to kepe well his swer //
de and the scawberde ^ scholde be stolyn by a woman frome
hym that he moste trusted // Also he tolde kyng **Arthure**
that he scholde mysse hym . And yett had ye levir than all
youre londis have me agayne // A sayde the kyng syn ye
knowe of youre evil adventure purvey for hit and putt
hit a way by youre craufts that mysse adventure / Nay seyde
M[erlion] hit woll not be .

^ the scribe omitted: for he told hym how the swerde and the scawberde

(Facsimile from BM Add MS 59678 f. 45, and also in *English Literary Manuscripts*, Hilton Kelliher and Sally Brown, The British Library, 1986)

SO aftir thes questis of Syr Gawayne Syr
Tor and kynge Pellynore Than hit be felle that Merly
on felle in dotage on the damesell that kynge Pellynore
brought to courte and she was one of the damesels of the lady of the
lake that hyght Nenyve But Merlion wolde nat lette her have
no reste but all wayes he wolde be wyth her And eu she made
M good chere tylle sche had lerned of hym all maner of thyng
that sche desyred and he was assoted uppon hir that he
myght nat be from hir So on a tyme he tolde to kynge
Arthure that he scholde nat endure longe but for all
his craftes he scholde be putte in to the erthe quyk and so
he tolde the kyng many thyngis that scholde befalle
but allwayes he warned the kyng to kepe well his swer
de and the scawberde scholde be stolyn by a woman frome
hym that he moste trusted Also he tolde kyng Arthure
that he scholde mysse hym And yett had ye levir than all
youre londis have me agayne A sayde the kyng syn ye
knowe of youre evil adventure purvey for hit and putt
hit away by youre crauftes that mysse adventure Nay seyde
M. hit woll not be.

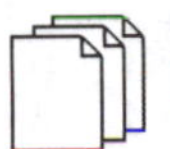

Activity 8.6

The first six lines of the facsimile were written by the principal scribe, while the rest was written by a second scribe. The handwriting is clearly different. Does the second scribe's spelling differ from that of the first?

8.6 Late fifteenth century London dialect

A collection of letters and memoranda of the Cely family, written in the 1470s and 1480s, gives us authentic handwritten evidence of London English a century after Thomas Usk's, and contemporary with the later Paston letters.

The Celys were wool merchants, or staplers. They bought woollen fleeces in England and sold them on the Continent in Calais and Bruges. The letters and accounts provide historians with direct evidence of the workings of a medieval English firm. They also give language students plenty of examples of late medieval commercial English, as well as evidence of the speech and writing habits of middle-class Londoners of the period.

The collection contains letters by 40 different people, but most are from two generations of the Cely family, father and sons. Like the Paston letters, they show that there was as yet no standardised written English. The spelling is not good evidence for the pronunciation of spoken English, partly because we do not know the sounds given to particular letters, but also because the spelling of the different writers is so irregular. Individual writers show many inconsistencies of spelling.

The following three texts consist of facsimiles and transcriptions, followed by versions in MnE spelling and punctuation.

TEXT 66 – George Cely in Calais to Richard Cely in London, 12 March 1478

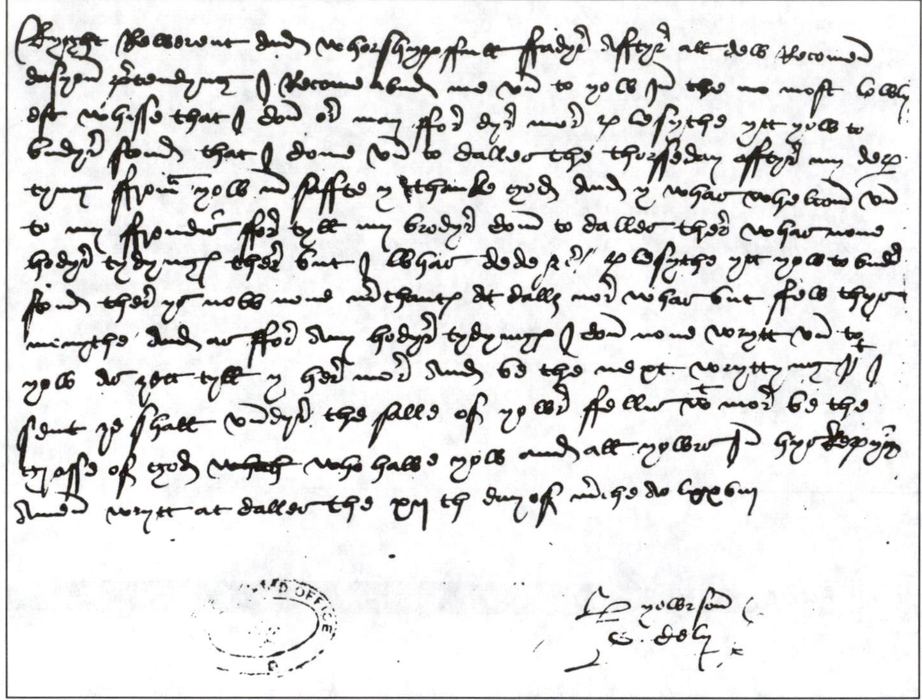

Transcription

Ryght rewerent and whorshypffull ffadyr affytyr all dew recomen
dasyon p^{r}tendyng I recomeavnd me vn to yow in the ~~mo~~ most lowly
est whisse that I con or may ffor dyr mor plesythe ytt yow to
vndyr stond that I come vn to calles the thorsseday affytyr my dep
tyng ffrom yow in saffte y thanke god and y whas whelcom vn
to my ffrendis ffor tyll my brodyr com to calles ther whas none
hodyr tydyng ther but I whas dede // etc // plesythe ytt yow to vnd^{r}
stond ther ys now none m^{r}chants at callȝ nor whas but ffew thys
monythe / and as ffor any hodyr tydyngs I con none wrytt vn to
yow as ȝett tyll y her mor and be the next wryttyng þ^{t} I
sent ȝe shall vndyr the salle of yowr ffellis w^{t} mor be the
grasse of god ~~whah~~ who hawe yow and all yowrs in hys kepy^{n}g
amen wrytt at calles the xij th day of mche a lxxviij

p yowr son
G cely

Version with modernised spelling/punctuation

Right reverent and worshipful father, after all due recommen-
dation pretending (= *having been given*), I recommend me unto you in the most lowliest wise that I can or may. Furthermore, pleaseth it you to
understand that I came unto Calais the Thursday after my dep(ar)-
ting from you, in safety I thank God, and I was welcome un
to my friends, for till my brother came to Calais there was none
other tidings there but (= *except*) I was dead etc. Pleaseth it you to understand there is now none merchants at Calais nor was but few this
month, and as for any other tidings, I can none write unto
you as yet till I hear more, and by the next writing that I
send ye shall under(stand) the sale of your fells (= *wool fleeces*) with more, by the
grace of God, who have you and all yowrs in his keeping,
amen. Writ at Calais the 12th day of March, a(nno) 78.

per (= *by*) your son,
G Cely

TEXT 67 – Richard Cely (the father) in London to Agnes, Richard and George Cely in Essex, 12 August 1479

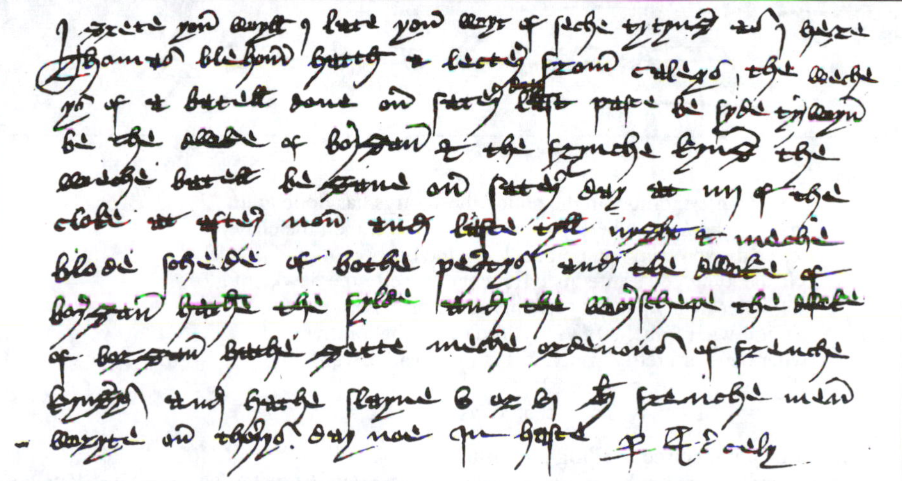

Transcription

I grete you wyll I late you wyt of seche tytyng as I here
Thomas blehom hatth a letter from caleys the weche
ys of a batell done on sater^{day} last paste be syde tyrwyn
be the dwke of borgan & the frynche kyng the
weche batell be gane on sater day at iiij of the
cloke at after non and laste tyll nyght & meche
blode schede of bothe pertys and the dwke of
borgan hathe the fylde and the worschepe the dwke
of borgan hathe gette meche ordenons of frenche
kyngys and hathe slayne v or vj ml frensche men
wryte on thorys day noe in haste

p Rc cely

Version with modernised spelling/punctuation

I greet you well. I let you wit of such tiding as I hear.
Thomas Blehom hath a letter from Calais, the which
is of a battle done on Saturday last past beside Tirwin
by the Duke of Burgundy and the French king, the
which battle began on Saturday at 4 of the
clock at afternoon, and lasted till night, and much
blood shed of both parties, and the Duke of
Burgundy hath the field, and the worship. The Duke
of Burgundy hath got much ordnance of (the) French
king's and hath slain 5 or 6 thousand Frenchmen.
Writ on Thursday now in haste.

per Richard Cely

The following text is not a letter, but a jotted down note of political events and rumours in the troubled times preceding the deposition of Edward V and the accession of the Duke of Gloucester as Richard III. The first five items are written as facts; the rest, beginning with 'If ...', are rumours. The jottings were written on the back of an old memorandum and are not always grammatically clear.

Lord Hastings, the Lord Chamberlain, had been executed in June 1483. The Chancellor was Thomas Rotherham, Archbishop of York. 'my lorde prynsse' was the Duke of York, Edward V's brother. The Earl of Northumberland and John Howard were supporters of the Duke of Gloucester. 'movnsewr sent jonys' (Monsieur St John) is a pseudonym, to disguise the name, for Sir John Weston, from whom George Cely presumably got the rumours.

TEXT 68 – Note of events and memoranda, George Cely, June 1483

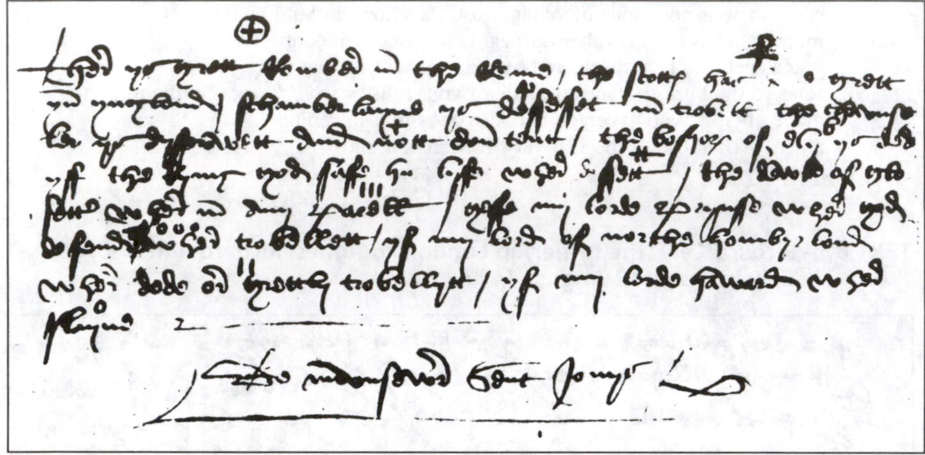

Transcription

Ther ys grett romber in the reme / the scottys has done grett
yn ynglond / schamberlayne ys dessesset in trobell the chavnse
ler ys dyssprowett and nott content / the boshop of ely ys dede
yff the kyng god ssaffe his lyffe wher dessett / the dewke of glo
sett wher in any parell / geffe my lorde prynsse wher god
defend wher trobellett / yf my lord of northehombyrlond
wher dede or grettly trobellytt / yf my lorde haward wher
slayne

De movnsewer sent jonys

Version with modernised spelling/punctuation

There is great romber (= *disturbance*, *upheaval*) in the realm. The Scots has done great
in England. (The Lord) Chamberlain is deceased in trouble. The
Chancellor is disproved (= *proved false*) and not content. The Bishop of Ely is dead.
If the King, God save his life, were deceased. (If) the Duke of
Gloucester were in any peril. If my Lord Prince were, God
defend, were troubled (= *molested*). If my Lord of Northumberland
were ded or greatly troubled. If my Lord Howard were
slain.

From monsieur Saint John

Activity 8.7

(i) Write versions of the letters in an acceptable MnE style.
(ii) Examine the facsimiles and write out the letter forms of the alphabet used in the letters.
(iii) List the principal lexical and grammatical features of the Cely's London English that mark its difference from MnE.

9. Early Modern English II – the sixteenth century

In Chapter 8, we saw how the private letters of the Pastons and the Celys written in the fifteenth century give us some idea of everyday speech at that time. Another large collection, the Lisle letters, from the early sixteenth century, provides us with examples of the language 50 years on.

Writers at that time were not using a nationally standardised form of spelling, but this does not mean that their spelling was haphazard, or that they 'wrote as they spoke'. There were inconsistencies, especially in the use of a redundant final <e> on many words, but they had clearly learned a system of spelling. Variations occurred because there were no dictionaries or spelling books to refer to until later in the sixteenth century.

9.1 The Lisle letters

These letters were written to and by Lord Lisle, his family, friends and staff, when he was Governor of Calais for King Henry VIII, from 1533 to 1540. The French town was at that time an English possession. The letters provide examples of a wide range of correspondence, both formal and informal, and are therefore first-hand evidence of the state of the language then.

Here is an example of a letter by a 14-year-old boy. George Bassett was Lady Lisle's son by her first marriage, and as part of his education he was 'put to service' in the household of Sir Francis Bryan. The letter is 'purely formal: the boy has nothing to say and he says it in the approved Tudor manner' (Muriel St Clare Byrne, editor of *The Lisle Letters*).

Activity 9.1

Describe 'the approved Tudor manner' of writing a formal letter, which the following letter illustrates.

TEXT 69 – George Bassett to his parents Lord and Lady Lisle, 1 July 1539

Ryht honorable and my most dere and singler goode lorde
and ladye / in my most humble man[ner] I recõmaunde me unto yow
besechynge to have yor dailye blessynge / and to here of yor goode
and prospus helth / fore the conservatione of whiche / I praye
dailye unto almyghty godde. I certifye youe by theys my
rude l[ett]res that my Maister and my Ladye be in goode helthe /
to whome I am myche bounde. ffurthe^{r}more I beseche
yor lordeshipe and ladishipe to have me hertilye recõmẽdyde
unto my Brothe^{r} and Systers. And thus I praye godde to conserve
yor lordshipe and ladishipe eve^{r} in goode / longe / and
prosperus helthe w^{t} hono^{r}. ffrom Woburn the
firste daye of Julye

By yor humble and
owne Son George
Bassette

(*The Lisle Letters*, Vol. 3 No. 549, Muriel St Clare Byrne (ed.))

George Bassett's formal 'duty letter' to his parents does not tell us much about him, except that he can write very competently in beautiful handwriting. He uses the **strike** or **virgule** (/) as a mark of punctuation, and the occasional full-stop, then called a **prick**. There are some conventional abbreviations, similar to those you will have noticed in the Cely and Paston letters. One that was commonly used both in handwriting and printing was the **tilde** (~) over the vowel preceding one of the nasal consonants <n> or <m>, especially if the consonant was double. Another was sometimes writing post-vocalic <r> as a superscript. Additional writing and spelling conventions can be observed in later texts.

The next letter is from Sir William Kingston, who was a member of the King's Privy Council and Constable of the Tower at the time. It is an interesting example of an educated man's style of writing which, at first glance, would be unacceptable today in its presentation because there is no punctuation. It mentions the names of several birds used in hawking, or falconry.

TEXT 70 – Sir William Kingston to Lord Lisle, 26 September 1533

... my lord to
advertyse you of newes here be nonne ȝit for now thay be
abowt the pesse (= *peace*) in the marches of scotland & with goddes
grace all shalbe well & as ȝit the kynges grace hathe
hard now word from my lord of Wynchester & so the
kyng hawkes evry day with goshawkes (= *goshawks*) & other hawkes
that ys to say layners (= *lanners*) sparhawkes (= *sparrowhawks*) and merlions
(= *merlins*) both affore
none & after yf the wether serve I pray you my lord yf
ther be hony gerfawken (= *gerfalcon*) or yerkyn (= *jerkin*) to help ^me to both yf it
may be & for lak of bothe to have wun & to send me
worde of the charges ther of & then your lordshyp dose meche
for me I & my wyfe both ryght hartely recõmaunde hus
unto my gud lady & we thanke my lady for my token for it
cam to me in the church of the blake freres (= *friars*) & my wyf
wase desposed to have offerd it to saynt loy (= *St Eligius*) (th)at hyr horse
shuld not halt & he never went up ryght syne (= *since*) I be(see)che your
lordshyp to have me in your reymembrance to master porter
& my lady & to master mershall & my lady ...

(*The Lisle Letters*, Vol. 1 No. 52, Muriel St Clare Byrne (ed.))

Activity 9.2

(i) Rewrite the letter using today's spelling and punctuation. Is it fully grammatical?
(ii) What did the following phrases mean in 1533: *to advertyse you of newes*, *yf the wether serve*?
(ii) Examine the spelling of the words in the letter and discuss any that seem unusual to you. Is the spelling significantly irregular or inconsistent? How many words have more than one spelling?

On 17 January 1536, Sir Thomas Audley wrote to Lord Lisle, Governor of Calais, for a post (called a 'Spear') in the Retinue on behalf of Robert Whethill. Whethill's father Richard had been Mayor of Calais and still lived there. He was constantly at loggerheads with Lord Lisle, who had to reply very diplomatically to Audley's letter.

Here is Lord Lisle's response, written on the back of Audley's letter. It would have been copied and tidied up before being sent, and is an interesting example of the first draft of a letter.

TEXT 71 – Draft of Lord Lisle's reply to a letter, 1536

> Ryght honorabyll aft^{r} my most humbylyst wyse I com̃end me vnto you & have reseyvyd yor jentyll lett^{r} in the favor of R whethyll cõs^{r}nyng the next speris rome within myn offyce her hit shall plesse yor good lordshype that ther is not the trustist s^{r}vãt in yor hovse nother in yngland that shall gladlyer do yor cõmandment & plessur then I wold w owght desemylassion as eu^{r} devryng my lyffe shall aper toward you & yo^{r}s thys whethill & his father orderyd me opynly at lantern gate w word & covntenans that I neu^{r} sofferyd so mvche of no degre sens I whas xvj yer̉ old notwstandyng I woll at yor cõmandement forget all

(*The Lisle Letters*, Vol. 3 No. 633a, Muriel St Clare Byrne (ed.))

Activity 9.3

(i) Rewrite the draft with modern spelling and punctuation, filling out the abbreviated words.
(ii) Comment on the grammar of *most humbylyst*, *hit* and *xvj yer old*.

9.2 Formal prose in the 1530s

An example of formal written language contemporary with the Lisle letters is Sir Thomas Elyot's *The boke named the Gouernour*, printed in London in 1531. Its dedication was:

vnto the moste noble & victorious prince
kinge Henry the eyght kyng of Eng-
lande and Fraunce / defender of
the true faythe / and lorde
of Irelande.

Elyot's purpose was 'to describe in our vulgare tunge/the fourme of a iuste publike weale' – for *weale* or *weal*, now an archaic word, we would use *welfare* or *prosperity*. He named it *The Gouernour* 'for as moch as this present boke treateth of the education of them/that hereafter may be demed worthy to be gouernors of the publike weale'. He wrote it in English, but in common with all educated men he regarded Latin and Greek as the essential languages of education and learning, as the following short extracts show.

The first chapter of the book deals with:

The significacion of a publike
weale / and why it is called
in latin *Respublica*

TEXT 72 – Sir Thomas Elyot's *The Gouernour*, 1531 (i)

A publike weale is a body lyuyng/cōpacte Publyke
or made of ſondry aſtates and degrees of weale.
men/ whiche is diſpoſed by the ordre of e-
quite/and gouerned by the rule and mode-
ration of reaſon. In the latin tonge hit is
called Reſpublica/ of the whiche the worde Reſpub-
Res/hath diuers ſignifications/ & dothe nat lica.
only betoken that/ that is called a thynge/
whiche is diſtincte from a perſone/ but alſo
ſignifieth aſtate/ condition/ ſubſtance/ and
Plebs. profite. In our olde vulgare/ ꝓfite is called
weale: And it is called a welthy contraye/
wherin is all thyng that is profitable: And
he is a welthy man/ that is riche in money
and ſubſtance. Publike (as Varro ſaith) is
diriuied of people: whiche in latin is called Populus. wherfore hit ſemeth that men
haue ben lōge abuſed in calling Rempublicā a
cōmune weale. And they which do ſuppoſe
it ſo to be called for that/ that euery thinge
ſhulde be to all men in cōmune/ without di-
ſcrepance of any aſtate or condition/ be ther
to moued more by ſenſualite/ than by any
good reaſon or inclinatiō to humanite. And
that ſhall ſone appere vnto them that wyll
be ſatiſfied either with autorite/ or with naturall ordre and example.

Fyrſt the ꝓpre & trewe ſignification of the
wordes publike & cōmune/ whiche be borowed of the latin tonge for the inſufficiēcie of
our owne lāgage/ ſhal ſufficiētly declare the
blyndenes of them/ whiche haue hitherto
holden and maynteyned the ſayde opiniōs.

Elyot refers to 'the insufficiencie of our owne langage' when defining the words *publike* and *commune* 'whiche be borowed of the latin tonge'. Elyot's *commune* is MnE *common* and is used in the sense of the word *commoner* as against *noble*. We now know that both words had been taken from OF during the ME period, but their source was Latin *publicus* and *communis*, and Elyot, like other scholarly writers of the period, Englished many Latin and Greek words in order to express his meaning.

Sir Thomas Elyot sets out a programme of education for young noblemen in which learning Latin begins before the age of seven.

TEXT 73 – Sir Thomas Elyot's *The Gouernour*, 1531 (ii)

The ordre of lernynge that a noble man
shulde be trayned in before he come
to thaige of seuen yeres. Cap.v.

But there can be nothyng moꝛe conuenient/than by litle and litle to trayne and exercise them in ſpekyng of latyne: infourmyng them to knowe firſt the names in latine of all thynges that cometh in ſyghte/ and to name all the partes of theyꝛ bodies:

It is clear that in Elyot's day, just as today, strong feelings could be aroused over accent and pronunciation. In the following text, he is recommending the kind of nurse and serving woman that a young nobleman under seven should have.

TEXT 74 – Sir Thomas Elyot's *The Gouernour*, 1531 (iii)

hit ſhall be expedient/that a noble mannes ſonne in his infancie haue with hym continually/onely ſuche/as may accuſtome hym by litle and litle to ſpeake pure and elegant latin. Semblably the nouriſes ⁊ other women aboute hym/if it be poſſible/to do the ſame: oꝛ at the leſte way/that they ſpeke none engliſſhe but that/ whiche is cleane/ polite/ perfectly/ and articulately pꝛonounced/omittinge no lettre oꝛ ſillable/ as foliſſhe women often times do of a wantonneſſe/wherby diuers noble men/and gẽtilmennes chyldꝛen (as I do at this daye knowe) haue attained coꝛrupte and foule pꝛonuntiation.

These texts from *The Gouernour* are not only of interest with regard to their subject matter and style, but also to observe those features of grammar and lexis which clearly mark Elyot's language as still archaic in terms of MnE, although it is much closer to our Standard English than the earlier texts we have studied.

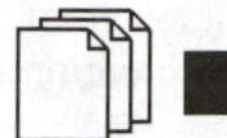

Activity 9.4

(i) Explain the few alternative spellings in the texts: hit/it, latin/latine/latyne, onely/only, pronounced/pronuntiation, saith/sayde, shal/shall, significacions/signification, ther/there, thinge/thyng/thyng, which/whiche.
(ii) Compare Elyot's system of punctuation with present-day conventions.
(iii) Use a dictionary to identify some of the words that were borrowed from French, Latin or Greek during the sixteenth century.
(iv) What was the meaning of the following words in the 1530s: vulgare, astates, equite, diuers, betoken, abused, discrepance, sensualite?
(v) Do any verb inflections differ from those in Standard English today?
(vi) How do the grammatical features of the following phrases or word sequences differ from Standard English today: body lyuyng; all thing; of the whiche, them whiche, they which; them that, that that; do suppose; whiche be borrowed?

9.3 A different view on new words

Sir Thomas Elyot expressed a scholar's view on the superiority of the resources of Latin and Greek, from which hundreds of words were 'Englished'. These words were disparagingly referred to as 'inkhorn terms' – words coming from the scholar's horn of ink and therefore pedantic – and there was a lot of controversy over this. For example, George Puttenham called the introduction of Latin and Greek words 'corruption' of language, the result of the 'peeuish affectation of clerks and scholers', because it introduced polysyllabic words into English.

TEXT 75 – George Puttenham's *The Arte of English Poesie*, 1589

but now I muſt recant and con-
feſſe that our Normane Engliſh which hath growen ſince *William*
the Conquerour doth admit any of the auncient feete, by reaſon of the many *polyſillables* euen to ſixe and ſeauen in one word,
which we at this day vſe in our moſt ordinarie language: and
which corruption hath bene occaſioned chiefly by the peeuiſh affectation not of the Normans them ſelues, but of clerks and ſcho-
lers or ſecretaries long ſince, who not content with the vſual Normane or Saxon word, would conuert the very Latine and Greeke
word into vulgar French, as to ſay innumerable for innombrable,
reuocable, irreuocable, irradiation, depopulatiõ & ſuch like, which
are not naturall Normans nor yet French, but altered Latines, and
without any imitation at all: which therefore were long time de-
ſpiſed for inkehorne termes, and now be reputed the beſt & moſt
delicat of any other.

auncient feete means the verse rhythms of the classical Latin and Greek poets. A *foot* is a unit of rhythm.

peeuish is here used as an adjective of dislike: 'expressing rather the speaker's feeling than any quality of the object referred to' (*OED*).

But there were those who did not accept Sir Thomas Elyot's view on 'the insufficiencie of our own langage', and who disliked any borrowing from other languages, not just the creation of 'inkhorn terms'. Richard Verstegan described them in 1605.

TEXT 76 – Richard Verstegan's *A Restitution of Decayed Intelligence*, 1605

Since the tyme of *Chaucer*, more Latin & French, hath bin mingled with our toung then left out of it, but of late wee haue falne to ſuch borowing of woords from, Latin, French, and other toungs, that it had bin beyond all ſtay and limit, which albeit ſome of vs do lyke wel and think our toung thereby much bettred, yet do ſtrangers therefore carry the farre leſſe opinion thereof, ſome ſaying that it is of it ſelf no language at all, but the ſcum of many languages, others that it is moſt barren, and that wee are dayly faine to borrow woords for it (as though it yet lacked making) out of other languages to patche it vp withall, and that yf wee were put to repay our borrowed ſpeech back again, to the languages that may lay claime vnto it; wee ſhould bee left litle better then dumb, or ſcarſly able to ſpeak any thing that ſhould bee ſencible.

Our toung diſcredited by our language-borrowing.

9.4 'English Dictionaries & other bookes written by learned men'

During the sixteenth century, the first dictionaries, spelling books and grammars of English were published. The writers were responding to a growing sense that the language needed an agreed form of spelling, grammar and vocabulary. People saw that the letters of the alphabet were too few to match the sounds of English, and that the spelling of many words did not match their pronunciation. A common description of the language was that it was 'corrupted'.

One of the earliest books that advocated a reform of English spelling was John Hart's *An Orthographie*, published in 1569. In the following extract, he is justifying the need for his new spelling system, 'the new maner'.

TEXT 77 – John Hart's *An Orthographie*, 1569 (i)

Which is vppon the conſideration of the ſeuerall voices of the ſpeach, and the vſe of their ſeuerall markes foꝛ them, which we cal letters. But in the moderne & pꝛeſent maner of wꝛiting (aſwell of certaine other languages as of our Engliſh) there is ſuch confuſion and diſoꝛder, as it may be accounted rather a kinde of ciphꝛing, oꝛ ſuch a darke kinde of wꝛiting, as the beſt and readieſt wit that euer hath bene, could, oꝛ that is oꝛ ſhalbe, can oꝛ may, by the only gift of reaſon, attaine to the ready and perfite reading thereof, without a long and tedious labour, foꝛ that it is vnfit and wꝛong ſhapen foꝛ the pꝛopoꝛtion of the voice. Whereas the new maner hereafter (thoughe it ſéeme at the firſt very ſtraunge, hard and vnpꝛofitable) by the reading only therof, will pꝛoue it ſelfe fit, eaſie and delectable, and that foꝛ whatſoeuer Engliſh may be wꝛittẽ in that oꝛder.

Activity 9.5

Discuss what an ideal alphabetic system of spelling should be like and give some examples of what Hart calls 'confusion and disorder' in our present system, which is largely unchanged since Hart's time in its essentials. For example:

(i) How many letters are there in the Roman alphabet used today?
(ii) How many contrastive sounds (phonemes) are there in English today?
(iii) What are some of the ways in which the mismatch between phonemes (Hart's *voices*) and letters (Hart's *markes*) has been dealt with in our spelling system?
(iv) Which of them had developed in ME before the sixteenth century?

Hart's argument begins with the 'fiue differing simple soundes or voyces' – that is, the five vowels <a e i o u>. They should each represent one sound, but 'they haue bene and are abused in diuers soundes'. He illustrates their proper pronunciation with this sentence:

> The pratling Hosteler hath dressed, curried, and rubbed our horses well.

and adds:

> ... none of the fiue vowels is missounded, but kept in their proper and auncient soundes.

As you read the sentence, remember two things. Firstly, the present-day RP and Southern pronunciation of *curried* and *rubbed*, with the short vowel /ʌ/, did not exist then. The vowel was /ʊ/. Secondly, the <r> in *horses* was pronounced.

Hart pointed out two spelling conventions which are still part of the modern English system, but which he did not use in his reformed spelling. The first was the use of a final <e> to mark a preceding *long* vowel, as in MnE *hate/hat* and *site/sit*. The second was the use of double consonants to mark a preceding *short* vowel, as in MnE *matting/mating* and *robbing/robing*. He preferred to use a dot under the letter to mark a long vowel:

> I leaue also all double consonants: hauing a mark for the long vowell, there is therby sufficient knowledge giuen that euerye unmarked vowell is that ...

The interest of Hart's book for us is not so much in the reformed alphabet that he invented, but the authentic evidence it indirectly provides about changes in the pronunciation of English. Here is a facsimile of the opening of the first two pages of the second part of the book, which is printed in Hart's new spelling, followed by a transcription into MnE spelling.

TEXT 78 – John Hart's *An Orthographie*, 1569 (ii)

*An exersịz ov dat huich iz sẹd: huer-in iz de-
clard, hou de rest ov de consonants ar mad
bei dinstruments ov de mouth: huich
uaz omited in de premisez, for dat
ui did not much abiuz
dem. Cap. vij.*

In dis tịtl abuv-uritn, ei konsider ov de ị, in exersịz, & ov de u, in instruments: de leik ov de ị, in tịtl, huich de kómon man, and mani lernd, du found in de diphthongs ei, and iu: iet ei uld not think it mịt to ureit dem, in doz and leik ụrds, huer de sound ov de voël ọnli, mẹ bi as uel álouëd in our spịch, as dat ov de diphthong iuzd ov de riud: and so fár ei álou observasion for derivasions. / hierbei iu mẹ persẹv, dat our singl sounding and ius of letters, mẹ in proses ov teim, bring our hol nasion tu ọn serten, perfet and zeneral ʃpẹking. / huer-in ʃi must bi riuled bei de lernd from teim tu teim. / and ei kan not blạm ani man tu think dis maner ov niu ureiting stranz, for ei du konfés it iz stranz tu mei self, dob befọr ei hạv ended de ureiting, and iu de rịding ov diz bụk, ei dout not bọd iu and ei ʃal think our lạburs uel bestoëd. / and not-uid-standing dat ei hạv devịzd dis niu maner ov ureiting for our /ingliʃ, ei miẹn not dat /latin ʃuld bi-uritn in dez leters, no mọr den de /grik or /hebriu, neder uld ei ureit t'ani man ov ani stranz nasion in dez léters, but huen az ei-uld ureit /ingliʃ. / and az ei-uld gladli konterfet hiz ʃpịch uid mei tung, so-uld ei hiz ureiting uid mei hand. / iet huo kuld let mi t'iuz mei pén de best ei kuld, derbei t'átẹn de sụner tu de perfet pronunsiasion, ov ani stranz ʃpịch: but ureiting /ingliʃ, ui mẹ (az is sẹd) iuz for evri stranz ụrd, de sạm marks or léters ov de voises huich ui du feind in ʃpịch, uidout ani-uder regard tu ʃiọ bei-ureiting huens de-ụrd iz boroëd; den az ui du-in ʃpẹking. / for such kuriozite in superfluz léters, for derivasion or diferens, and so furth, iz de disordring and konfounding, ov ani-ureiting: kontrari tu de lau-ov de perfeksion derof, and agenst aul rẹzon: huer-bei, it ʃuld bi obedient untu de pronunsiasion, az tu hir lạdi and mistres: and so, ád or diminiʃ az ʃi ʃaul in sukses ov teim kómaund. /

Version with MnE spelling

An exercise of that which is said: wherein is declared, how the rest of the consonants are made by th'instruments of the mouth: which was omitted in the premisses, for that we did not much abuse them. Chapter vii.

In this title above-written, I consider of the <i> in exercise, & of the <u>, in instruments: the like of the <i>, in title, which the common man, and many learned, do sound in the diphthongs <ei>, and <iu>: yet I would not think it meet to write them, in those and like words, where the sound of the vowel only, may be as well allowed in our speech, as that of the diphthong used of the rude: and so far I allow observation for derivations. ~ / Whereby you may perceive, that our single sounding and use of letters, may in process of time, bring our whole nation to one certain, perfet and general speaking. ~ / Wherein she must be ruled by the learned from time to time. ~ / And I can not blame any man to think this manner of new writing strange, for I do confess it is strange to my self, though before

I have ended the writing, and you the reading of this book, I doubt not but you and I shall think our labours well bestowed. ~ / And not-with-standing that I have devised this new manner of writing for our /English, I mean not that /Latin should be written in these letters, no more then the /Greek or /Hebrew, neither would I write t'any man of any strange nation in these letters, but when as I would write /English. ~ / And as I would gladly counterfeit his speech with my tongue, so would I his writing with my hand. ~ / Yet who could let me t'use my pen the best I could, thereby t' attain the sooner to the perfect pronunciation, of any strange speech: but writing /English, we may (as is said) use for every strange word, the same marks or letters of the voices which we do find in speech, without any other regard to show by writing whence the word is borrowed, then as we do in speaking. ~ / For such curiosity in superfluous letters, for derivation or for difference, and so forth, is the disordering and confounding, of any writing: contrary to the law of the perfection thereof, and against all reason: whereby, it should be obedient unto the pronunciation, as to her lady and mistress: and so, add or diminish as she shall in success of time command. ~

Activity 9.6

Identify the sound changes that Hart describes in this extract from his book.

In Text 78, John Hart refers to some of his objections to the current spelling system:

- **Superfluous letters** – some of the letters of the Roman alphabet are redundant and could be dropped.
- **Derivation** – he rejects the argument that the original spelling of words borrowed from other languages should be retained because it shows their derivation. He advocates the use of English spelling conventions once a word is assimilated.
- **Difference** – he also rejects the use of different spelling for words that are pronounced alike. If there is no confusion when we speak them, then there can be none when we write them.

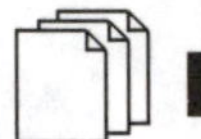

Activity 9.7

Give some examples of each of these three 'abuses' of spelling in present-day English.

9.5 Changes in English pronunciation – the Great Vowel Shift

Between the time of Chaucer in the late fourteenth century and Shakespeare in the late sixteenth century, all the long vowels in English spoken in the Midlands and South of England shifted their pronunciation. We don't know why it happened, and no similar shift is known to have taken place at other times. It has therefore been called the **Great Vowel Shift**. John Hart's reference to the <i> vowel in *exercise* – that it was being pronounced as a diphthong by some speakers – is contemporary evidence of the shift taking place.

The shift was not complete in 1569, and there was variation between regional and social dialect speakers, but in time all the long vowels were either raised or became diphthongs. In spite of Hart and other reformers up to the present day, our spelling system has never been altered to fit the changed pronunciations. Consequently, the sound of the short vowels, represented by the letters <a> <e> <i> <o> <u>, has remained more or less the same, while the sounds of the long vowels no longer match the letters.

Here is a simplified list of the changes (there are a lot of irregularities and variations which make this topic very complex to study in detail):

Short vowels

ME vowel	Letter	MnE word	MnE pronunciation
/i/	<i>	think	/ɪ/
/e/	<e>	pen	/ɛ/
/a/	<a>	add	/æ/
/o/	<o>	common	/ɒ/
/u/	<u>	but	/ʊ/ or /ʌ/

Long vowels before and after the Great Vowel Shift

ME vowel	Letter	MnE word	MnE pronunciation
/iː/	<i>	find	/aɪ/
/eː/	<e> <ee>	we, geese	/iː/
/ɛː/	<e> <ea>	speak	/iː/
/aː/	<a>	lady	/eː/ or /eɪ/
/ɔː/	<o> <oa>	oak	/oː/ or /əʊ/
/oː/	<o> <oo>	do, goose	/uː/
/uː/	<u> <ou> <ow>	cow, house	/aʊ/

Notice that there were two pairs of contrasting long front and back vowels, /eː/ and /ɛː/, /oː/ and /ɔː/. This can be seen in the facsimile of the letters in an 'amendment of ortography' by another spelling reformer, William Bullokar, in 1580. These vowels were represented in traditional spelling (but not consistently) by the digraphs <ee>, <ea>, <oo> and <oa> respectively. Bullokar provides a separate letter for each of the four sounds.

The names of the letters according to this amendment of ortography, appéere in this Table, by the which ye may name the letters in the written Copies following.

a / a	b / b	cé / c	kæ / c	ché / ch	d / d	e : ea / e : æ	é / e
f / f	gé / g	ga / g turn a into e.	hé / h	i / i	k / k	l / l	yl / l
m / m	ym / m	n / n	yn / n	o / o	between o : ø : v / ω	p / p	phé / ph
qué / q	r / r	er / r	ſ / ſ	ſhé / ſh	t / t	thé / th	thæ / th
v / v	ou / v	vé / v	wæ / w	whé / wh	x / x	yæ / y	zé / z

Here haue ye, gentle Reader, the vse of this amended ortography, in the Romaine, Italian, Chauncerie, and Secretarie handes, by the examples of which, any other hande may easily be framed with this ortography: assuring you that the same hands, being written with the pen, doe excell these printed. which written hands, and the Court hand also, you may at any time herafter sée, at the house of the Printer of this worke, who (as also the Author of this worke) desireth to be borne withall for a time, if any figure or letter be not in his perfectnesse, for the charge is not small, that bringeth all thinges to perfectnes in such cases. Hereafter (by the grace of God and your good accepting of this) greater charges shall not want to the full perfecting hereof

Examples of words with long vowels in the two pages of Hart's new spelling have been sorted into sets below, using Hart's subscript 'prick' to mark a long vowel as one criterion (although it is not printed consistently). Only one possible ME spelling is given as an example. The column of Hart's spellings does not reproduce his new letters for <th>, <sh> and <ch>.

(A more detailed description of the Great Vowel Shift, and the evidence for it as shown in Hart's *An Orthographie*, is given in Commentary 13 of the *Text Commentary Book*.)

Changes to long vowels and diphthongs from ME to MnE

Only one possible ME spelling is given as an example. The column of Hart's spellings does not reproduce his new letters for <th>, <sh>, <ch>.

Source (OE/OF)	**ME**	**Hart's spelling**	**MnE**
1		<ei>	
OE tīma /**i:**/	tīme /**i:**/	**teim** = /əɪ/	time /**ai**/
2		<i>	
OF exercīse /**i:**/	exercīsen /**i:**/	**exersiz** = /**i:**/	exercise /**ai**/
3		<i>	
OE mē /**e:**/	me /**e:**/	**mi** = /**i:**/	me = /**i:**/
OE rǣdan /**æ:**/	rēden /**e:**/	**rid** = /**i:**/	read = /**i:**/
OE spēc /**e:**/	spēche /**e:**/	**spich** = /**i:**/	speech = /**i:**/
4		<e>	
OE specan /**ɛ**/	spēken /**ɛ:**/	**spek** = /**e:**/	speak /**i:**/
OF perceivre /**ɛ**/	perceiven /**ɛ:**/	**persev** = /**e:**/	perceive /**i:**/
		<e>	
OE mæg /**æɣ**/	mai /**aɪ**/	**me** = /**e**/	may /**eɪ**/
5		<a>	
OF blamer /**a**/	blāmen /**a:**/	**blam** = /**a:**/	blame /**eɪ**/
OE hlǣfdige /**æ:**/	lādi /**a:**/	**ladi** = /**a:**/	lady /**eɪ**/
OE macode /**a**/	māde /**a:**/	**mad** = /**a:**/	made /**eɪ**/
6		<o>	
OE ānlic /**ɑ:**/	ōnli /**ɔ:**/	**onli** = /**o:**/	only /**o:**/ or /**əʊ**/
		<o>	
OE ān /**ɑ:**/	ōn /**ɔ:**/	**on** = /**o:**/	one /**wʌn**/ or /**wʊn**/
7		<u>	
OE dōn /**o:**/	dōn /**o:**/	**du** = /**u:**/	do /**u:**/
		<u>	
OE bōc /**o:**/	bōk /**o:**/	**buk** = /**u:**/	book /**ʊ**/
8		<ou>	
OE mūþ /**u:**/	mōūth/muth /**u:**/	**mouth** = /əʊ/	mouth /**aʊ**/
OE ūre /**u:**/	ōūre/ure /**u:**/	**our** = /əʊ/	our /**aʊ**/

Activity 9.8

Use the preceding list of words, which gives their pronunciation in ME, the sixteenth century (from John Hart's book) and in MnE, to answer the questions.

(i) What evidence is there of a shift, by the 1560s, in the pronunciation of long vowels, according to Hart's evidence?
(ii) Have any vowels not yet begun to shift?
(iii) List some words from the text which show that the pronunciation of short vowels was not changing.

9.6 Punctuation in sixteenth century texts

The facsimiles of written and printed texts that you have already read will have shown some obvious differences from present-day conventions in punctuation. A useful summary of conventions in the 1560s is provided by John Hart.

TEXT 79 – John Hart's *An Orthographie* (iii)

At laſt, to be readye to enter into my newe maner of writing, I will brieflye write of diſtinction or pointing, which (well obſerued) maye yeelde the matter, much the readier to the ſenſes, as well to the eie as to the eare. For it ſheweth vs how to reſt: when ÿ ſentence continueth, and when it endeth: how to vnderſtande what is written, and is not needefull to the ſentence: what ſome tranſlatour or new writer of a worke, doth adde more than the Author did at firſt write: and alſo what ſentence is aſking: and what is wondring: their number is ſeuen, whoſe figures folow. The firſt marked thus , the Greekes call comma, for which the Latines and other vulgares haue vſed a ſtrike thus / or thus, / & called it inciſum, and is in reading the ſhorteſt reſt, neare the time of a Trachet in muſicke, alwayes ſignifying the ſentence vnfiniſhed which we commonly nowe marke thus , for that the vſe thereof is ſo often to be ſeene, I forbeare to giue you any other example therof.

The ſecond marked thus : ÿ Greekes call colon, which the Latines interprete artus membrorum or internodium, which is the ſpace, or the bone, fleſhe and ſkinne betwixt two ioyntes, and ſo (accompting a full ſentence, as a complete bodie) theſe two prickes may well ſignifie a great part therof, : as of the body, may be taken from the ancle ioint to the knee, and from the knee to the huckle or buttock ioynt: and knowing thereby that there is more to come, whereas the other firſt reſt or comma, doth but in maner deuide the ſmall parts (betwixt the ioynts) of the hands and feete.

And the laſt of theſe three is a pricke thus . to ſignifie the ende of a full and perfite ſentence, as the head and feete are the extreeme endes of a body, which prick the Greekes and Latines with many other nations doe vſe:

Hart goes on to speak of the **parenthesis** ( ), the **interrogatiue** ? and the **admiratiue** !

9.7 The development of the standard language

In Chapters 4 to 7, we saw that there was no ME standard language, but a number of interrelated dialects of the language. English today consists of interrelated dialects, spread throughout the world, but in England people now tend to regard the Standard English dialect as 'the English language', and look on the other regional and social dialects as substandard or inferior. Hence they talk of 'good English' or 'correct English', and devalue the status of the regional dialects.

This point of view is not new: we have seen evidence of concern over the differences between the dialects at least as far back as the fourteenth century, in John of Trevisa's discussion of the language (see Texts 29 and 30). Both Chaucer in the 1380s and Caxton in the 1480s refer to the 'diversity' of the English language.

A written standard was the first to develop. Educated men and women wrote in the standard but continued to speak in the dialect of their region. John Aubrey, writing in the mid-seventeenth century, says of Sir Walter Raleigh (1552–1618):

> Old Sir Thomas Malett, one of the Justices of the King's bench *tempore Caroli I et II*, knew Sir Walter, and I have heard him say, that notwithstanding his so great Mastership in Style and his conversation with the learnedest and politest persons, yet he spake broad Devonshire to his dying day.

Aubrey implies that this was unusual, and that gentlemen in his time did not speak in regional dialects at court. There is also the hint that the dialect does not somehow fit with learning and polite behaviour.

Standard vocabulary and grammar eventually spread to spoken English as well as written. We have already noted in Chapter 8 how, by the end of the fifteenth century, there is less and less evidence in printed books and in manuscripts of the range of dialects of English. Regional and social varieties still flourished, but the evidence for them is much more difficult to find. There are no written records of colloquial speech as authentic as sound recording makes possible for present-day English. The language of informal letters or the dialogue of characters in prose drama is probably the nearest we can get to everyday speech of the time.

9.7.1 'The best and most perfite English'

John Hart in *An Orthographie* insisted that writing should represent speech: 'we must be ruled by our speech'. But he also recognised the problem that the diversity of dialects posed in using his new alphabet to write English as it sounded – whose dialect do you choose?

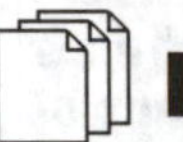

Activity 9.9

Read the following paragraph from Hart's book and discuss his solution to the problem of choice of dialect.

TEXT 80 – John Hart's *An Orthographie* (iv)

Notwithſtanding, he ſhould haue a wrong opinion of me, that ſhould thinke by the premiſſes, I ment any thing ſhoulde be printed in London in the maner of Northerne or Weſterne ſpeaches: but if any one were minded at Newcaſtell vppon Tine, or Bodman in Cornewale, to write or print his minde there, who could iuſtly blame him for his Orthographie, to ſerue hys neyghbours according to their mother ſpeach, yea, though he wrate ſo to London, to whomſoeuer it were, he could be no more offended to ſee his writing ſo, than if he were preſent to heare him ſpeake: and there is no doubt, but that the Engliſh ſpeach, which the learned ſort in the ruled Latin, togither with thoſe which are acquainted with the vulgars Italian, French, and Spaniſh doe vſe, is that ſpeach which euery reaſonable Engliſh man, will the neareſt he can, frame his tongue therevnto: but ſuch as haue no conference by the liuely voice, nor experience of reading, nor in reading no certaintie how euery letter ſhoulde be ſounded, can neuer come to the knowledge and vſe, of that beſt and moſte perfite Engliſh: which by Gods grace I will the néereſt I can follow, leauing manye an Inckhorne terme (which I could vſe) bicauſe I regarde for whoſe ſake I doe it.

Text 80 is clear evidence of the advocacy of educated London speech as 'the best and most perfite', spoken by 'euery reasonable English man'.

9.7.2 'The vsuall speach of the Court'

George Puttenham's advice to writers about choosing the best variety of English was briefly quoted in Section 7.1. Here is a longer extract which illustrates Puttenham's awareness of the range of available regional and social varieties before Standard English was a fully accepted and defined variety.

TEXT 81 – George Puttenham's *The Arte of English Poesie*, 1589

But after a ſpeach is fully faſhioned to the common vnderſtanding, & accepted by conſent of a whole countrey & natiõ, it is called a language, & receaueth none allowed alteration, but by extraordinary occaſions by little & little, as it were inſenſibly bringing in of many corruptiõs that creepe along with the time: This part in our maker or Poet muſt be heedyly looked vnto, that it be naturall, pure, and the moſt vſuall of all his countrey: and for the ſame purpoſe rather that which is ſpoken in the kings Court, or in the good townes and Cities within the land, then in the marches and frontiers, or in port townes, where ſtraungers haunt for traffike ſake, or yet in Vniuerſities where Schollers vſe much peeuiſh affectation of words out of the primatiue languages, or finally, in any vplandiſh village or corner of a Realme, where is no reſort but of poore ruſticall or vnciuill people: neither ſhall he follow the ſpeach of a craftes man or carter, or other of the inferiour ſort, though he be inhabitant or bred in the beſt towne and Citie in this Realme, for ſuch perſons doe abuſe good ſpeaches by ſtrange accents or ill ſhapen ſoundes, and falſe ortographie. But he ſhall follow generally the better brought vp ſort, ſuch as the Greekes call [*charientes*] men ciuill and graciouſly behauoured and bred. Our maker therfore at theſe dayes ſhall not follow *Piers plowman* nor *Gower* nor *Lydgate* nor yet *Chaucer*, for their language is now out of vſe with vs: neither ſhall he take the termes of Northern-men, ſuch as they vſe in dayly talke, whether they be noble men or gentlemen, or of their beſt clarkes all is a matter: nor in effect any ſpeach vſed beyond the riuer of Trent, though no man can deny but that theirs is the purer Engliſh Saxon at this day, yet it is not ſo Courtly nor ſo currant as our Southerne Engliſh is, no more is the far Weſterne mãs ſpeach: ye ſhall therfore take the vſuall ſpeach of the Court, and that of London and the ſhires lying about London within lx. myles, and not much aboue. I ſay not this but that in euery ſhyre of England there be gentlemen and others that ſpeake but ſpecially write as good Southerne as we of Middleſex or Surrey do, but not the common people of euery ſhire, to whom the gentlemen, and alſo their learned clarkes do for the moſt part condeſcend, but herein we are already ruled by th'Engliſh Dictionaries and other bookes written by learned men, and therefore it needeth none other direction in that behalfe.

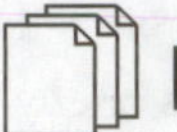

Activity 9.10

(i) Describe the assumptions about language that are evident in the text. Comment particularly on the following:
   (a) His use of the word *corruptions* to describe changes in a language.
   (b) The reference to a language that is *naturall, pure and the most vsuall.*
   (c) His contrasting of *good townes and Cities* with other places.
   (d) His references to *the inferiour sort* of men and women.
   (e) The attitude implied in *any speach vsed beyond the riuer of Trent.*

(ii) Are Puttenham's attitudes still current today?

Puttenham was expressing a point of view that is probably common in all societies. There is evidence earlier in the sixteenth century in the books on spelling and grammar, which Puttenham mentions, that 'diversity' in the language worried writers and scholars. The implications of this point of view are, however, more serious, because it is not limited simply to specifying a choice of language for writers:

- Varieties of the language are marked by social class and education. Social classes speak differently and can be recognised by their speech. Written and spoken English have **prestige varieties.**
- Once a written standard language becomes the norm for speech in the educated class, the division between that class and regional dialect speakers is complete.

Such differences of language are a part of every society. Standardisation of language is a necessary development in a society, but brings with it social consequences.

This development of a standard is, therefore, the background to our continuing study of the development of EMnE in the sixteenth and seventeenth centuries.

9.8 Evidence for some sixteenth century varieties of English

9.8.1 National dialects

The dialogue of characters in plays cannot be taken as completely authentic evidence of the spoken language, but may indicate the more obvious dialectal features of speech. In Shakespeare's *The Life of Henry the Fift*, there are comic episodes involving four captains – Gower, Fluellen, Mackmorrice and Iamy. Their names give them away as an Englishman, a Welshman, an Irishman and a Scotsman.

Activity 9.11

Describe the dialectal features of the characters' speech which is indicated by the spelling, vocabulary and syntax of the dialogue in Text 82.

TEXT 82 – Shakespeare's *The Life of Henry the Fift*

Enter Gower.

Gower. Captain *Fluellen*, you muſt come preſently to the Mines; the Duke of Gloucester would ſpeak with you.

Flu. To the Mines? Tell you the Duke, it is not ſo good to come to the Mines: for look you, the Mines are not according to the Diſciplines of War; the Concavities of it is not ſufficient: for look you, th' athverſary, you may diſcuſs unto the Duke, look you, is digt himſelf four yards under the Countermines: by *Cheſhu*, I think a will plow up all, if there is not better directions.

Gower. The Duke of *Glouceſter*, to whom the Order of the Siege is given, is altogether directed by an Iriſh man, a very valiant Gentleman, I'faith.

Welch. It is Captain *Makmorrice*, is it not?

Gower. I think it be.

Welch. By *Cheſhu* he is an Aſs, as in the World, I will verifie as much in his Beard: he ha's no more directions in the true diſciplines of the Wars, look you, of the *Roman* diſciplines, than is a Puppy-dog.

Enter Makmorrice, *and Captain* Jamy.

Gower. Here a comes, and the *Scots* Captain, Captain *Jamy*, with him.

Welch. Captain *Jamy* is a marvellous valorous Gentleman, that is certain, and of great expedition and knowledge in th'aunchiant Wars, upon my particular knowledge of his directions; by *Cheſhu* he will maintain his Argument as well as any Militarie man in the World, in the Diſciplines of the priſtine Wars of the *Romans*.

Scot. I ſay gudday, Captain *Fluellen*.

Welch. Godden to your Worſhip, good Captain *James*.

Gower. How now, Captain *Makmorrice*, have you quit the Mines? have the Pioners given o're?

Iriſh. By Chriſh, Law, tiſh ill done: the Work iſh give over, the Trompet ſound the Retreat. By my Hand I ſwear, and my father's Soul, The Work iſh ill done: it iſh give over: I would have blowed up the Town, ſo Chriſh ſave me, law, in an hour. O tiſh ill done, tiſh ill done: by my Hand tiſh ill done.

Welch. Captaine *Makmorrice*, I beſeech you now, will you vouchafe me, look you, a few diſputations with you, as partly touching or concerning the diſciplines of the War, the *Roman* Wars, in the way of Argument, look you, and friendly communication: partly to ſatisfie my Opinion, and partly for the ſatisfaction, look you, of my Mind, as touching the direction of the Military diſcipline, that is the Point.

Scot. It ſall be vary gud, gud feith, gud Captens bath, and I ſall quit you with gud leve, as I may pick occaſion: that ſal I marry.

Iriſh. It is no time to diſcourſe, ſo Chriſh ſave me: The day is hot, and the Weather, and the Wars, and the King, and the Duke: it is not time to diſcourſe, the Town is beſeech'd: and the Trumpet calls us to the Breach, and we talk, and by Chriſh do nothing, 'tis ſhame for us all: ſo God ſa'me 'tis ſhame to ſtand ſtill, it is ſhame by my hand: and there is Throats to be cut, and Works to be done, and there iſh nothing done, ſo Chriſt ſa'me law.

Scot. By the Mes, ere theiſe eyes of mine take themſelves to ſlomber, ayle de gud ſervice, or Ile ligge i'th' grund for it; ay, or go to death: and Ile pay't as valorouſly as I may, that ſal I ſurely do, the breff and the long; marry, I wad full fain heard ſome queſtion 'tween you tway.

9.8.2 Using *thou/thee* and *ye/you*

In OE, there were both singular and plural forms of the 2nd person pronoun, *þu/þe/þin* and *ge/eow/eower*. This was at first a simple contrast of number – *þu* was used to address one person and *ge* more than one – or of case – *þu/ge* as subject, *þe/eow* as object and *þin/eower* as possessive. However, it developed into a means of marking the relationship between the speaker and the listener which the language has now lost, and so it is difficult for us to respond to the **social connotations** of *thee/thou/thine* and *ye/you/your* in ME and EMnE writing.

The pronoun *ye/you/your* came to be spoken to a single person to mark a relationship that was either formal or one of superiority of rank, and *thou/thee/thine* of informality and intimacy. A master or mistress used *thou* to a servant, but the servant replied with *ye*. It remained conventional to address God as *thou*, as in the Church of England's *Book of Common Prayer*, from the 1540s. The 1611 translation of the Bible preserved the contrasting use of *thou* and *you* as singular and plural, which remained familiar to readers and church goers until the 1960s (when the *New English Bible* began to be used), long after *thou* had ceased to be used in speech.

(Note that the distinction between *ye* as subject and *you* as object became confused during the sixteenth century, so that they were virtually interchangeable. You can find plenty of examples in Shakespeare.)

The choice between using *thou* or *you* was part of a quite complex way of charting the course of a relationship, and if we are not aware of this, then we miss something important in, for example, Shakespeare's plays, as the extract from *The Tragedie of King Lear* (see Text 84) shows. Section 10.3.2 shows how the Quaker George Fox used *thou* in a way that appeared to insult others.

This social meaning of *thou* and *ye* had been established well before the sixteenth century. Here is an example from the 1390s in Chaucer's 'The Knight's Tale'. Arcite, in prison, addresses the gods Mars and Juno at first with *thow* as individuals and then with *youre* as a pair. Immediately, he goes on to address his absent love Emelye, whom he has seen but not yet met, with *ye*. He is the suppliant and she is far above him in his estimation, so *thow* would not be appropriate, as it would mark an established intimacy.

Allas **thow** felle Mars, allas Iuno,
Thus hath **youre** ire oure lynage al fordo ... lines 1561–2

Ye sleen me with **youre** eyen, Emelye,
Ye been the cause wherfore that I dye ... lines 1569–70

Elsewhere in *The Canterbury Tales*, the Host addresses the Cook with *thou*:

Now tel on, gentil Roger, by **thy** name
But yet I praye **thee** be nat wrooth for game ... lines 4345–6

but uses *ye* to the Monk, his social superior:

Now telleth **ye**, sire monk, if that **ye** konne ... line 3114

In English today, we have only one 2nd person pronoun, *you/your*, which is used to address both one and more than one person, and carries no connotations of power or intimacy. The former singular forms *thou/thee/thine* are archaic.

9.8.3 Regional dialects

By the end of the sixteenth century, the educated language of London was clearly established as the standard for writing in England, so that there is little evidence of the regional dialects apart from occasional references. Here is another extract from Richard Verstegan's *A Restitution of Decayed Intelligence* (see Text 76) which gives us just a little information about regional dialects. He is discussing 'alteration and varietie' in related languages like Danish, Norwegian and Swedish, and is saying that they do not borrow 'from any extrauagant language' (the word *extrauagant* here meant *outside the boundaries*, that is, *foreign*).

TEXT 83 – Richard Verstegan's *A Restitution of Decayed Intelligence*, 1605

This is a thing that eaſely may happen in ſo ſpatious a toung as this, it beeing ſpoken in ſo many different countries and regions, when wee ſee that in ſome ſeueral partes of *England* it ſelf, both the names of things and pronountiations of woords are ſomwhat different, and that among the countrey people that neuer borrow any woords out of the Latin or French, and of this different pronountiation one example in ſteed of many ſhal ſuffiſe, as this: for pronouncing according as one would ſay at *London*, I would eat more cheeſe yf I had it/the northern man ſaith, Ay ſud eat mare cheeſe gin ay hadet/and the weſterne man ſaith: Chud eat more cheeſe an chad it. Lo heer three different pronountiations in our own countrey in one thing, & heerof many the lyke examples might be alleaged.

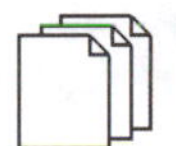

Activity 9.12

Identify and describe the differences between the three dialectal sentences quoted in Text 83.

There is little evidence of contemporary regional dialect in Shakespeare's plays, but an example can be found in *The Tragedie of King Lear*. Edgar, the Duke of Gloucester's son, banished by King Lear, disguises himself as a madman – a Tom a Bedlam. The speech he assumes is often inconsequential but not obviously dialectal, for example:

> Away, the fowle fiend followes me, thorough the sharpe
> hathorne blowes the cold wind, goe to thy cold bed and warme
> thee.

but at one point, defending his blinded father, his speech becomes clearly dialectal for one short episode.

In the following extract, Gloster does not recognise Edgar as his son, and cannot see him. The Steward believes Edgar to be a beggar. The facsimile is taken from the folio of 1685.

TEXT 84 – Shakespeare's *The Tragedie of King Lear*

Glou. Now good Sir, what are you?
Edg. A moſt poor man, made tame to fortunes blows
Who, by the Art of known, and feeling ſorrows,
Am pregnant to good pitty. Give me your hand,
I'le lead you to ſome biding.
Glou. Hearty thanks:
The bounty, and the benizon of Heaven
To boot, and boot.

Enter Steward.

Stew. A proclaim'd prize: moſt happy:
That eyeleſs head of thine, was firſt fram'd fleſh
To raiſe my fortunes. Thou old, unhappy traitor,
Briefly thy ſelf remember: the Sword is out
That muſt deſtroy thee.
Glou. Now let thy friendly hand
Put ſtrength enough to't.
Stew. Wherefore, bold Peazant,
Darſt thou ſupport a publiſh'd traitor? hence,
Leſt that th'infection of his fortune take
Like hold on thee. Let go his Arm.
Edg. Chill not let go Zir,
Without vurther caſion.
Stew. Let go, Slave, or thou dy'ſt.
Edg. Good Gentleman go your gate, and let poor volk paſs: and'chud ha'been zwagged out of my life, 'twould ha'been zo long as 'tis, by a vortnight. Nay, come not near th'old man: keep out che vor'ye, or ice try whither your Coſtard, or my Ballow be the harder; chill be plain with you.
Stew. Out Dunghil.
Edg. Child pick your teeth Zir: come, no matter vor your foyns.
Stew. Slave thou haſt ſlain me: villain, take my purſe;
If ever thou wilt thrive, bury my body,
And give the Letters which thou find'ſt about me,
To *Edmud* Earl of *Gloſter*: ſeek him out
Upon the Engliſh party. Oh untimely death, death.
Edg. I know thee well. A ſerviceable Villain,
As duteous to the vices of thy Miſtris,
As badneſs would deſire.
Glou. What, is he dead?
Edg. Sit you down Father: reſt you.

(A detailed description can be found in Commentary 14 of the *Text Commentary Book*.)

Activity 9.13

(i) Which of Richard Verstegan's examples of dialect in Text 83 does Edgar's speech resemble?
(ii) The scene of the play is set in Kent. The words *ice try* stand for *I sal try*. *Sal* for *shall* and *gate* for *way* are both northern forms. Is Shakespeare accurately reproducing a regional dialect?
(iii) Describe the differences in Edgar's language, when he is talking to Gloster and the Steward, which mark it as a dialect.
(iv) Explain the changing use of the 2nd person pronouns *thou/thee/thine* and *ye/you/your.*

9.9 English at the end of the sixteenth century

Reading texts from the sixteenth century onwards, we find fewer and fewer features of vocabulary and grammar that are archaic and unfamiliar, and it becomes more difficult to specify exactly what differences there are between older and contemporary English. This is especially so if the spelling of older texts is modernised. Facsimiles or exact reproductions make the language look more unfamiliar than it really is. But it is worth trying to sum up the principal differences between English in 1600 and Standard English today. Most of them have already been described in relation to the printed texts.

9.9.1 Spelling and punctuation

OE and ME <þ> was no longer in use, except in the conventional abbreviations for *the* and *that*, <y^{e}> and <y^{t}>.

<u> and <v> were still used for both vowel /u/ and consonant /v/, determined by their position in the written or printed word. Similarly, long and short <s> continued to be written according to their position in the word.

Letter <j> was not yet in general use for the consonant, only as a variant of letter <i>. Letters <i> and <y> were generally interchangeable for the vowel /i/.

The redundant final <e> was still added to many words, long after the unstressed vowel /ə/ had disappeared.

The comma <,>, colon <:> and full stop (prick) <.> were used, with question and exclamation marks <?>, <!>. The virgule or strike </> was no longer in general use by 1600. The apostrophe <'> to mark the possessive had not yet appeared.

9.9.2 Pronunciation

The raising or diphthongisation of long vowels in the South and Midlands (the Great Vowel Shift) had taken place, but was not yet complete. For some time, until after the sixteenth century, there were no words with the long back vowel /ɑ:/.

<ee> words were generally pronounced /i:/, <ea> words /e:/, <oo> words /u:/ and <oa> words /o:/, but there was considerable irregularity and variation between dialects. Many words spelt with <ea> and <oo> were pronounced with either a long or a short vowel in different dialects. This diversity led to a growing demand for regularity and standardisation.

9.9.3 Vocabulary

The adoption of large numbers of Latin words into the written language had been made easy because of the previous adoption of hundreds of French words. At the same time, a number of new prefixes and suffixes were also adopted into the language and used with English words; for example:

circum-	non-	-able	-ant/-ent
co-	pre-	-acy	-ate
dis-	re-	-age	-ess
en/em-	semi-	-al	-ician
inter-	sub-	-ance	-ise
		-ancy/-ency	-let

Words were also adopted from other languages, some through travel and exploration, others from foreign literature and culture. For example, the following list contains a very small selection of words adopted before 1600 from Latin, Greek, French, Italian, Spanish, Low German, Scandinavian, Scots Gaelic, Persian and Arabic. Many were adopted indirectly, via another language. Greek words were often adopted through their use in Latin, for instance.

Activity 9.14

Find the source of the following words from an etymological dictionary.

almanac	carnival	medium	serviette
armada	chorus	milliner	silt
arsenic	cipher	pickle	slogan
batten (vb)	galleon	plaid	taffeta
bog	genius	redeem	traffic
bonnet	jasmine	rhythm	vacuum
buoy	lemon	scrag	waggon

9.9.4 Grammar

In general terms, the grammar of sixteenth century English is the same as that of ME; only a few features mark it as an earlier form.

Personal pronouns

Both 2nd person pronouns were still in use, *thou/thee/thy/thine* and *ye/you/your* (see Section 9.8.2), and the neuter pronoun *hit/his*.

The unstressed form *a* was written for *he*, as in Shakespeare's *The Life of Henry the Fift*, when Mistress Quickly describes Falstaff's death:

> .. **a** made a finer end, and went away and it had beene any Christome Childe: **a** parted eu'n iust betweene Twelue and One ... and **a** babeld of greene fields ... so **a** cryed out, God, God, God, three or foure times ... so **a** bad me lay more Clothes on his feet ...

Relative pronouns

That and *which* were most common. *Which* was used with a human subject – *Our Father which art in heaven ...* – but *who/whom* began to be used in the late sixteenth century.

Verbs

In the verb phrase, the **modal system** was established, with the verbs *will/would*, *shall/should*, *can/couthe~coude*, *dare/durst*, *may/might~mought* and *mote/must*.

The passive was fully in use.

Perfect aspect was expressed with *have*, and also with *be* when the verb was intransitive, as in *I am come*. Some complex verb phrases were recorded but they were still to develop in general use.

The 3rd person singular present tense was marked by both <-eth> (the southern form) and <-s> (the northern form); for example:

Beautie **doth** varnish Age, as if new borne,
And **giues** the Crutch the Cradles infancie.
O tis the Sunne that **maketh** all thinges shine.

but <-s> eventually became standard. The King James Bible of 1611 kept the old-fashioned <-eth> suffix, as the translation was based on the early sixteenth century translations of Tyndale and Coverdale. Poets continued to use both forms, because they provided different metrical and syllabic patterns. There is evidence in William Bullokars' *Booke at Large* that both the <-eth> and <-s> suffixes were acceptable:

And, s, for, eth, may chaũged be
to yield som vers his grace truly.

Interrogatives and negatives

The inversion of subject and verb in the simple present and past for the interrogative was still common – *knowest thou?*, *came he?* – but the MnE form with *do* had also come into use – *dost thou know?*, *did he come?*

Similarly, the negative *not* was still used with inversion – *I know not* – but was now also used with *do* – *I do not know*.

It is at about this time that the multiple negative ceased to be standard usage, although it was and still is normal usage in the dialects.

There and it

The filling of the subject slot in a clause with the 'dummy' *there* or *it* had been established well before the beginning of the century, as in the following extract from Chaucer:

With vs **ther** was a doctour of phisik
In al this world ne was **ther** noon hym lik ...

It is nat honeste, **it** may noght auance
For to deelen with no swich poraille ...

and this led to the loss of the OE and ME impersonal verb constructions without a subject, such as:

Me thynketh it acordant to resoun ...

A yeman he hadde and seruantz namo
At that tyme for **hym liste** ryde so.

which were replaced with *It seems to me* ... and *It pleased him to ride so*.

Nouns

The plural with <-s> or <-es> was the regular form, and most <-en> forms like *eyren* (*eggs*) and *shoon* (*shoes*) had gone.

10. Early Modern English III – the seventeenth century

In Chapters 7 to 9, we followed the establishment of educated London English as a standard language. Although all varieties of seventeenth and twentieth century writing are clearly contrasted in style, the underlying grammatical differences between seventeenth century and present-day English are relatively small, so there are fewer developments in the grammar to record. As the spelling of words becomes more and more regular, the look of the printed page becomes more familiar, although we still find less conformity to a standard spelling and punctuation in handwriting. The vocabulary is, of course, always losing and gaining words according to the needs of communication.

The remaining chapters of the book therefore consist of a series of texts that provide some typical examples of the uses of the language – ordinary uses, letters and diaries for example, and examples of literary prose, both colloquial and rhetorical, together with a section on some of the evidence for changes in pronunciation during the century.

10.1 More evidence for changes in pronunciation

All living languages are in a constant state of change in their vocabulary and grammar. A standard language, however, changes more slowly, because new forms tend to be resisted, and the very fact of it being standard means that it is regarded as fixed and unchangeable.

At the same time as the establishment of a standard in vocabulary and grammar, social standards of pronunciation are also set up, and the speech of those with prestige or authority is imitated by others. In this way, there is a polarisation of opinion in attitudes to language use, which is derived from differences of social class. In the seventeenth century, rural and artisan speech was referred to as *barbarous*, meaning *uncultured* or *unpolished* as against *polite* or *civilised*. In England today, if a man or woman is said to have 'a good accent', we would understand what is meant, although we might find it hard to describe objectively. It is commonly asserted that such speech 'has no accent', but to say of someone that 'she speaks with an accent' is to imply a non-standard or regional way of speaking.

The evidence for pronunciation is not as easy to interpret as that for vocabulary, spelling and grammar, in spite of a series of books on spelling and pronunciation in the seventeenth century, because, unlike today, there was no International Phonetic Alphabet (IPA) to provide an agreed reference for the relationship of sounds to letters. We shall study some of this evidence in Section 10.9.

Other evidence comes from a study of the rhymes in poetry (see an earlier example from Chaucer in the late fourteenth century in Section 7.3.3); some of the rhymes in John Dryden's verse, written at the end of the seventeenth century, are examined in Section 10.10.3.

10.1.1 Occasional spellings in handwritten sources

Another indirect source of knowledge about changing pronunciation is in the spelling of written manuscripts. Printers in the seventeenth century tended to regularise spelling more and more, even though there were still variations and no fixed standard of spelling had been established. In letters, however, even educated writers sometimes used 'phonetic' spellings, and these provide some clues to their pronunciation. The concept of a 'spelling mistake' had not yet been established.

In what follows, we consider a small selection of 'occasional spellings' which are evidence of differences in pronunciation. The range of differences in dialectal pronunciation would have been much greater then than now. People moved from all parts of the country into London and their varieties of dialectal accent were in competition with each other for acceptability. Sometimes it was the 'vulgar' speech that eventually became the social standard.

The following activity is designed to show the kind of evidence that scholars draw upon in building up their knowledge of changes in the language. The words do not come from any one particular dialect. The ME source, the spelling found in a written seventeenth century source and the MnE reflex are given for each word.

Activity 10.1

What changes in the pronunciation of the vowels do the spellings of each group show?

ME	Written form	MnE reflex
/a:/		/eɪ/
came	ceme	came
cradel	credyll	cradle
take	teke	take
/e:/		/i:/
semed	symed	seemed
stepel	stypylle	steeple
/ɛ:/		/i:/
discrete	discrate	discreet
retrete	retrate	retreat
/ɔi/		/ɔɪ/
joinen	gine	join
puisun/poisoun	pyson	poison
rejoissen	regis	rejoice
/i:/		/aɪ/
defiled/defyled	defoyled	defiled
/er/		/ɜ:/
certein	sarten	certain
derþe	darth	dearth
diuert	divart	divert
lernen	larne	learn
merci	marcy	mercy
persoun	parson	person/parson

Although consonants are more stable than vowels, there have been a number of changes for which there is evidence in written letters.

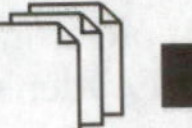

Activity 10.2

Describe any changes of pronunciation in the consonants indicated by the spelling in the following words.

ME	Written word	MnE reflex
doughter	dafter	daughter
boght	boft	bought
fasoun	fessychen	fashion
instruccion	instrocshen	instruction
issu/issue	ishu	issue
suspecious	suspishious	suspicious
seute/siute	sheute	suit
morsel	mosselle	morsel
persoun	passon	person/parson
portion	posshene	portion
scarsliche	skasely	scarcely
excepte	excep	except
often	offen	often
wastcotte (16th C)	wascote	waistcoat
linnene	lynand	linen
los	loste	loss
syns	synst	since
vermine	varment	vermin

(Data from *Studies in English Rhymes from Surrey to Pope*, H. C. Wyld, 1923)

10.1.2 Evidence of change from musical settings

Sir Walter Raleigh's poem *What Is Our Life?* was set to music by Orlando Gibbons in 1612. The first two lines are:

> What is our life? a play of passion,
> Our mirth the music of division ...

The music sets *passion* to three syllables on separate notes, *pas/si/on*, and *division* to four, *di/vi/si/on*, so the pronunciation of the last two syllables of each word must have been /-si**'on**/ and /-zi**'on**/, with **secondary stress** on the final syllable /on/, as well as **primary stress**, as in today's pronunciation, /**'pæ**ʃən/ and /di'**vi**ʒən/. This loss of secondary stress in many words marks one of the differences between sixteenth and seventeenth century pronunciation and today's.

10.1.3 Evidence of change from verse

Hundreds of lines of verse were written in the late sixteenth and early seventeenth centuries by William Shakespeare, Ben Jonson and other dramatists, using the iambic pentameter line, which in its regular form consisted of ten syllables of alternating unstressed and stressed syllables, as in Raleigh's poem and in these lines of Shakespeare:

> What **say** / you, **can** / you **loue** / the **Gen** / tle**man**?
> This **night** / you **shall** / be**hold** / him **at** / our **feast**

This gives us the patterning of stressed syllables in words of two or more syllables, and shows whether the distribution of stress has since changed. For example, the word *proportion* in these lines:

> I thought King Henry had resembled thee,
> In Courage, Courtship, and *Proportion*:

must have four syllables to complete the line:

> In **Cour**- / age **Court**- / ship **and** / pro**por**- / ti- **on**

and reinforces the musical evidence about the pronunciation of *passion* and *division*.

■ Activity 10.3

What is the stress pattern of the italicised words in the following lines from Shakespeare, and in present-day speech?

TEXT 85 – Shakespeare

1 ... I do coniure thee,
Who art the Table wherein all my thoughts
Are visibly *Character'd*,
2 Ay, and peruersly, she *perseuers* so:
3 Goe to thy Ladies graue and call hers thence,
Or at the least, in hers, *sepulcher* thine.
4 Madam: if your heart be so *obdurate*:
Vouchsafe me yet your Picture for my loue,
5 Nephew, what meanes this passionate *discourse*?
6 She beares a Dukes *Reuenewes* on her back,
And in her heart she scornes our Pouertie:
7 *Pernitious* Protector, dangerous Peere ...
8 Away: Though parting be a fretfull *corosiue*,
It is *applyed* to a deathfull wound.
9 Close vp his eyes, and draw the Curtaine close,
And let vs all to *Meditation*.
10 Is it for him you do *enuie* me so?

10.2 Sir Thomas Browne

10.2.1 *Religio Medici*

Sir Thomas Browne (1605–82), after studying medicine on the Continent, practised as a physician in Norwich for the rest of his life, but he is remembered today as a writer. His first book *Religio Medici* ('the faith of a doctor') had been written as 'a private Exercise directed to myself', but a pirated edition had been published 'in a most depraved Copy', so he decided to publish his own version.

The book explores the tension that existed then between religious faith and new scientific ideas. This conflict had been expressed earlier by John Donne in 1611 in *An Anatomy of the World*:

> And new Philosophy calls all in doubt,
> The Element of fire is quite put out;
> The Sun is lost, and th'earth, and no mans wit
> Can well direct him where to looke for it ...
> 'Tis all in peeces, all coherence gone;
> All just supply, and all Relation.

The following short extract from *Religio Medici* expresses Sir Thomas Browne's religious faith.

TEXT 86 – Sir Thomas Browne's *Religio Medici*, 1642

> As for those wingy Mysteries in Divinity, and airy subtleties in Religion, which have unhing'd the brains of better heads, they never stretched the *Pia Mater* (= *a membrane in the brain*) of mine. Methinks there be not impossibilities enough in Religion for an active faith; the deepest Mysteries ours contains have not only been

> illustrated, but maintained, by Syllogism (= *a logical argument consisting of two propositions and a conclusion*) and the rule of Reason. I love to lose my self in a mystery, to pursue my Reason to an *O altitudo*!. 'Tis my solitary recreation to pose my apprehension with those involved Ænigma's and riddles of the Trinity, with Incarnations, and Resurrection. I can answer all the Objections of Satan and my rebellious reason with that odd resolution I learned of *Tertullian, Certum est quia impossibile est* (= Latin for *It is certain because it is impossible*).

Students of literature value Browne's writings for their style rather than for their content, and style is of interest to students of language too, in showing how a writer exploits and expands the resources of the language of the time.

10.2.2 *Vulgar Errors*

Sir Thomas Browne's learning is illustrated in the volumes of *Pseudodoxia Epidemica,* or *Enquiries into very many received tenents and commonly presumed truths*, which are more popularly known as *Vulgar Errors* – *vulgar* in the sense of *common*. He examines a variety of beliefs that were commonly held in the light of authority (what had been written about the subject), rational thought and experience. The outcome is often, to a modern reader, quaint and amusing, but the book gives us valuable insights into the 'world view' of the early seventeenth century, which was still largely a late medieval view in spite of the beginnings of scientific experiment at that time.

The following extract shows the alternation of direct observation and appeal to antiquarian authorities (now long since forgotten), which he applies to the problem 'what is Sperma-ceti?', a substance found in whales and used both in medicine and the manufacture of candles. Notice also his literal acceptance of the Old Testament account of Jonah and the whale. As a point of minor interest, he uses the phrases *sixty foot* and *two pound*, which today are arguably non-standard (for the OE origins of this construction see Section 2.7.3).

TEXT 87 – Sir Thomas Browne's *Vulgar Errors* (i)

> What Sperma-Ceti is, men might justly doubt, since the learned *Hofmannus* in his work of Thirty years, saith plainly, *Nescio quid sit* (Latin for *I do not know what it is*). And therefore need not wonder at the variety of opinions; while some conceived it to be *flos maris* (Latin for *a flower of the sea*), and many, a bituminous substance floating upon the sea.
>
> That it was not the spawn of the Whale, according to vulgar conceit, or nominal appellation (= *name given without reference to fact*) Phylosophers have always doubted, not easily conceiving the Seminal humour (= *sperm, humour = body fluid*) of Animals, should be inflamable; or of a floating nature.
>
> That it proceedeth from a Whale, beside the relation of *Clusius*, and other learned observers, was indubitably determined, not many years since by a Sperma-Ceti Whale, cast upon our coast of *Norfolk*. Which, to lead on further inquiry, we cannot omit to inform. It contained no less then sixty foot in length, the head somewhat peculiar, with a large prominency over the mouth; teeth only in the lower Jaw, received into fleshly sockets in the upper. The Weight of the largest about two pound: No gristly substances in the mouth, commonly called Whale-bones; Only two short finns seated forwardly on the back; the eyes but small, the pizell large, and prominent. A lesser Whale of this kind above twenty years ago, was cast upon the same shore.
>
> The discription of this Whale seems omitted by *Gesner*, *Rondeletius*, and the first Editions of *Aldrovandus*; but describeth the latin impression of *Pareus*, in the Exoticks of *Clusius*, and the natural history of *Nirembergius*; but more amply in Icons and figures of *Johnstonus* ...
>
> Out of the head of this Whale, having been dead divers days, and under putrifaction, flowed streams of oyl and Sperma-Ceti; which was carefully taken up and preserved by the Coasters. But upon breaking up, the Magazin of Sperma-Ceti, was found in the head lying in folds and courses, in the bigness of goose eggs, encompassed with large flakie substances, as large as a mans head, in form of hony-combs, very white and full

of oyl ... And this many conceive to have been the fish which swallowed *Jonas*. Although for the largeness of the mouth, and frequency in those seas, it may possibly be the *Lamia*.

Some part of the Sperma-Ceti found on the shore was pure, and needed little depuration (= *purifying*); a great part mixed with fetid oyl, needing good preparation, and frequent expression, to bring it to a flakie consistency. And not only the head, but other parts contained it. For the carnous parts being roasted, the oyl dropped out, an axungious (= *greasy*, *like lard*) and thicker parts subsiding; the oyl it self contained also much in it, and still after many years some is obtained from it ...

(A full analysis of the text is given in Commentary 15 in the *Text Commentary Book*.)

Activity 10.4

(i) Discuss how the vocabulary and grammatical structures that Browne uses in Text 87 tend to make the style of his writing formal and unlike ordinary speech.
(ii) Identify those parts of the text in which Browne appeals to either authority, reason or experience.

It was a 'vulgar error' of the times that a badger's legs were longer on one side than the other, and Browne discusses this also.

TEXT 88 – Sir Thomas Browne's *Vulgar Errors* (ii)

That a Brock or badger hath the legs on one side shorter then of the other, though an opinion perhaps not very ancient, is yet very general; received not only by Theorists and unexperienced believers, but assented unto by most who have the opportunity to behold and hunt them daily. And for my own part, upon indifferent enquiry, I cannot discover this difference, although the regardable side be defined, and the brevity by most imputed unto the left.

Again, It seems no easie affront unto reason, and generally repugnant unto the course of Nature; for if we survey the total set of Animals, we may in their legs, or Organs of progression, observe an equality of length, and parity of Numeration; that is, not any to have an odd legg, or the supporters and movers of one side not exactly answered by the other. Perfect and viviparous quadrupeds, so standing in their position of proneness, that the opposite points of Neighbour-legs consist in the same plane; and a line descending from their Navel intersects at right angles the axis of the Earth ...

(There is a complete list of the vocabulary of Text 88, and a commentary on the activity, in Commentary 15 in the *Text Commentary Book*.)

Activity 10.5

Discuss the distribution of words of OE, French and Latin derivation in Text 87 or 88, and their effect upon the formality and style of the writing.

10.3 George Fox's journal

George Fox (1624–91) was the son of a Leicestershire weaver. He experienced a religious conversion, an intense spiritual conviction of 'the Inner Light of Christ', and left home in 1643 to become a preacher and the founder of the Society of Friends, or Quakers. At this time, however, failure to conform to the doctrines and practice of the Church meant civil penalties and often persecution. He was imprisoned many times, and it was during his long stay in Worcester jail between 1673 and 1674 that he dictated an account of his experiences to his fellow prisoner Thomas Lower, who was Fox's son-in-law.

Fox's journal is not only a moving account of his life but also, for students of language, an insight into everyday spoken language of the late seventeenth century, as it was taken down from Fox's spoken narrative.

Some extracts follow in which Fox speaks of some of his many clashes with individuals and institutions.

10.3.1 The origin of the name 'Quaker'

The name 'Quaker' was originally a term of abuse, but it has since been adopted by the Friends and its original connotations lost. Fox and his followers called themselves Children of the Light, Friends of Truth or simply Friends. George Fox explains in his journal how the name Quaker came about:

> ... this was Justice Bennett of Darby y^t first called Us Quakers because wee bid y^m tremble att ye Word of God & this was in ye year 1650.

Fox referred to this in a letter addressed to Justice Bennett and reproduced in his journal.

TEXT 89 – *The Journal of George Fox*, 1650

Collonell Bennett that called the servants of the Lord Quakers
G.F. paper to him: Collonell bennett of darbe 1650

... thou wast the first man in the nation that gave the people of god the name quaker
And Called them quakers, when thou Examinest George in thy house att Derbey
(which they had never the name before) now A Justice to wrong name people, what
may the brutish people doe, if such A one A Justice of peace give names to men,
but thou art Lifted upp proud and haughty and soe turnest Against the Just
one given upp to misname the saints, and to make lyes for others to beeleve.

Thus saith the LORD, The heaven is my throne, and the earth is my footstool: where is the house that ye build unto me? and where is the place of my rest? For all those things hath mine hand made, and all those things have been, saith the LORD: but to this man will I look, even to him that is poor and of a contrite spirit, **and trembleth at my word**. (Isaiah 66: 1–2)

(*The Journal of George Fox*, Norman Penney (ed.), Cambridge UP, 1911)

The spelling and punctuation of the written journal are typical of the time in their lack of conformity to the developing printed standard, but if a transcription is made using present-day spelling and punctuation, it becomes easier to examine the features of vocabulary and grammar that mark the narrative style.

Transcription

... Thou wast the first man in the nation that gave the people of God the name 'Quaker', and called them 'Quakers', when thou examine(d)st George (Fox) in thy house at Derby (which they had never the name before). Now, a Justice to wrong name people! What may the brutish people do, if such a one – a Justice of Peace – give names to men? But thou art lifted up proud and haughty, and so turnest against the just. (Thou art) one given up to misname the saints, and to make lies for others to believe ...

There can be no doubt that this is a record of speech, with its exclamation 'now A Justice to wrong name people', and the verb *wrong name*, but its only marked difference from MnE is the use of *thou* in addressing the Justice, which Fox insisted upon.

10.3.2 Saying *thou* to people

The use of *thee/thou/thine* became old-fashioned and out of date in polite society during the seventeenth century. For example, in Section 10.5, you will see that Dorothy Osborne always uses *you* when writing to her future husband, in the 1650s. The grammarian John Wallis in 1653 considered that the use of *thou* was 'usually contemptuous, or familiarly caressing' and that 'custom' required the plural *you* when addressing one person.

George Fox took a different view and published a pamphlet in 1660 called:

> A Battle-Door for Teachers and Professors to Learn Singular and Plural; *You* to many and *Thou* to *One*: Singular *One*, *Thou*; Plural *Many*, *You*

He believed that the use of *thou* to address one person was a mark of equality between people, whereas it had long been used to mark social superiority or inferiority.

TEXT 90 – George Fox's *A Battle-Door for Teachers*, 1660

> For all you Doctors, Teachers, Schollars, and School-masters, that teach people in your Hebrew, Greek, Latine, and English Grammars, Plural and Singular; that is, *Thou* to one, and *You* to many, and when they learn it, they must not practice it: what good doth your teaching do them? for he is a Novice, and an Ideot, and a fool called by *You*, that practises it; Plural, *You* to many; and Singular, *Thou* to one.
>
> Now People, What good doth all your giving money to these Schoolmasters, Teachers, and Doctors, to teach your children Singular and Plural, in their Accidence, and Grammars? ... If your childe practice that which he hath learned at School, which you have paid for, he is called a Clown, and unmannerly, and ill bred ...

Activity 10.6

(i) Rewrite the following two extracts from Fox's journal using present-day spelling and punctuation. (Text 91 describes events at Patrington in the East Riding of Yorkshire; Text 92 describes what happened when Fox was brought before a JP.)

(ii) Why was the woman 'something strange' and why did the JP ask whether Fox was not 'Mased or fonde'?

(iii) Explain Fox's use of the word *meate* when referring to milk and cream.

(iv) Explain the use of letter <y> in the words *ye* and *y*[t].

TEXT 91 – *The Journal of George Fox*, 1651 (i)

> ... And afterwards I passed away through ye Country & att night came to an Inn: & there was a rude Company of people & I askt ye woman if shee had any Meate to bringe mee some: & shee was somethinge strange because I saide thee & thou to her: soe I askt her if shee had any milke but shee denyed it: & I askt her if shee had any creame & shee denyed y[t] also though I did not greatly like such meate but onely to try her.
>
> And there stoode a churne in her house: & a little boy put his hande Into ye churne & pulled it doune: & threw all ye creame In ye floore before my eyes: & soe Itt manifested ye woman to bee a lyar: & soe I walkt out of her house after ye Lord God had manifested her deceite & perversenesse: & came to a stacke of hay: & lay in ye hay stacke all night: beinge but 3 days before ye time caled Christmas in snowe & raine.

TEXT 92 – *The Journal of George Fox*, 1652 (ii)

> ... & before I was brought in before him ye garde saide It was well if ye Justice was not drunke before wee came to him for hee used to bee drunke very early: & when I was brought before him because I did not putt off my hatt & saide thou to him hee askt ye man whether I was not Mased or fonde: & hee saide noe: Itt was my principle: & soe I warned him to repent & come to ye light y^t Christ had enlightened him withall y^t with it hee might see all his evill words & actions y^t hee had donne & acted & his ungodly ways hee had walked in & ungodly words hee had spoaken ...

10.3.3 The steeplehouse

The use of a particular word may cause offence when its connotations are not shared. For George Fox, the *Church* meant the *people* of God; he refused to use the word for the *building* in which religious worship took place. This, like much of Fox's preaching, his use of *thee* and *thou*, and his principled refusal to remove his hat before a magistrate, caused offence. Here is one of many references to this in his journal. In Fox's view, a *professor* is one who pretends to be religious but is not truly so.

TEXT 93 – *The Journal of George Fox*, 1652 (iii)

> ... And when I was at Oram before in ye steeplehouse there came a professor & gave me a push in ye brest in ye steeplehouse & bid me gett out of ye Church: alack poore man saide I dost thou call ye steeplehouse ye Church: ye Church is ye people whome God has purchased with his bloode: & not ye house.

10.3.4 George Fox persecuted

Fox's journal is full of accounts of violent attacks on Fox and his followers for their faith and preaching. The following extract is typical. Barlby is about 12 miles south of York and Tickhill is about six miles south of Doncaster.

TEXT 94 – *The Journal of George Fox*, 1652 (iv)

> ... then we went away to Balby about a mile off: & the rude people layde waite & stoned us doune the lane but blessed be ye Lorde wee did not receive much hurte: & then ye next first day (= *Fox's term for Sunday*) I went to Tickill & there ye freinds (= *members of the Society of Friends*) of y^t side gathered togeather & there was a meetinge (= *Quaker term for a religious service*).
>
> And I went out of ye meetinge to ye steeplehouse & ye preist & most of ye heads of ye parish was gott uppe Into ye chancell & soe I went uppe to y^m & when I began to speake they fell upon mee & ye Clarke uppe with his bible as I was speakinge & hitt mee in ye face y^t my face gusht out with bloode y^t I bleade exceedingely in ye steeplehouse & soe ye people cryed letts have him out of ye Church as they caled it: & when they had mee out they exceedingely beate mee & threw me doune & threw mee over a hedge: & after dragged mee through a house Into ye street stoneinge & beatinge mee: & they gott my hatt from mee which I never gott againe.
>
> Soe when I was gott upon my leggs I declared to y^m ye worde of life & showed to y^m ye fruites of there teachers & howe they dishonored Christianity.
>
> And soe after a while I gott Into ye meetinge againe amongst freinds & ye preist & people comeinge by ye house I went foorth with freinds Into ye Yarde & there I spoake to ye preist & people: & the preist scoffed at us & caled us Quakers: but ye Lords power was soe over y^m all: & ye worde of life was declared in soe much power & dreade to y^m y^t ye preist fell a tremblinge himselfe y^t one saide unto him looke howe ye preist trembles & shakes hee is turned a Quaker alsoe.

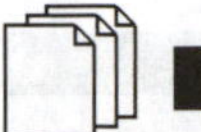

Activity 10.7

Examine the grammatical structure of the narrative in Text 94 and describe those features that mark the text as written down from dictation, in contrast to, for example, Sir Thomas Browne's prose in Section 10.2. (A description of the grammar and vocabulary can be found in Commentary 16 in the *Text Commentary Book*.)

10.4 John Milton

George Fox gave offence to the religious and civil authorities both during the Commonwealth under Oliver Cromwell in the 1650s and the Restoration of Charles II after 1660. John Milton (1608–74), on the other hand, devoted years of political activity to the Puritan cause in the 1640s and 1650s, writing books and pamphlets on behalf of, for example, religious liberty (against bishops), domestic liberty (for divorce) and civil liberty (against censorship).

One of his best-known pamphlets was *Areopagitica* (the *Areopagus* was the highest civil court of Ancient Athens), 'A Speech of Mr John Milton for the Liberty of Vnlicenc'd Printing, to the Parlamant of England, Printed in the Yeare 1644'. It is called a speech although in fact it was printed, and uses the rhetorical model of Greek and Latin oratory – as if it were written to be spoken. Its style is in complete contrast to the artless narrative of George Fox.

TEXT 95 – John Milton's *Areopagitica* (i)

be aſſur'd, Lords and Commons, there can no greater teſtimony appear, then when your prudent ſpirit acknowledges and obeyes the voice of reaſon from what quarter ſoever it be heard ſpeaking; and renders ye as willing to repeal any Act of your own ſetting forth, as any ſet forth by your Predeceſſors.

If ye be thus reſolv'd, as it were injury to thinke ye were not, I know not what ſhould withhold me from preſenting ye with a fit inſtance wherein to ſhew both that love of truth which ye eminently profeſſe, and that uprightneſſe of your judgement which is not wont to be partiall to your ſelves; by judging over again that Order which ye have ordain'd *to regulate Printing. That no Book, pamphlet, or paper ſhall be henceforth Printed, unleſſe the ſame be firſt approv'd and licenc't by ſuch*, or at leaſt one of ſuch as ſhall be thereto appointed.

I deny not, but that it is of greateſt concernment in the Church and Commonwealth, to have a vigilant eye how Bookes demeane themſelves as well as men; and thereafter to confine, impriſon, and do ſharpeſt juſtice on them as malefactors: For Books are not abſolutely dead things, but doe contain a potencie of life in them to be as active as that ſoule was whoſe progeny they are; nay they do preſerve as in a violl the pureſt efficacie and extraction of that living intellect that bred them. I know they are as lively, and as vigorouſly productive, as thoſe fabulous Dragons teeth; and being ſown up and down, may chance to ſpring up armed men. And yet on the other hand unleſſe warineſſe be us'd, as good almoſt kill a Man as kill a good Book; who kills a Man kills a reaſonable creature, Gods Image; but hee who deſtroyes a good Booke, kills reaſon it ſelfe, kills the Image of God, as it were in the eye. Many a man lives a burden to the Earth; but a good Booke is the pretious life-blood of a maſter ſpirit, imbalm'd and treaſur'd up on purpoſe to a life beyond life.

Activity 10.8

Using the following checklist, comment on the stage of development in spelling and grammar by the 1640s, as illustrated in this text, and contrast it with the sixteenth century texts of Chapter 9.

Spelling and punctuation

(i) The distribution of the letters <u> and <v>, and <i> and <j>.
(ii) The use of <-y> in the spelling of *testimony, injury*, etc.
(iii) What does the spelling <'d> in *assur'd*, *treasur'd*, etc., imply about pronunciation?
(iv) What was the probable pronunciation of *armed*?
(v) Comment on these spellings:
  (a) *Bookes* and *Books*, *Booke* and *Book*.
  (b) *Dragons teeth* and *Gods Image*.
  (c) *testimony*, *injury*, etc., but *potencie* and *efficacie*.

Grammar

(i) Comment on the grammar of:
  (a) *ye*.
  (b) *I know not/I deny not*.
  (c) *doe contain/do preserve*.
  (d) **who** *kills a Man kills a reasonable creature*.
  (e) *that order* **which** *ye have ordain'd*/**whose** *progeny they are*/*hee* **who** *destroyes*.
(ii) What is the inflection of the 3rd person singular present tense of verbs?

The second text from *Areopagitica* is often quoted as an example of the 'high style' of rhetorical writing, and for Milton's vision of an approaching Golden Age in England. Its content and imagery derive largely from the older medieval world view.

The 'spirits' and the 'vital and rational faculties' refer to the belief that the human body contained both a 'vegetable soul', which conducted unconscious vital bodily processes, and a 'rational soul', which controlled understanding and reason.

The comparison of the Nation to an eagle depends on an ancient 'vulgar error' which Sir Thomas Browne did not in fact discuss. Medieval descriptions of animals, real and legendary, were collected in books called **bestiaries**, and the description of the eagle in a thirteenth century bestiary can be found in Section 3.7.

TEXT 96 – John Milton's *Areopagitica* (ii)

For as in a body, when the blood is freſh, the ſpirits pure and
vigorous, not only to vital, but to rationall faculties, and thoſe in
the acuteſt, and the perteſt operations of wit and ſuttlety, it argues
in what good plight and conſtitution the body is, ſo when the
cherfulneſſe of the people is ſo ſprightly up, as that it has, not only
wherewith to guard well its own freedom and ſafety, but to ſpare,
and to beſtow upon the ſolideſt and ſublimeſt points of controver-
ſie, and new invention, it betok'ns us not degenerated, nor droo-
ping to a fatall decay, but caſting off the old and wrincl'd skin of
corruption to outlive theſe pangs and wax young again, entring
the glorious waies of Truth and proſperous vertue deſtin'd to became great and honourable in theſe latter ages. Methinks I ſee in
my mind a noble and puiſſant Nation rouſing herſelf like a ſtrong
man after ſleep, and ſhaking her invincible locks: Methinks I ſee
her as an Eagle muing her mighty youth, and kindling her undazl'd
eyes at the full midday beam; purging and unſcaling her long abuſed ſight at the fountain it ſelf of heav'nly radiance; while the
whole noiſe of timorous and flocking birds, with thoſe alſo that
love the twilight, flutter about, amaz'd at what ſhe means, and in
their envious gabble would prognoſticat a year of ſects and ſchiſms.

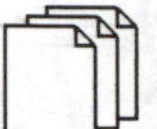

Activity 10.9

Discuss the style and rhetoric of this extract. (A stylistic analysis can be found in Commentary 17 of the *Text Commentary Book*.)

10.5 Dorothy Osborne's letters

Dorothy Osborne (1627–95) met William Temple in 1648 (1628–99). They married in 1654, after much opposition from their families in the intervening years, during which they wrote many letters to each other. Most of Dorothy's letters to William from 1652 to 1654 have survived. They give a lively and personal picture of the life and manners of the times, and contain a moving portrait of her constancy at a time when other suitors were urged upon both of them by their families. It was not fashionable to marry for love, and marriages for men and women in landed wealthy families were more often than not arranged for them, as this paragraph written by William Temple's sister explains.

> S^r^ W T went imediately into England with the hopes of being soon happy in seing the end of soe long a persuit, though against the consent of most of her friends, & dissatisfaction of some of his, it haveing occasion'd his refusall of a very great fortune when his famely was most in want of it, as she had done of many considerable offers of great estates & Famelies.
>
> (*The Letters of Dorothy Osborne to William Temple*, G. C. Moore Smith (ed.), OUP, 1928)

Dorothy believed that letters should be 'as free and easy as one's discourse', so they provide us with an authentic account of mid-seventeenth century informal English, as if we were overhearing her speak.

At the time of the following letter, William Temple was in London and Dorothy was at her family home, Chicksands, in Essex. Temple's diary for Friday 18 March 1653 records: 'R Squire carried Jane to London to goe for Guarnsey'.

'Your fellow servant' refers to Dorothy's servant, her companion and friend Jane Wright. William Temple is also a 'servant' of Dorothy's because he is in love with her, so he called Jane a 'fellow servant'. Jane delivered the letter to Temple on her way to Guernsey.

TEXT 97 – Dorothy Osborne's letter to William Temple, 17 March 1653

> S^r^
> Your fellow servant upon the news you sent her is goeing to Looke out her Captain. In Earnest now shee is goeing to sea, but 'tis to Guarnesey to her freinds there. her goeing is soe sudden that I have not time to say much to you, but that I Longe to heare what you have done, & that I shall hate my selfe as Longe as I live if I cause any disorder between your father and you, but if my name can doe you any service, I shall not scruple to trust you with that, since I make none to trust you with my heart. she will dirrect you how you may sende to mee, and for god sake though this bee a short Letter let not yours bee soe, tis very late & I am able to hold open my Eyes noe longer, good night. if I were not sure to meet you againe by and by, I would not Leave you soe soone.
> Your

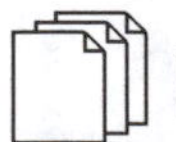

Activity 10.10

Comment on the way that Dorothy makes a definite promise to marry William Temple if he wishes it.

The following text is the last page of a letter that provides evidence of the marriage market of the landed gentry in seventeenth century society.

TEXT 98 – Dorothy Osborne's letter to William Temple, 25 March 1653

had had lesse reason; but in my life
I never heard a man say more, nor
Lesse to the purpose, and if his Brother
have not a better Guift in Courtship
hee will owe my Ladys favour to his
fortune rather then to his advise.
My Lady Anne Wentworth I heare is
marryeing but I cannot learne to whome
nor is it easy to guesse whoe is worthy
of her, in my Judgment she is without
dispute the finest Lady I know (one always
excepted) not that she is at all handsome
but infinitly vertuous and discreet, of a sober
and a very different humor from most
of the young People of these times, but
has as much wit and is as good company
as any body that ever I saw; what would
you give that I had but the Witt to know
when to make an End of my letters never
any body was persecuted with such long
Epistles but you will pardon my unwilling-
nesse to leave you; and notwithstanding
all your little doubts, beleeve that I am
very much

March ye 25th

Your faithfull friend
& humble servant

Osborne

Activity 10.11

Discuss the conventions of punctuation used by Dorothy Osborne in her letters.

The next letter is complete. Dorothy asked William to send her copies of the diary he was compiling: her reference to 'your first Chapter' is evidence to the fact. An *ague* was a malarial type of fever, with alternate 'fits' of high temperature and shivering.

TEXT 99 – Dorothy Osborne's letter to William Temple, 30 April 1653

S[r]
I am sory my last letter frighted you soe, twas now part of my intention it should. but I am more sory to see by your first Chapter that your humor is not alway's soe good as I could wish it, 'twas the only thing I ever desyr'd wee might differ in and (therfore) I think it is deny'd mee. whilest I read the discription on't I could not believe but y[t] I had writt it my self, it was soe much my owne. I pitty you in Earnest much more then I doe my self, and yet I may deserve yours when I shall have told you, that besyd's all that you speake of I have gotten an Ague that with two fitts has made mee soe very weak that I doubted Extreamly yesterday whether I should be able to sit up to day to write to you. but you must not bee troubled at this, that's the way to kill mee indeed, besydes it is imposible I should keep it long for heer is my Eldest Brother and my Cousen Molle & two or three more of them that have great understanding in Agues and they doe so tutor & governe mee that I am neither to eate drink nor sleep without theire leave, and sure my Obedience derserv's they should cure mee or else they are great Tyrants to very litle purpose. You cannot imagin how Cruel they are to mee and yet will perswade mee tis for my good, I know they mean it soe and therfore say nothing but submitt, and sigh to to think those are not heer that would bee kinder to mee. but you were Cruell your self when you seem'd to aprehende I might Oblige you to make good your last offer*. Alasse if I could purchase the Empire of the world at that rate I should think it much too deare ... for god sake write mee all that you heare or can think of that I may have something to Entertaine my self withall. I have a scurvy head that will not let mee write longer.

I am

Your

* Dorothy and William were informally engaged to each other, and he had offered to release her from the engagement.

Activity 10.12

Identify any lexical and grammatical features of the letters which show the language to be of the seventeenth century.

Henry Osborne, Dorothy's brother, kept a diary, in which the following entry occurs in 1654:

Dec 25, Munday. Being Christmasse day my sister was married.

William Temple's sister Martha (later Lady Giffard) wrote a *Life of Sir William Temple*; her account gives us a little more information about Dorothy Osborne's marriage with William Temple. (William Temple was in Ireland in early 1654.)

TEXT 100 – Martha Temple's *Life of Sir William Temple*

... He staid there six months, & in y^t time Mrs Osborne came to be at liberty by the loss of her Father, & S^r W T went imediately into England with the hopes of being soon happy in seing the end of soe long a persuit, though against the consent of most of her friends, & dissatisfaction of some of his, it haveing occasion'd his refusall of a very great fortune when his Famely was most in want of it, as she had done of many considerable offers of great Estates & Famelies. But the misfortunes of this amour were not yet ended. The week before they were to be marryed she fell soe desperately ill there was little hopes* of her life and nothing, the Doctors said, but its proveing the small pox could have sav'd her. He was happy when he saw y^t secure, his kindness haveing greater tyes then that of her beauty though that Loss was too great to leave him wholy insensible. He saw her constantly while she was ill, & maried her soon after. They past ye year at the House of one of their friends in the Country, where at the end of it she was brought to bed of a son & the beginning of the next they made a visitt to his Father and Famely, y^t were then in Ireland.

*The plural form of the word was used as a singular.

By the 1680s, after Sir William Temple's retirement, they had only two children living, seven others having died in infancy. One of these two, also called Dorothy, died of small pox in 1684. The following letter from Dorothy to her father has survived, although the date is not known.

TEXT 101 – Dorothy Temple's letter to her father, c.1680

Sir, – I defer'd writing to you till I could tell you that I had receaved all my fine things, which I have just now done; but I thought never to have done giueing you thanks for them – they have made me soe very happy in my new closet, and euery body that comes dose admire them aboue all things, but yett not soe much as I think they deserue; and now, if Papa was heare I should think myself a perfect pope, though I hope I should not be burnt as there was one at Nell guin's doore the 5th of November, who was sat in a great cheare, with a red nose half a yard long, with some hundreds of boys throwing squibs at it. monsieur gore and I agree mighty well, and he makes me belieue I shall come to something at last: that is if he stays, which I don't doubt but he will, because all the faire ladys will petition for him. we are got rid of the workmen now, and our howse is redy to entertain you come when you please, and you will meet with no body more glad to see you then

S^r

your most obedient

and dutiful daughter,

D. Temple

(*Letters from Dorothy Osborne to Sir William Temple*, E. A. Parry (ed.), p. 278, Dent n.d.)

10.6 John Evelyn's diary

John Evelyn (1620–1706) travelled widely on the Continent and had a great variety of interests – he published books on engraving, tree-growing, gardening, navigation and commerce, and architecture, but is now best known for his diary, which covers most of his life.

During the Civil Wars of the 1640s, Evelyn was a royalist in sympathy. After the execution of King Charles I in 1649, a Commonwealth was set up, with Oliver Cromwell later named Lord Protector. One of the many ordinances or regulations imposed by the Puritan regime abolished the celebration of Christmas and other Church festivals. On Christmas Day 1657, John Evelyn went with his wife to the chapel of Exeter House in the Strand, London, where the Earl of Rutland lived. He recorded in his diary what happened.

TEXT 102 – John Evelyn's diary for 25 December 1657

I went with my Wife &c: to *Lond*: to celebrate *Christmas day*. Mr. *Gunning* preaching in *Excester* Chapell on *7*: *Micha 2*. Sermon Ended, as he was giving us the holy Sacrament, The Chapell was surrounded with Souldiers: All the Communicants and Assembly surpriz'd & kept Prisoners by them, some in the house, others carried away: It fell to my share to be confined to a roome in the house, where yet were permitted to Dine with the master of it, the Countesse of *Dorset*, *Lady Hatton* & some others of quality who invited me: In the afternoone came *Collonel Whaly*, *Goffe* & others from *Whitehall* to examine us one by one, & some they committed to the *Martial (= Marshal, title of a senior Army officer)*, some to Prison, some Committed: When I came before them they tooke my name & aboad, examind me, why contrary to an Ordinance made that none should any longer observe the superstitious time of the *Nativity* (so esteem'd by them) I durst offend, & particularly be at *Common prayers*, which they told me was but the *Masse* in *English*, & particularly pray for *Charles stuard*, for which we had no Scripture: I told them we did not pray for *Cha*: *Steward* but for all *Christian Kings*, *Princes & Governors*: They replied, in so doing we praied for the K. of *Spaine* too, who was their Enemie, & a *Papist*, with other frivolous & insnaring questions, with much threatening, & finding no colour to detaine me longer, with much pitty of my Ignorance, they dismiss'd me: These were men of high flight, and above Ordinances: & spake spitefull things of our B: Lords nativity: so I got home late the next day blessed be God: These wretched miscreants, held their muskets against us as we came up to receive the Sacred Elements, as if they would have shot us at the Altar, but yet suffering us to finish the Office of Communion, as perhaps not in their Instructions what they should do in case they found us in that Action:

(*The Diary of John Evelyn*, Vol. III, E.S. de Beer (ed.), OUP, 1955)

The object of the raids on churches was political as well as religious, as the authorities were afraid of royalist plots against the government. A newspaper, *The Publick Intelligencer*, printed an account on 28 December 1657.

TEXT 103 – *The Publick Intelligencer*, 28 December 1657

This being the day commonly called *Christmas*, and divers of the old Clergymen being assembled with people of their own congregating in private to uphold a superstitious observation of the day, contrary to Ordinances of Parliament abolishing the observation of that and other the like Festivals, and against an express Order of his Highness and his Privy-Council, made this last week; for this cause, as also in regard of the ill Consequences that may extend to the Publick by the Assemblings of ill-affected persons at this season of the year wherein disorderly people are wont to assume unto themselves too great a liberty, it was judged necessary to suppress the said meetings, and it was accordingly performed by some of the Soldiery employed to that end; who at *Westminster* apprehended one Mr *Thiss cross**, he being with divers people met together in private; In *Fleet street* they found another meeting of the same nature, where one Dr *Wilde* was Preacher; And at Exeter-house in the Strand they found the grand Assembly, which some (for the magnitude of it) have been pleased to term *the Church of England*; it being (as they say) to be found no where else in so great and so compact a Body, of which Congregation one Mr *Gunning* was the principal Preacher, who together with Dr *Wilde*, and divers other persons, were secured, to give an account of their doings: Some have since been released, the rest remain in custody at the White-Hart in the Strand, till it shall be known who they are:

*The paper's version of *Thurcross*. Timothy Thurcross was a Doctor of Divinity and a priest.

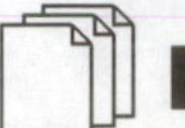

Activity 10.13

Compare the language of Evelyn's account of the events with that of the newspaper. (A stylistic analysis can be found in Commentary 18 in the *Text Commentary Book*.)

The following entry in Evelyn's diary describes a whale that was stranded in the Thames Estuary. It is an interesting contrast to Sir Thomas Browne's account in Text 87.

TEXT 104 – John Evelyn's diary for 2 and 3 June 1658

> 2 An extraordinary storme of haile & raine, cold season as winter, wind northerly neere 6 moneths. 3 A large *Whale* taken, twixt my Land butting on $\overset{e}{y}$ *Thames* & *Greenwich*, which drew an infinite Concourse to see it, by water, horse, Coach on foote from *Lon'd*, & all parts: It appeared first below *Greenwich* at low-water, for at high water, it would have destroyed all $\overset{e}{y}$ boates: but lying now in shallow water, incompassd wth boates, after a long Conflict it was killed with the harping yrons, & struck in $\overset{e}{y}$ head, out of which spouted blood and water, by two tunnells like Smoake from a chimny: & after an horrid grone it ran quite on shore & died: The length was 58 foote: 16 in height, black skin'd like Coach-leather, very small eyes, greate taile, small finns & but 2: a piked (= *pointed*) snout, & a mouth so wide & divers men might have stood upright in it: No teeth at all, but sucked the slime onely as thro a grate made of y^{t} bone wch we call Whale bone: The throate yet so narrow, as woud not have admitted the least of fishes: The extreames of the *Cetaceous* bones hang downewards, from $\overset{e}{y}$ upper jaw, & was hairy towards the Ends, & bottome withinside: all of it prodigious, but in nothing more wonderfull then that an Animal of so greate a bulk, should be nourished onely by slime, thrû those grates:

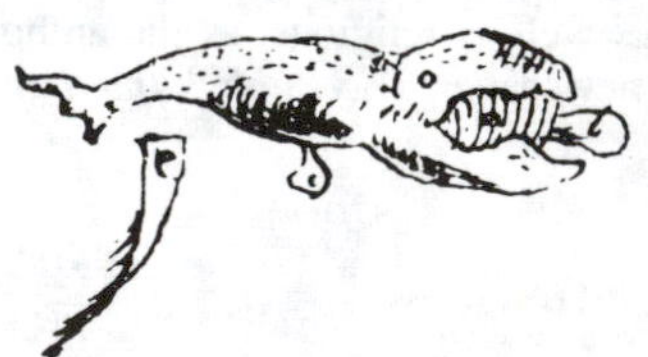

> a) The bones making $\overset{e}{y}$ grate.
> b) The Tongue, c. $\overset{e}{y}$ finn: d $\overset{e}{y}$ Eye:
> e) one of $\overset{e}{y}$ bones making the grate (a) f $\overset{e}{y}$ Tunnells thrû which shutting $\overset{e}{y}$ mouth, the water is forced upward, at least 30 foote, like a black thick mist. &c:

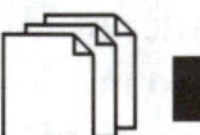

Activity 10.14

Compare John Evelyn's description of the whale with that of Sir Thomas Browne's, which was written less than 20 years earlier. Discuss the differences in content and style – the choices of vocabulary and grammatical structure.

10.6.1 The Royal Society and prose style

The Royal Society of London for the Improving of Natural Knowledge, usually called just The Royal Society, was founded in 1662 under the patronage of King Charles II, who had been restored to the throne in 1660. Evelyn was a founder member of the society, whose members met regularly to present and discuss scientific papers. The poet John Dryden was also a member, and two verses of a poem called *Annus Mirabilis – The Year of Wonders 1666* contain what he called an 'Apostrophe to the Royal Society'. (An **apostrophe** is a term in rhetoric which means 'a figure in which a writer suddenly stops in his discourse, and turns to address some other person or thing'.)

This I fore-tel, from your auspicious care,
  Who great in search of God and nature grow:
Who best your wise Creator's praise declare,
  Since best to praise his works is best to know.

O truly Royal! who behold the Law,
  And rule of beings in your Makers mind,
And thence, like Limbecks, rich Ideas draw,
  To fit the levell'd use of humane kind.

Evelyn's diary entry on the whale shows his interest in the detailed scientific observation of natural phenomena, expressed obliquely in Dryden's poem as 'the Law and Rule of beings in your Makers mind'.

Members of The Royal Society like John Evelyn and John Dryden were dedicated to new ways of scientific thinking and experiment, and the style of writing that they began to adopt in the 1660s also changed. The following statement, about the prose style being developed by members of the society in their scientific papers, was written by Thomas Sprat, Secretary of The Royal Society, in 1667.

TEXT 105 – Thomas Sprat's *The History of The Royal Society*, 1667

And, in few words, I dare ſay; that of all the Studies of men, nothing may be ſooner obtain'd, than this vicious abundance of *Phraſe*, this trick of *Metaphors*, this volubility of *Tongue*, which makes ſo great a noiſe in the World.

They have therefore been moſt rigorous in putting in execution,the only Remedy,that can be found for this *extravagance* : and that has been, a conſtant Reſolution, to reject all the amplifications, digreſſions, and ſwellings of ſtyle: to return back to the primitive purity, and ſhortneſs, when men deliver'd ſo many *things*, almoſt in an equal number of *words*. They have exacted from all their members, a cloſe, naked, natural way of ſpeaking; poſitive expreſſions; clear ſenſes; a native eaſineſs: bringing all things as near the Mathematical plainneſs, as they can: and preferring the language of Artizans, Countrymen, and Merchants, before that, of Wits, or Scholars.

10.7 John Bunyan

John Bunyan (1628–88) was the son of a Bedfordshire brass-worker; he followed his father's trade after learning to read and write in the village school at Elstow. He served in the Parliamentary army during the Civil War in the 1640s, and joined a non-conformist church in Bedford in 1653 and preached there. His first writings were against George Fox and the Quakers. He too came into conflict with the authorities in 1660 for preaching without a licence, and spent 12 years in Bedford jail, during which time he wrote nine books. In 1672, he returned to the same church and was again imprisoned for a short time in 1676, when he finished the first part of *The Pilgrim's Progress*. The book was published in 1678, and a second part in 1684.

The Pilgrim's Progress is an allegory, in which personifications of abstract qualities are the characters. The story is in the form of a dream, in which the narrator tells of Christian's progress 'from this World to that which is to come'.

The following text, reproduced in facsimile, is from the first edition of the book published in 1678. Christian's religious doubts have caused him to lose hope and fall into despair. In the terms of the allegory, he and his companion Hopeful have been caught by Giant Despair and thrown into the dungeon of Doubting Castle.

Bunyan's use of the language brings us close to hearing the colloquial, everyday speech of the 1670s. It is 'the language of artisans, countrymen and merchants', not of 'wits and scholars', that Thomas Sprat commended.

The text shows us that spelling in printed books was by now standardised in a form that has hardly changed since. There are only a few unfamiliar conventions, like the use of long <s>, the capitalising of some nouns and adjectives, and the use of italics to highlight certain words.

TEXT 106 – John Bunyan's *The Pilgrim's Progress*

Now there was not far from the place where they lay, a *Caſtle*, called *Doubting Caſtle*, the owner whereof was *Giant Deſpair*, and it was in his grounds they now were ſleeping; wherefore he getting up in the morning early, and walking up and down in his Fields, caught *Chriſtian* and *Hopeful* aſleep in his grounds. Then with a *grim* and *ſurly* voice he bid them awake, and asked them whence they were? and what they did in his grounds? They told him, they were Pilgrims, and that they had loſt their way. Then ſaid the *Giant*, You have this night treſpaſſed on me, by trampling in, and lying on my grounds, and therefore you muſt go along with me. So they were forced to go, becauſe he was ſtronger then they. They alſo had but little to ſay, for they knew themſelves in a fault. The *Giant* therefore drove them before him, and put them into his Caſtle, into a very dark Dungeon, naſty and ſtinking to the ſpirit of theſe two men: Here then they lay, from *Wed-*
Pſ. 88. 18. *neſday* morning till *Saturday* night,

He finds them in his ground, and carries them to Doubting *Caſtle.*

The Grievouſneſs of their Impriſonment

cont ...

without one bit of bread, or drop of drink, or any light, or any to ask how they did. They were therefore here in evil caſe, and were far from friends and acquaintance. Now in this place, *Chriſtian* had double ſorrow, becauſe 'twas through his unadviſed haſte that they were brought into this diſtreſs.

Well, on *Saturday* about midnight they began to *pray*, and continued in Prayer till almoſt break of day.

Now a little before it was day, good *Chriſtian*, as one half amazed, brake out in this paſſionate Speech, *What a fool, quoth he, am I thus to lie in a ſtinking Dungeon, when I may as well walk at liberty?* I have a *Key* in my boſom, called *Promiſe*, that will, I am perſuaded, open any Lock in *Doubting Caſtle*. Then ſaid *Hopeful*, That's good News; good Brother pluck it out of thy boſom and try: Then *Chriſtian* pulled it out of his boſom, and began to try at the Dungion door, whoſe bolt (as he turned the Key) gave back, and the door flew open with eaſe, and *Chriſtian* and *Hopeful* both came out. Then he went to the outward door that leads into the *Caſtle yard*, and with his *Key*

A Key in **Chriſtians,** ***boſom called Promiſe, opens any Lock in*** **Doubting** ***Caſtle.***

opened the door alſo. After he went to the *Iron* Gate, for that muſt be opened too, but that Lock went *damnable* hard, yet the Key did open it; then they thruſt open the Gate to make their eſcape with ſpeed, but that Gate, as it opened, made ſuch a creaking, that it waked *Giant Deſpair*, who haſtily riſing to purſue his Priſoners, felt his Limbs to fail, ſo that he could by no means go after them. Then they went on, and came to the Kings high way again, and ſo were ſafe, becauſe they were out of his Juriſdiction.

Activity 10.15

Discuss some of the evidence of informal and colloquial language in Bunyan's text.

Bunyan was not a scholar of the universities in Latin and Greek. His own use of the language was influenced by his reading of the King James Bible of 1611, but at the same time, as we have seen, it reflects popular everyday usage. We can therefore use *The Pilgrim's Progress* with reasonable confidence as evidence of ordinary language use in the 1670s.

Although there has been little change in the basic grammatical patterns of the language since the seventeenth century, there are many superficial features, part of the idiom and usage of that period, that date it. A list of selected quotations from *The Pilgrim's Progress* follows to illustrate this, but you could extend this activity yourself by examining any suitable seventeenth century text.

TEXT 107 – John Bunyan's *The Pilgrim's Progress*

1

a his reason was, for that the Valley was altogether without *Honour*;
b ... but he could not be silent long, because that his trouble increased.
c So the other told him, that by that he was gone some distance from the Gate, he would come at the House of the *Interpreter* ...

2

a (we) shall miserably come to ruine: except (the which yet I see not) some way of escape can be found ...
b ... all is not worth to be compared with a little of that that I am seeking to enjoy.
c ... to be bestowed at the time appointed, on them that diligently seek it.

3 (*3rd person singular present tense inflections*)

a ... by reason of a burden that lieth hard upon me:
b The shame that attends Religion, lies also as a block in their way:
c Why came you not in at the Gate which standeth at the beginning of the way?
d How stands it between God and your Soul now?

4 (*perfective aspect*)

a ... but the ground is good when they are once got in at the Gate.
b I thought so; and it is happened unto thee as to other weak men.
c So when he was come in, and set down, they gave him something to drink;
d There was great talk presently after you was gone out ...

5 (*negatives*)

a Then said *Pliable*, Don't revile;
b My Brother, I did not put the question to thee, for that I doubted of the truth of our belief my self ...
c Well then, did you not know about ten years ago, one *Temporary*?
d Nay, methinks I care not what I meet with in the way ...
e Why came you not in at the Gate which standeth at the beginning of the way?

6 (*interrogatives*)

a But my good Companion, do you know the way ...?
b ... dost thou see this narrow way?
c Wherefore dost thou cry?
d But now we are by our selves, what do you think of such men?
e ... how many, think you, must there be?
f Know you not that it is written ...?
g Whence came you, and whither do you go?

7 (*colloquialisms*)

a Oh, did he light upon you?
b Know him! Yes, he dwelt in *Graceless* ...
c I thought I should a been killed there ...
d If this Meadow lieth along by our way side, lets go over into it.
e But did you tell them of your own sorrow? Yes, over, and over, and over.
f ... the remembrance of which will stick by me as long as I live.
h Joseph was hard put to it by her ...
i ... but it is ordinary for those ... to give him the slip, and return again to me.
j He said it was a pitiful low sneaking business for a Man to mind Religion.
k ... let us lie down here and take one Nap.

8

a I beshrow him for his counsel;
b ... and he wot not what to do.
c Who can tell how joyful this Man was, when he had gotten his Roll again!
d The Shepherds had them to another place, in a bottom, where was a door in the side of an Hill.
e He went on thus, even untill he came at a bottom ...
f ... out of the mouth of which there came in an abundant manner Smoak, and Coals of fire, with hideous noises.
g And did you presently fall under the power of this conviction?
h But is there no hopes for such a Man as this?
i They was then asked, If they knew the Prisoner at the Bar?

9
a ... but get it off my self I cannot.
b ... abhor thy self for hearkening unto him

10 (*punctuation*)
a The hearing of this is enough to ravish ones heart.
b A Lot that often falls from bad mens mouths upon good mens Names.

■ Activity 10.16

Identify any features of the language of these quotations that mark it as belonging to the seventeenth century. (Some are included as a contrast to others and may not show such features.)

10.8 John Aubrey

John Aubrey lived from 1626 to 1697. He was an antiquary, archeologist and biographer, but only one book of stories and folklore, *Miscellanies*, was published in his lifetime in 1696. He finished none of his many other books and deposited all his manuscripts in the Ashmolean Museum in Oxford in 1693, including a collection of 'lives' of sixteenth and seventeenth century notable men and women entitled *Brief Lives*.

The 426 'lives' range in length from two to 23 000 words, so any published version is an edited selection. Aubrey himself wrote:

> I hope, hereafter it may be an Incitement to some Ingeniose and publick-spirited young Man, to polish and compleat, what I have delivered rough hewn.

Some of the 'lives' are in no more than note form, but the longer ones are examples of writing that give the impression of spoken narrative – 'a record of his unselfconscious gossip with his friends'. Consequently, they provide an example of standard educated English of the seventeenth century in its informal and colloquial style.

TEXT 108 – John Aubrey's *Brief Lives*

> Mr Gore. He is a fidling peevish fellow.
>
> Thomas Willis, M.D. was middle stature: darke brindle haire (like a red pig) stammered much.
>
> William Sanderson dyed at Whitehall (I was then there): went out like a spent candle: died before Dr. Holder could come to him with the Sacrament.
>
> William Outram was a tall spare leane pale consumptive man; wasted himself much, I presume, by frequent preaching.
>
> Mrs. Abigail Sloper borne at Broad Chalke, near Salisbury, A.D. 1648. Pride; lechery; ungratefull to her father; married; runne distracted; recovered.
>
> Richard Stokes, M.D. His father was Fellow of Eaton College. He was bred there and at King's College. Scholar to Mr. W. Oughtred for Mathematiques (Algebra). He made himselfe mad with it, but became sober again, but I feare like a crackt-glasse. Became a Roman-catholique: married unhappily at Liege, dog and catt. etc. Became a Sott. Dyed in Newgate, Prisoner for debt April 1681.
>
> Thomas Fuller was of middle stature; strong sett; curled haire; a very working head, in so much that, walking and meditating before dinner, he would eate-up a penny loafe, not knowing that he did it. His naturall memorie was very great, to which he added the Art of Memorie: he would repeat to you forwards and backwards all the signes from Ludgate to Charing-crosse.

(*Aubrey's Brief Lives*, 3rd edn, Oliver Lawson Dick (ed.), Secker and Warburg, 1958)

The 'lives' were anecdotal, each one a collection of facts and stories that Aubrey had gathered about his subject – 'he was sometimes inaccurate, it is true, but he was never untruthful'. The following example is from Aubrey's *Life of Richard Corbet* (1582–1635), who was Bishop firstly of Oxford and then of Norwich. It is typical of the amusing stories that Aubrey remembered and recorded about his subjects.

TEXT 109 – John Aubrey's *Life of Richard Corbet*

> ... His conversation was extreme pleasant. Dr. Stubbins was one of his Cronies; he was a jolly fatt Dr. and a very good house-keeper; parson in Oxfordshire. As Dr. Corbet and he were riding in Lob Lane in wett weather ('tis an extraordinary deepe, dirty lane) the coach fell; and Dr. Corbet sayd that Dr. Stubbins was up to the elbowes in mud, he was up to the elbowes in Stubbins.
>
> He was made Bishop of Oxford, and I have heard that he had an admirable, grave and venerable aspect.
>
> One time, as he was Confirming, the country-people pressing in to see the Ceremonie, sayd he, *Bear off there, or I'le confirm yee with my Staffe*. Another time, being to lay his hand on the head of a man very bald, he turns to his chaplaine, Lushington, and sayd, *Some Dust, Lushington* (to keepe his hand from slipping). There was a man with a great venerable Beard: sayd the Bishop, *You, behind the Beard*.
>
> His Chaplain, Dr. Lushington, was a very learned and ingeniose (= *intelligent*) man, and they loved one another. The Bishop sometimes would take the key of the wine-cellar, and he and his Chaplaine would goe and lock themselves in, and be merry. Then first he layes downe his Episcopall hat – *There lyes the Doctor*. Then he putts off his gowne – *There lyes the Bishop*. Then 'twas *Here's to thee, Corbet*, and *Here's to thee, Lushington ...*
>
> The last words he sayd were, *Good night, Lushington*.

10.9 Christopher Cooper's *The English Teacher*

Christopher Cooper, 'Master of the Grammar School of Bishop-Stortford in Hartfordshire', published *The English Teacher* or *The Discovery of the Art of Teaching and Learning the English Tongue* in 1687. He has been described as 'the best phonetician and one of the fullest recorders of pronunciation that England (and indeed modern Europe) produced before the nineteenth century, the obscure schoolmaster of a country town' (*English Pronunciation 1500–1700*, E. J. Dobson, 1968). An examination of Christopher Cooper's book will therefore provide good evidence of the pronunciation of English in his time.

Cooper's description of the relationship of letters to sounds is, like that of all the orthoepists of the sixteenth and seventeenth century, not always easy to follow, because there was no phonetic alphabet at that time to act as a reference for the sounds. His first concern was the spelling of the vowels and consonants, to which he relates the variety of sounds that they represent. He made no proposals for spelling reform, but aimed at teaching the spelling system in general use at that time.

There was still a clear distinction of **quantity** between short and long vowels with the same **quality**, as in OE and ME, but this had become complicated as a result of the Great Vowel Shift (see Section 9.5), which was not fully complete until about the end of the seventeenth century. As the shift of the long vowels took place in the South of England, and not in the North, the educated speech of London and the Home Counties – the emerging standard language – was affected by it. This meant that the same vowel letter now represented *different* sounds.

Activity 10.17

Examine the following lists in turn (Texts 110–115), taken from Cooper's *The English Teacher*. Discuss the evidence they show of:

(a) Cooper's pronunciation in the 1680s and any change from ME as a result of either the shift of the long vowels or other causes.
(b) Later changes that have taken place in the pronunciation of any of the words.

(A description with the etymologies of an extended vocabulary can be found in Commentary 19 of the *Text Commentary Book*.)

10.9.1 'Of the Vowel a'

Cooper described the letter <a> as having three sounds: a short, a long and *a* slender. In the IPA today, they would be written /a/, /a:/ or /æ:/, and /ɛ:/ respectively.

TEXT 110 – Christopher Cooper's *The English Teacher*, 1687 (i)

a ſhort	a long	a ſlender
Bar	*Barge*	*Bare*
blab	*blaſt*	*blazon*
cap	*carking*	*cape*
car	*carp*	*care*
cat	*caſt*	*caſe*
daſh	*dart*	*date*
flaſh	*flasket*	*flake*
gaſh	*gaſp*	*gate*
grand	*grant*	*grange*
land	*lance*	*lane*
maſh	*mask*	*maſon*
pat	*path*	*pate*
tar	*tart*	*tares*

Cooper distinguished as different the vowels in certain pairs of words which today are identical **homophones** in RP and other dialects. These words, however, have remained different in parts of the North and East Anglia, for example, *pane* with a pure vowel /pe:n/ and *pain* with a diphthong /pɛIn/ (see *Accents of English*, 1, Chapter 3 Section 3.1.5, J. C. Wells, CUP, 1982), although the contrast is not the same as that in Cooper's speech. He describes the difference in the following way (Cooper's 'u guttural' was the short vowel /ə/).

TEXT 111 – Christopher Cooper's *The English Teacher*, 1687 (ii)

ai pronounced gently hath the ſound of *a* pure, as in *cane*, but where *a* onely is written *u* guttural is ſounded after it; as

Bain	*Hail*	*Maid*
bane	*hale*	*made*
main	*lay'n*	*pain*
mane	*lane*	*pane*
plain	*ſpaid*	*tail*
plane	*ſpade*	*tale*

10.9.2 'Of the Vowel e'

The purpose of the digraph <ea> was to distinguish the more open of the two long front vowels /ɛ:/ from the closer vowel /e:/, usually spelt <ee> (see Section 9.5). Here is the evidence from Cooper's book (his 'long *e*' was the vowel /ɛ:/):

That sound which is taken for the long *e* is exprest by putting a after it; as *men*, *mean*.

10.9.3 'Of the Vowel o'

TEXT 112 – Christopher Cooper's *The English Teacher*, 1687 (iii)

o oa ou in theſe following is ſounded *oo*.

A-board	*con-courſe*	*court-ſhip*	*ſourſe*	*whom*
ac-cou-tred	*could*	*force*	*ſword*	*whore*
af-ford	*courſe*	*forces*	*ſworn*	*who-ſo-e-ver*
be-hoves	*courſes*	*move*	*tomb*	*womb*
boar	*court*	*mourn*	*two*	*worn*
born	*cour-ti-er*	*ſcourſe*	*un-couth*	*would*
bourn	*court-li-neſs*	*ſhould*	*who*	

In all others this ſound is written *oo*; as *look*, *roof*. But *Board*, *forth*, *prove*, *ſloup*, are better written *boord*, *foorth*, *proove*, *ſloop*.

10.9.4 'Improper diphthongs'

Cooper differentiated diphthongs in pronunciation from digraphs in writing. He did not, however, use the word *digraph* but the phrase *improper diphthong* for pairs of letters that represented only one sound.

In the following extract, '*e* short' meant /ɛ/, '*e* long' /ɛ:/, 'ee' /i:/, 'ɑ' /ɛ:/ and 'a' /a:/. Only a selection from Cooper's lists of words is printed here.

TEXT 113 – Christopher Cooper's *The English Teacher*, 1687 (iv)

Of the improper Diphthongs *ea*, *oa*, *eo*, *ie*. In which one Vowel alone is pronounced; to which may be added *ui*, as it is commonly taken.

Rule 1. Of *ea*.

Ea is put 1. For *e* short. 2. For *e* long. 3 For *ee*. 4 for ɑ and *a*.

(*e*) short (= /ɛ/)	(*e*) long (= /ɛ:/)	(*ee*) (= /i:/)	(ɑ) (= /ɛ:/)
bread	break	dear	learn
dearth	clean	blear-ey'd	scream
earth	leaf	ear-wig	swear
ready	sea	near	(*a*) (=/a:/)
tread	wear	weary	hearth

10.9.5 'Barbarous speaking'

The pronunciation of rural and urban dialects has always been regarded as inferior by those who consider themselves to be in a superior social class. Cooper, as a teacher, shows this in his chapter 'Of Barbarous Speaking', in which he implies that a person's pronunciation will determine his spelling.

Activity 10.18

(i) Read the two pages 'Of Barbarous Dialects' in Text 114.
(ii) Are any of the 'barbarous' pronunciations to be heard today in (a) RP or (b) any of our regional dialects?
(iii) Does this provide any evidence that some features of RP, the socially prestigious accent of English today, have derived from regional accents?

TEXT 114 – Christopher Cooper's *The English Teacher*, 1687 (v)

HE, that would write more exactly,muſt avoid a Barbarous Pronunciation ; and conſider for facility, or thorow miſtake,many words are not ſounded after the beſt dialect : Such as

A.	E.	I.
	Ex-tre, **axle-tree**	***Im-poſſable***, **im poſſible ;**
	eend, **end**	
	e'nt, **is it not**	

cont ...

B.

Buſhop, Biſhop
Bellis, bellows

C.

Chimly, Chimney
Chorles, Charles

D.

Dud, did
Dander, *dandruffe*, dandraffe

F.

Frankamcenſe, —incenſe
Firmity, frumenty
Fut, foot
Fâw, few

G.

Gurgians, *gurgions*, grudgings; *gem me*, *gim me*, give me; *gove*, *gov*, gave; *griſt*, graſt, graff; *git*, get.

H.

Hundurd, hundred
howſomever, *howz-ever*, howſoever; *Hild*, held; *hanke-cher*, handkerchief.

K.

L.

Lat, let;
leece, lice

M.

Mought, *med*, might; *Maracle*, miracle; *meece*, mice;

N.

Nother, neither

O.

Ommoſt, almoſt
Wuts, Oats
Op, up
Wun, one.

P.

Q.

Quawm, qualm

R.

Reddiſh, Raddiſh

S.

Sez, ſayes; *ſed*, ſaid; (*ſh*) for (*ſ*) before (*u*) as *Shure*, *Shugar*, &c. *Stomp*, Stamp; *skim-mer*, ſcummer; *ſcurge*, ſcourge. *ſcru-pe-lous*, ſcrupulous; *ſhet*, ſhut; *ſarvice*, ſervice.

T.

Terrable, terrible; *Tunder*, tinder; *Thraſh*, threſh; *Thair*, *there*, thare; *Truel*, trowel;

V.

Vitles, Victuals.

W.

Widſt, *wudſt*, wouldſt; *wull*, will; *wuth*, with; *wumme*, *wuth me*, with me; *whutter*, hotter; *whuther*, whether; *wuſted*, worſted; *wurry*, weary; *wont*, will not.

Y.

Yerb, herb; *yerth*, earth; *yau*, you; *yeuſleſs*, *yeuſary*, &c. uſeleſs, &c.

10.9.6 'Words that have the same pronunciation'

Other lists in Cooper's book are useful in a study of changing pronunciation. For example, there are several pages of 'Words that have the same pronunciation, but different signification and manner of writing'. Most of them are pronounced alike today, although not necessarily with the same vowels as in the seventeenth century. For example, *seas* and *seize* are homophones today, /si:z/, but would have been pronounced /sɛ:z/ or /se:z/ in Cooper's time, the final raising to /i:/ not yet having taken place.

Some of the words confirm changes since ME. For example, the pairing of *rest/wrest*, *right/wright* and *ring/wring* shows the loss of <w> from the OE and ME initial consonant group <wr> to be complete. John Hart's *An Orthographie* written in the sixteenth century showed that <w> was still pronounced.

Here are a few of the pairs that have remained homophones:

altar/alter	chewes/chuse	in/inn
assent/ascent	dear/deer	lesson/lessen
bare/bear	hair/hare	pair/pare/pear

Others show that at least one word in each pair or group has changed since the 1680s, for example, the pronunciation of *are*, *one*, the *-ure* of *censure*, *gesture* and *tenure*, the *oi* of *oil* and *loin*, and the *ea* of *flea*, *heard*, *least*, *rear*, *reason*, *shear* and *wear*.

TEXT 115 – Christopher Cooper's *The English Teacher*, 1687 (vi)

are/air/heir/ere
ant/aunt
bile/boil
censer/censor/censure
coat/quote
comming/cummin
cool'd/could
coughing/coffin
car'd/card
doe/do/dow (= dough)
flea/flay
fit/fight (= did fight)
jester/gesture
hard/heard/herd
i'le/isle/oil
jerkin/jerking
kill/kiln
least/lest
line/loin
mile/moil (= hard labour)
nether/neither
own/one
pastor/pasture
pick't her/picture
pour/power
rare/rear
raisins/reasons
share/shear
shoo (*shoe*)/shew (*show*)
stood/stud
tenor/tenure
to/two/toe
war/wear/ware
woo/woe
yea/ye

10.9.7 Words spelt with <oi>

The study of sound changes is complex. Here, we consider briefly one particular change, in which two sets of words with different vowels in ME and MnE fell together for a time.

From the evidence of the preceding list, *boil*, *oil*, *loin* and *moil* had the same pronunciation as *bile*, *isle*, *line* and *mile*. This can be checked in the poetry of the seventeenth and early eighteenth centuries, in which many similar pairs of words consistently rhyme together (see Section 10.10.3 on John Dryden). However, this did not mean that their pronunciation at that time was either /bail/ or /bɔil/.

<boil>

The verb *boil*, like many other words spelt with the <oi> digraph, came from French and was pronounced /bʊɪl/ in ME, although it was usually spelt with <oi>. The diphthong was 'unrounded' during the seventeenth century and changed to /ʌɪ/.

We saw evidence in John Hart's *An Orthographie* of the shift of the long vowel /i:/ to the diphthong /əɪ/, which was almost the same in sound as /ʌɪ/ by the 1560s. As a result, words formerly with /i:/ and /ʊɪ/ fell together, and both were pronounced with the diphthong /əi/.

After about 1700, the first element of the diphthong shifted further to its present-day pronunciation /aɪ/ in words like *bile*. Why, then, do we pronounce *boil* (and similar words) today as /bɔɪl/ and not /baɪl/?

The reason is that, in ME, there was a second set of words spelt with <oi>, for example, *choice* and *noise*, with a diphthong pronounced /ɔɪ/, not /ʊɪ/. Evidence from the orthoepists suggests that /ʊɪ/ words were also pronounced /ɔɪ/ by some speakers. Eventually, helped by the spelling, all words spelt with <oi> came to be pronounced /ɔɪ/, so that *bile*, by then pronounced /baɪl/, ceased to rhyme with *boil*, pronounced /bɔɪl/.

10.10 John Dryden

John Dryden (1631–1700), one of the great writers in the English literary tradition, was a poet, dramatist and critic. He was largely responsible for the 'cherished superstition that prepositions must, in spite of the incurable English instinct for putting them late, ... be kept true to their name & placed before the word they govern' (H. W. Fowler, 1926). Dryden 'went through all his prefaces contriving away the final prepositions that he had been guilty of in his first editions' (*ibid*). This is incidental, however, to his recognised eminence as a prose writer, and it has been said that Modern English prose begins with Dryden.

10.10.1 Dryden as letter writer

This first example of his writing reveals the problems of being dependent on patronage at that time.

TEXT 116 – John Dryden's letter to Lawrence Hyde, Earl of Rochester, August 1683

My Lord
I know not whether my Lord Sunderland has interceded with your Lordship, for half a yeare of my salary: But I have two other Advocates, my extreame wants, even almost to arresting, & my ill health, which cannot be repaird without immediate retireing into the Country. A quarters allowance is but the Jesuites powder to my disease; the fitt will return a fortnight hence. If I durst I wou'd plead a little merit, & some hazards of my life from the Common Enemyes, my refuseing advantages offerd by them, & neglecting my beneficiall studyes for the King's service: But I onely thinke I merit not to sterve. I never applyd my selfe to any Interest contrary to your Lordship's; and, on some suasions, perhaps not known to you, have not been unserviceable to the memory & reputation of My Lord your father. After this, My Lord, my conscience assures me I may write boldly, though I cannot speake to you. I have three Sonns growing to mans estate, I breed them all up to learning beyond my fortune; but they are too hopefull to be neglected though I want. Be pleasd to looke on me with an eye of compassion; some small employment wou'd render my condition easy. The King is not unsatisfyed of me, the Duke has often promis'd me his assistance; & your Lordship is the Conduit through which their favours passe. Either in the Customes, or the Appeales of the Excise, or some other way; meanes cannot be wanting if you please to have the will. Tis enough for one Age to have neglected Mr Cowley, and sterv'd Mr Butler; but neither of them had the happiness to live till your Lordship's Ministry. In the meane time be pleasd to give me a gracious and speedy answer to my present request of halfe a yeares pension for my necessityes. I am goeing to write somewhat by his Majestyes command, & cannot stirr into the Country for my health and studies, till I secure my family from want. You have many petitions of this nature, & cannot satisfy all, but I hope from your goodness to be made an Exception to your generall rules; because I am, with all sincerity,

Your Lordship's most obedient
Humble Servant
John Dryden

Activity 10.19

List any features of spelling, punctuation, vocabulary or grammar in Text 116 that are not now standard and comment on their number in proportion to the whole letter.

10.10.2 Dryden on Chaucer

Dryden admired Chaucer's poetry, but some aspects of his assessment of Chaucer throw as clear a light on Dryden himself, and the way he and his contemporaries thought about language and writing, as it does on Chaucer. His summary of Chaucer's achievement is well known:

> 'Tis sufficient to say according to the Proverb, that here is God's Plenty.

Dryden's remarks on Chaucer's language are relevant to our survey of the development of Standard English, and of the attitudes to acceptable usage. The earliest English for us is OE, in texts as far back as the ninth century. Dryden was concerned with the idea of the 'purity' of English and the notion that it had reached a state of perfection in his day – 'From *Chaucer* the Purity of the *English* Tongue began ... *Chaucer* (lived) in the Dawning of our Language'. For Dryden, Chaucer's diction 'stands not on an equal Foot' with 'our present English'.

TEXT 117 – John Dryden on Chaucer's verse (i)

> The verse of *Chaucer*, I confess, is not harmonious to us ... They who liv'd with him, and some time after him, thought it Musical ... There is the rude Sweetness of a *Scotch* tune in it, which is natural and pleasing, though not perfect.

In the following text, Dryden criticises the editor of an earlier late sixteenth century printed edition of Chaucer.

TEXT 118 – John Dryden on Chaucer's verse (ii)

> ... for he would make us believe the Fault is in our Ears, and that there were really Ten Syllables in a Verse where we find but Nine: But this Opinion is not worth confuting; 'tis so gross and obvious an Errour, that Common Sense ... must convince the Reader, that Equality of Numbers in every Verse which we call *Heroick*, was either not known, or not always practis'd in *Chaucer's* Age. It were an easie Matter to produce some thousands of his Verses, which are lame for want of half a Foot, and sometimes a whole one, and which no Pronunciation can make otherwise ... *Chaucer*, I confess, is a rough Diamond, and must first be polish'd e're he shines.

Dryden's 'polishing' of Chaucer was done by reversifying some of the Canterbury tales, making his choice from those tales 'as savour nothing of Immodesty'. In his preface to the fables, he quotes from Chaucers's prologue, where the narrator 'thus excuses the Ribaldry, which is very gross...'. Dryden then goes on to discuss Chaucer's language.

TEXT 119 – John Dryden on Chaucer's verse (iii)

> You have here a *Specimen* of *Chaucer's* Language, which is so obsolete, that his Sense is scarce to be understood; and you have likewise more than one Example of his unequal Numbers, which were mention'd before. Yet many of his verses consist of Ten Syllables, and the Words not much behind our present *English*.

The following texts consist of the same extract from Chaucer's prologue to *The Canterbury Tales*, firstly as quoted by Dryden in 1700 from an early printed version as an example of Chaucer's 'obsolete' language and rough versification, and then in a modern edition based on the manuscripts.

TEXT 120 – John Dryden's version of Chaucer's prologue to *The Canterbury Tales*

But first, I pray you, of your courtesy,
That ye ne arrete it nought my villany,
Though that I plainly speak in this mattere
To tellen you her words, and eke her chere:
Ne though I speak her words properly,
For this ye knowen as well as I,
Who shall tellen a tale after a man
He mote rehearse as nye, as ever He can:
Everich word of it been in his charge,
All speke he, never so rudely, ne large.
Or else he mote tellen his tale untrue,
Or feine things, or find words new:
He may not spare, altho he were his brother,
He mote as well say o words as another.
Christ spake himself full broad in holy Writ,
And well I wote no Villany is it.
Eke *Plato* saith, who so can him rede,
The words mote been Cousin to the dede.

TEXT 121 – Modern Edition of Text 120

But first I pray yow of youre curteisye
That ye n'arette it noght my vileynye
Though that I pleynly speke in this mateere
To telle yow hir wordes and hir cheere
Ne thogh I speke hir wordes proprely.
For this ye knowen al so wel as I
Whoso shal telle a tale after a man
He moot reherce as ny as euere he kan
Euerich a word if it be in his charge
Al speke he neuer so rudeliche and large,
Or ellis he moot telle his tale vntrewe
Or feyne thyng or fynde wordes newe.
He may nat spare althogh he were his brother
He moot as wel seye o word as another.
Crist spak hymself ful brode in hooly writ
And wel ye woot no vileynye is it.
Eek Plato seith, whoso that kan hym rede,
The wordes moote be cosyn to the dede.

Activity 10.20

(i) Study the two versions of Chaucer's prologue and comment on the difference between them.
(ii) Read Section 5.1.1, which briefly describes the pronunciation of Chaucer's verse.
(iii) Discuss the possible reasons for Dryden's criticism of Chaucer's 'unequal Numbers'; that is, his belief that many of Chaucer's lines have fewer than the ten syllables that verses should have.
(iv) What was 'obsolete' for Dryden in Chaucer's vocabulary and grammar?

10.10.3 Dryden and rhymes

When you read poetry from the sixteenth to the eighteenth centuries, you will often find pairs of words that should rhyme, but do not do so in present-day pronunciation. We have already looked at rhymes in our study of the language, as evidence of changes in the pronunciation and structure of words up to the end of the fourteenth century (see Section 7.3.3 on Chaucer's rhymes). It is therefore interesting to examine a few examples from the end of the seventeenth century and to relate them to what we have learned about pronunciation from the two orthoepists, John Hart in the sixteenth century (see Chapter 9) and Christopher Cooper in the seventeenth century (see Section 10.9).

These rhymes from John Dryden's translation of Virgil's Latin *Aeneis* occur many other times in the translation, and thus are not single examples that might be explained as false or eye rhymes.

TEXT 122 – John Dryden's *Aeneis*

<ea>

appear
Amidst our course Zacynthian Woods **appear**;
And next by rocky Neritos we **steer**: III 351

At length, in dead of Night, the Ghost **appears**
Of her unhappy Lord: the Spectre **stares**,
And with erected Eyes his bloody Bosom **bares.** I 486

Sea
He calls to raise the Masts, the Sheats **display**;
The Chearful Crew with diligence **obey**;
They scud before the Wind, and sail in open **Sea**. V 1084

Long wandring Ways for you the Pow'rs **decree**:
On Land hard Labours, and a length of **Sea**. II 1058

Then, from the South arose a gentle **Breeze**,
That curl'd the smoothness of the glassy **Seas**: V 997

Year
When rising Vapours choak the wholsom **Air**,
And blasts of noisom Winds corrupt the **Year**. III 190

Laocoon, *Neptune's* Priest by Lot that **Year**,
With solemn pomp then sacrific'd a **Steer**. II 267

<i>

Wind
His Pow'r to hollow Caverns is **confin'd**,
There let him reign, the Jailor of the **Wind**. I 199

<oi>
For this are various Penances **enjoyn'd**;
And some are hung to bleach, upon the **Wind**; VI 1002

Did I or *Iris* give this mad **Advice**,
Or made the Fool himself the fatal **Choice**? X 110

The passive Gods behold the *Greeks* **defile**
Their Temples, and abandon to the **Spoil**
Their own Abodes ... II 471

But that o'reblown, when Heav'n above 'em **smiles**,
Return to Travel, and renew their **Toils**: X 1144

... Resolute to **die**,
And add his Fun'rals to the fate of **Troy**: II 862

<a>
The rest, in Meen, in habit, and in **Face**,
Appear'd a *Greek*; and such indeed he **was**. III 778

Yet one remain'd, the Messenger of **Fate**;
High on a craggy Cliff *Celæno* **sate**,
And thus her dismall Errand did **relate**. III 321

cont ...

Then, as her Strength with Years increas'd, **began**
To pierce aloft in Air the soaring **Swan**:
And from the Clouds to fetch the heron and the **Crane**. XI 868

<ar> O more than Madmen! you your selves shall **bear**
The guilt of Blood and Sacrilegious **War**: VII 821

Loaded with Gold, he sent his Darling, **far**
From Noise and Tumults, and destructive **War**:
Committed to the faithless Tyrant's **Care**. III 73

<oo> She seem'd a Virgin of the *Spartan* **Blood**:
With such Array *Harpalice* **bestrode**
Her *Thracian* Courser, and outstri'd the rapid **Flood** I 440

His Father *Hyrtacus* of Noble **Blood**;
His Mother was a Hunt'ress of the **Wood**: IX 223

... The Brambles drink his **Blood**;
And his torn Limbs are left, the Vulture's **Food**. VIII 855

Resume your ancient Care; and if the **God**
Your Sire, and you, resolve on Foreign **Blood**: VII 516

<oa> His knocking Knees are bent beneath the **Load**:
And shiv'ring Cold congeals his vital **Blood**. XII 1308

Maids, Matrons, Widows, mix their common **Moans**:
Orphans their Sires, and Sires lament their **Sons** XI 329

<-y> *Acestes*, fir'd with just Disdain, to **see**
The Palm usurp'd without a **Victory**;
Reproch'd *Entellus* thus ... V 513

The Pastor pleas'd with his dire **Victory**,
Beholds the satiate Flames in Sheets ascend the **Sky**: X 573

... the Coast was **free**
From Foreign or Domestick **Enemy**: III 168

He heav'd it at a Lift: and poiz'd on **high**,
Ran stagg'ring on, against his **Enemy**. XII 1304

Activity 10.21

(i) Study the pairs of rhymes in Text 122 and discuss their probable pronunciations.
(ii) How can we explain the fact that several words appear to have two pronunciations?

It seems odd at first that *enemy* could apparently rhyme with either *free*, MnE /fri:/, and *high*, MnE /haɪ/. But the vowel of *high* was still in the process of shifting, in Dryden's time, from /i:/ to /aɪ/, and the vowel of *free* from /e:/ to /i:/, and pronunciations varied.

This explains the following word-play in Shakespeare's *The Two Gentlemen of Verona* a century earlier. The dialogue is between Protheus, 'a gentleman of Verona', and Speed, 'a clownish seruant'. The word *Ay* (*yes*) is spelt *I*; *noddy* meant *foolish*.

TEXT 123 – Shakespeare's *The Two Gentlemen of Verona*

PROTHEUS	But what said she?
SPEED	(*Nods, then saies*) I.
PROTHEUS	Nod-I, why that's noddy.
SPEED	You mistooke Sir: I say she did nod; and you aske me if she did nod and I say I.
PROTHEUS	And that set together is noddy.

Activity 10.22

Explain the dialogue of Text 123.

10.11 North Riding Yorkshire dialect in the 1680s

It was said in an earlier chapter that from the late fifteenth century it becomes increasingly rare to find texts that provide evidence of regional forms other than those of the educated London dialect, which became established as the standard. Once the grammar and vocabulary of written English were standardised, other dialects were recorded only in texts written for the purpose of presenting dialects as different.

During the seventeenth century, there was a revival of interest in antiquarian studies and of language, two of the many topics discussed by members of The Royal Society. Writings on language included descriptions of the Saxon language of the past and of contemporary dialects.

One form that this interest in dialect took can be seen in George Meriton's *A Yorkshire Dialogue*, published in York in 1683. Meriton was a lawyer, practising in the North Riding town of Northallerton. Meriton's dialogue is a lively representation of a Yorkshire farming family, written in verse couplets, and is deliberately full of proverbial sayings. It is therefore only indirect evidence of the authentic spoken North Riding English of the time, but nevertheless gives us plenty of examples of dialectal and traditional vocabulary and grammar.

The spelling of written English in the seventeenth century had remained virtually unchanged, in spite of the efforts of spelling reformers like John Hart in the sixteenth century, and took no account of the shifts of pronunciation that had taken place since the fourteenth century. Consequently, the spelling of Standard English did not accurately indicate the 'polite' accent of the late seventeenth and early eighteenth centuries. But when writing in dialect, it was (and still is) usual to spell many of the words 'as they were spoken', so that features of dialectal pronunciation were shown as well as the vocabulary and grammar.

In the following short extract, the two young women in the family, Tibb the daughter and Nan the niece, talk about their sweethearts. There are no 'stage directions', so their movements have to be inferred from the dialogue.

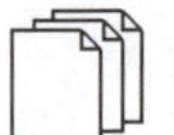

Activity 10.23

(i) List some of the probable dialectal pronunciations that the spellings in Text 124 suggest.
(ii) In what ways does the grammar of the dialect differ from the Standard English of the late seventeenth century?

TEXT 124 – George Meriton's *A Yorkshire Dialogue*, 1683

(The extract begins at line 155 of the original. The Yorkshire dialectal pronunciation of *the* is spelt in the *Dialogue* as *'th*.)

A York-shire DIALOGUE, In its pure Natural DIALECT: As it is now commonly Spoken in the North parts of *York-Shire* Being a Miscellaneous discourse, or Hotchpotch of several Country Affaires, begun by a Daughter and her Mother, and continued by the Father, Son, Uncle, Neese, and Land-Lord.

F. = Father, M. = Mother, D. = Daughter, N. = Niece.

F. What ails our *Tibb*, that she urles seay ith Newke,
Shee's nut Reet, she leauks an Awd farrand Leauke.

D. Fatther, Ive gitten cawd, I can scarce tawke,
And my Snurles are seay sayr stopt, I can nut snawke,

N. How duz my Cozen *Tibb* Naunt I mun nut stay,
I hard she gat a Cawd the other day,

M. Ey wallaneerin, wilta gang and see,
Shee's aboun 'ith Chawmber, Thou may Clim upth Stee.
Shee's on a dovening now gang deftly *Nan*,
And mack as little din as ee'r Thou can.

N. Your mains flaid, there's an awd saying you knawe
That there's no Carrion will kill a Crawe:
If she be nut as dead as a deaur Naile,
Ile mack her flyer and semper like Flesh Cael,
What *Tibb* I see, Thou is nut yet quite dead,
Leauke at me woman, and haud up thy head.

D. Ah *Nan* steeke'th winderboard, and mack it darke,
My Neen are varra sayr, they stoun and warke.
They are seay Gummy and Furr'd up sometime.
I can nut leauke at'th Leet, nor see a stime.

N. Come come, I can mack Thee Leetsome and blythe,
Here will be thy awd Sweet-heart here Belive.
He tell's me seay I say him but last night
O *Tibb* he is as fine as onny Kneet.

D. Nay *Nan* Thou dus but jest there's neay sike thing,
He woes another Lasse and gave her a Ring.

N. Away away great feaul tack thou neay Care,
He swears that hee'l love thee for evermare.
And sayes as ever he whopes his Saul to seave,
Hee'l either wed to Thee, or tull his greave ...

(*A Yorkshire Dialogue*, A. C. Cawley (ed.), Yorkshire Dialect Society, reprint II, 1959)

F. What ails our *Tibb*, that she crouches* so in the Nook,
She's not Right, she looks an Old fashioned Look.

D. Father, I've gotten (a) cold, I can scarce talk,
And my Nostrils are so sore stopped (up), I can not inhale,

N. How does my Cousin *Tibb* Aunt I must not stay,
I heard she got a Cold the other day,

M. Ey alas, wilt thou go and see,
She's above in the Chawmber, Thou may Climb up the Ladder.
She's in a doze now go gently *Nan*,
And make as little din as ever Thou can.

N. You're very worried, there's an old saying you know
That there's no Carrion will kill a Crow:
If she be not as dead as a door Nail,
I'll make her laugh and simper like Meat Broth,
What *Tibb* I see, Thou is not yet quite dead,
Look at me woman, and hold up thy head.

D. Ah *Nan* shut the window-board (= *shutter*), and make it dark,
My Eyes are very sore, they smart and ache.
They are so Gummy and Furr'd up sometime.
I can not look at the Light, nor see a thing.

N. Come come, I can make Thee Lightsome and blithe,
Here will be thy old Sweet-heart here Soon.
He tells me so I saw him but last night
O *Tibb* he is as fine as any Knight.

D. Nay *Nan* Thou dost but jest there's no such thing,
He woos another Lass and gave her a Ring.

N. Away away great fool take thou no Care,
He swears that he'll love thee for evermore.
And says as ever he hopes his Soul to save,
He'll either wed to Thee, or till his grave (= *die*).

**urles* cannot be accurately translated into one Standard English word. A contemporary gloss (1684) on the word was: '*To Vrle*, is to draw ones self up on a heap'; a later one (1808) was: 'to be pinched with cold'.

(A descriptive analysis can be found in Commentary 20 in the *Text Commentary Book*.)

11. Modern English – the eighteenth century

A standard language is achieved when writers use prescribed and agreed forms of the vocabulary and grammar, regardless of the dialectal variety of the language that each one may speak. As a result, regional and class dialects, which are themselves no less rule-governed and systematic than an agreed standard, tend to be regarded as inferior. This chapter presents some of the evidence about attitudes towards, and beliefs about, the standard language and the dialects in the eighteenth century. The linguistic changes that have taken place from the eighteenth century to the present day are relatively few and will be discussed in the next chapter.

11.1 Correcting, improving and ascertaining the language

11.1.1 'The continual Corruption of our English Tongue'

During the eighteenth century, many pamphlets, articles and grammar books were published on the topic of correcting, improving and, if possible, fixing the language in a perfected form. One word that recurred time and time again in referring to the state of the English language was *corruption*. You will find it in the following text, which is an extract from an article written by Jonathan Swift (1667–1745) in 1710 in the journal *The Tatler*. The complete article took the form of a supposed letter written to *Isaac Bickerstaff*, a pseudonym for Jonathan Swift.

TEXT 125 – *The Tatler*, 26 September 1710

> The following Letter has laid before me many great and manifest Evils in the World of Letters which I had overlooked; but they open to me a very busie Scene, and it will require no small Care and Application to amend Errors which are become so universal ...
>
> *To* Isaac Bickerstaff *Esq*;
>
> *SIR*,
>
> There are some Abuses among us of great Consequence, the Reformation of which is properly your Province, tho', as far as I have been conversant in your Papers, you have not yet considered them. These are, the deplorable Ignorance that for some Years hath reigned among our English Writers, the great depravity of our Taste, and the continual Corruption of our Style ...

These two Evils, Ignorance and Want of Taste, have produced a Third; I mean, the continual Corruption of our English Tongue, which, without some timely Remedy, will suffer more by the false Refinements of twenty Years past, than it hath been improved in the foregoing Hundred ...

But instead of giving you a List of the late Refinements crept into our Language, I here send you the Copy of a Letter I received some Time ago from a most accomplished person in this Way of Writing, upon which I shall make some Remarks. It is in these Terms.

> *SIR*,
> I *Cou'dn't* get the Things you sent for all *about Town*.... I *thôt* to *ha*' come down my self, and then *I'd ha' brôut 'um*; but I *han't don't*, and I believe I *can't do't*, that's *Pozz*.... *Tom* begins to *gi'mself Airs* because *he's* going with the *Plenipo's*.... 'Tis said, the *French* King will *bambooz'l us agen*, which *causes many Speculations*. The *Jacks*, and others of that *Kidney*, are very *uppish*, and *alert upon't*, as you may see by their *Phizz's*.... *Will Hazzard* has got the *Hipps*, having lost *to the Tune of* Five hundr'd Pound, *thô* he understands Play very well, *no body better*. He has promis't me upon *Rep*, to leave off Play; but, you know 'tis a Weakness *he's* too apt to *give into*, *thô* he has as much Wit as any Man, *no body more*. He has lain *incog* ever since.... The *Mobb's* very quiet with us now.... I believe you *thot* I *banter'd* you in my Last like a *Country Put*.... I *sha'n't* leave Town this Month, &c.

This Letter is in every Point an admirable Pattern of the present polite Way of Writing; nor is it of less Authority for being an Epistle ... The first Thing that strikes your Eye is the Breaks at the End of almost every Sentence; of which I know not the Use, only that it is a Refinement, and very frequently practised. Then you will observe the Abbreviations and Elisions, by which Consonants of most obdurate Sound are joined together, without one softening Vowel to intervene; and all this only to make one Syllable of two, directly contrary to the Example of the Greeks and Romans; altogether of the Gothick Strain, and a natural Tendency towards relapsing into barbarity, which delights in Monosyllables, and uniting of Mute Consonants; as it is observable in all the Northern Languages. And this is still more visible in the next refinement, which consists in pronouncing the first Syllable in a Word that has many, and dismissing the rest; such as *Phizz*, *Hipps*, *Mobb*, *Pozz*, *Rep*, and many more; when we are already overloaded with Monosyllables, which are the disgrace of our Language ...

The Third Refinement observable in the Letter I send you, consists in the Choice of certain Words invented by some Pretty Fellows; such as *Banter*, *Bamboozle*, *Country Put*, and *Kidney*, as it is there applied; some of which are now struggling for the Vogue, and others are in Possession of it. I have done my utmost for some Years past to stop the Progress of *Mobb* and *Banter*, but have been plainly borne down by Numbers, and betrayed by those who promised to assist me.

In the last Place, you are to take Notice of certain choice Phrases scattered through the Letter; some of them tolerable enough, till they were worn to Rags by servile Imitators. You might easily find them, though they were in a different Print, and therefore I need not disturb them.

These are the false Refinements in our Style which you ought to correct: First, by Argument and fair Means; but if those fail, I think you are to make Use of your Authority as Censor, and by an Annual *Index Expurgatorius* expunge all Words and Phrases that are offensive to good Sense, and condemn those barbarous Mutilations of

cont ...

Vowels and Syllables. In this last Point, the usual pretence is, that they spell as they speak; A Noble Standard for a Language! to depend upon the Caprice of every Coxcomb, who, because Words are the Cloathing of our Thoughts, cuts them out, and shapes them as he pleases, and changes them oftner than his Dress ... And upon this Head I should be glad you would bestow some Advice upon several young Readers in our Churches, who coming up from the University, full fraught with Admiration of our Town Politeness, will needs correct the Style of their Prayer Books. In reading the Absolution, they are very careful to say *pardons* and *absolves*; and in the Prayer for the Royal Family, it must be *endue 'um*, *enrich 'um*, *prosper 'um*, and *bring 'um*. Then in their Sermons they use all the modern Terms of Art, *Sham*, *Banter*, *Mob*, *Bubble*, *Bully*, *Cutting*, *Shuffling*, and *Palming* ...

I should be glad to see you the Instrument of introducing into our Style that Simplicity which is the best and truest ornament of most Things in Life ...

I am, with great Respect,

SIR,

Your, &c.

Activity 11.1

(i) Discuss what the word *corruption* implies as a metaphor of language. Is it a plausible and acceptable concept?

(ii) List the features of contemporary language use that Swift objected to.

(iii) Discuss Swift's argument and his own use of language, for example, his irony and the connotations of words like *Errors*, *Evils*, *Abuses*, *deplorable*, *Depravity*, *Corruption*, *suffer*, *Barbarity*, *Disgrace*, *betrayed*, *Mutilations*, *Coxcomb*.

(iv) Are there any significant differences between Swift's punctuation and present-day conventions? (The dots in the second Letter (....), quoted within the main letter addressed to 'Isaac Bickerstaff', are part of the punctuation which Swift objected to (*the Breaks at the End of almost every Sentence*). Elsewhere (...) they mark omissions from the original longer text.)

Some of the contracted or colloquial forms that Swift disliked were:

banter	humorous ridicule (n), to make fun of (vb) (origin unknown, regarded by Swift as slang)
Hipps/hip	hypochondria, depression
incog	incognito, concealed identity
Jacks	lads, chaps
Mobb/mob	originally shortened from *mobile*, from Latin *mobile vulgus*, the movable or excitable crowd, hence the rabble
Phizz	physiognomy, face
Plenipos	plenipotentiary, representative
Put	fool, lout, bumpkin (origin not known)
Poz	positive, certain
Rep	reputation

The Absolution in *The Book of Common Prayer*, which Swift referred to, contains the words *he pardoneth and absolveth*.

You can see that what Swift disliked was certain new colloquial words and phrases, and fashionable features of pronunciation – all part of spoken usage rather than written. He specifically condemned these as features of *Style*, that is, of deliberate choices of words and structures from the resources of the language. But at the same time, he referred in general to the *Corruption of our English Tongue*, an evaluative metaphor that implied worsening and decay, as if the style he disliked to hear could affect everyone's use of English, both written and spoken.

This attitude of condemnation, focusing on relatively trivial aspects of contemporary usage, was taken up time and time again throughout the eighteenth century, and has continued to the present day. It is important to study it and to assess its effects. One obvious effect is that non-standard varieties of the language tend to become stigmatised as *substandard*, while Standard English is thought of as the English language, rather than as the prestige dialect of the language.

The language and speech of educated men and women of the south-east, especially in London, Oxford and Cambridge, was, as we have already observed, the source of Standard English. This was John Hart's 'best and most perfite English' (see Section 9.7.1) and George Puttenham's 'vsuall speach of the Court, and that of London and the shires lying about London' (see Section 9.7.2). The following text from the 1770s illustrates the establishment of this choice.

TEXT 126 – James Beattie's *Theory of Language*, 1774

> Are, then, all provincial accents equally good? By no means. Of accent, as well as of ſpelling, ſyntax, and idiom, there is a ſtandard in every polite nation. And, in all theſe particulars, the example of approved authors, and the practice of thoſe, who, by their rank, education, and way of life, have had the beſt opportunities to know men and manners, and domeſtick and foreign literature, ought undoubtedly to give the law. Now it is in the metropolis of a kingdom, and in the moſt famous ſchools of learning, where the greateſt reſort may be expected of perſons adorned with all uſeful and elegant accompliſhments. The language, therefore, of the moſt learned and polite perſons in London, and the neighbouring Univerſities of Oxford and Cambridge, ought to be accounted the ſtandard of the Engliſh tongue, eſpecially in accent and pronunciation: ſyntax, ſpelling, and idiom, having been aſcertained by the practice of good authors, and the conſent of former ages.

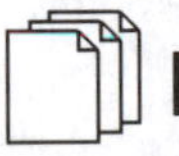

Activity 11.2

Discuss your response to James Beattie's assertions. Does his argument hold good for the present day?

11.1.2 Fixing the language

Swift's concern about the state of the language, as he saw it, was so great that he published a serious proposal for establishing some sort of 'academy' to regulate and maintain the standards of the English language, similar to the Académie Française which had been set up in France in 1634. The arguments used were similar to those expressed in *The Tatler* article of 1710, but Swift also introduced the idea of *ascertaining* the language (*fixing, making it certain*) so that it would not be subject to further change. Here are some extracts from Swift's proposal.

TEXT 127 – A Proposal for Correcting, Improving and Ascertaining the English Tongue; in a Letter to the Most Honourable Robert, Earl of Oxford, and Mortimer, Lord High Treasurer of Great Britain, 1712

My LORD; I do here, in the Name of all the Learned and Polite Perſons of the Nation, complain to Your LORDSHIP, as *Firſt Miniſter*, that our Language is extremely imperfect; that its daily Improvements are by no means in proportion to its daily Corruptions; that the Pretenders to poliſh and refine it, have chiefly multiplied Abuſes and Abſurdities; and, that in many Inſtances, it offends againſt every Part of Grammar.

I ſee no abſolute Neceſſity why any Language ſhould be perpetually changing;

BUT what I have moſt at Heart is, that ſome Method ſhould be thought on for *aſcertaining* and *fixing* our Language for ever, after ſuch Alterations are made in it as ſhall be thought requiſite. For I am of Opinion, that it is better a Language ſhould not be wholly perfect, than that it ſhould be perpetually changing; and we muſt give over at one Time, or at length infallibly change for the worſe:

BUT where I ſay, that I would have our Language, after it is duly correct,always to laſt; I do not mean that it ſhould never be enlarged: Provided, that no Word which a Society ſhall give a Sanction to, be afterwards antiquated and exploded, they may have liberty to receive whatever new ones they ſhall find occaſion for:

Activity 11.3

Comment on the possibility and desirability of *ascertaining* a language, and Swift's assertion that a language need not be 'perpetually changing'.

11.2 The perfection of the language

Dr Samuel Johnson (1709–84) published his *Dictionary* in 1755. In the preface to the dictionary he refers to the idea of fixing the language. He himself is sceptical of the possibility of success, although he believes in the idea of the perfection and decay of a language:

> Those who have been persuaded to think well of my design, will require that it should fix our language, and put a stop to those alterations which time and chance have hitherto been suffered to make in it without opposition. With this consequence I will confess that I have indulged expectation which neither reason nor experience can justify.
>
> ... tongues, like governments, have a natural tendency to degeneration; we have long preserved our constitution, let us make some struggles for our language.

Swift thought that the century from the beginning of Queen Elizabeth's reign in 1558 to the Civil Wars in 1642 was a kind of Golden Age of improvement in the language, although he did not believe that it had yet reached a state of perfection. The belief that languages could be improved and brought to a state of perfection was common (although we may not believe it today). Confusion between *language* and *language use* causes the one to be identified with the other, and a period of great writers is called a period of greatness for the language. We have already seen Swift identifying and associating a style that he disliked with corruption of the language.

11.2.1 The Augustan Age and Classical perfection

Some writers thought that the 'state of perfection' would be achieved some time in the future, but later eighteenth century grammarians placed it in the early and mid-eighteenth century language of writers like Addison, Steele, Pope and Swift himself. This period is known as the 'Augustan Age' (from the period of the reign of the Roman Emperor Augustus, 27 BC to AD 14, when great writers like Virgil, Horace and Ovid flourished). The language and literature of Classical Rome and Greece were still the foundation of education in the eighteenth century. Writers copied the forms of Classical literature, like the epic, the ode, and dramatic tragedy, while the Latin and Greek languages were models of perfection in their unchangeable state, which writers hoped English could attain. The influence of the sound of Latin and Greek helps to explain Swift's dislike of 'Northern' consonant clusters (see Text 125).

The vernacular Latin language of the first century had, of course, continued to change, so that after various centuries its several dialects had evolved into French, Italian, Spanish and the other Romance languages. But Classical Latin was fixed and ascertained, because its vocabulary and grammar were derived from the literature of its greatest period. This state seemed to be in complete contrast to contemporary English, and so, following Swift, many other writers and grammarians sought to improve the language. Somewhere, in the past or the future, lay the perfected English language.

11.3 'The Genius of the Language'

There are few references to the language of ordinary people by eighteenth century writers on language – the grammarians – 'it is beneath a grammarian's attempt' (Anselm Bayly in 1772). But even writers whom they admired were not necessarily taken as models of good English either. Authors' writings were subjected to detailed scrutiny for supposed errors. Grammarians sometimes spoke of 'the Genius of the Language' or 'the Idiom of the Tongue' as a criterion for judgement, the word *genius* meaning sometimes *character* or *spirit*, or simply *grammar*. But, in practice, this concept meant little more than the intuition of the grammarian; what he thought or felt sounded right, expressed in the Latin phrase *Ipse dixit* (*he himself says*). Sometimes this reliance on personal opinion was clearly stated:

> ... *to commute* to I look upon not to be English.
>
> It will be easily discovered that I have paid no regard to authority. I have censured even our best penmen, where they have departed from what I conceive to be the idiom of the tongue, or where I have thought they violate grammar without necessity. To judge by the rule of *Ipse dixit* is the way to perpetuate error.
>
> (*on the wrong use of prepositions*) ... even by Swift, Temple, Addison, and other writers of the highest reputation; some of them, indeed, with such shameful impropriety as one must think must shock every English ear, and almost induce the reader to suppose the writers to be foreigners.
>
> (*Reflections on the English Language*, Robert Baker, 1770)

Notice that Baker condemns *Ipse dixit* when applied to 'the best penmen', but not when applied to himself.

Often, appeals were made to *Reason*, or *Analogy* (a similar form to be found elsewhere in the language):

> In doubtful cases regard ought to be had in our decisions to the analogy of the language ... Of 'Whether he will or *no*' and 'Whether he will or *not*', it is only the latter that is analogical ... when you supply the ellipsis, you find it necessary to use the adverb *not*, '*Whether* he will *or* will *not*.'
>
> (*Philosophy of Rhetoric*, George Campbell, 1776)

Grammarians were not always consistent in their arguments, however. They recognised that the evidence for the vocabulary and grammar of a language must be derived from what people actually wrote and spoke, referred to sometimes as *Custom*:

> Reason permits that we give way to Custom, though contrary to Reason. Analogie is not the Mistress of Language. She prescribes only the Laws of Custom.
>
> (*Art of Speaking*, 1708)

This point of view is argued in greater detail in the following text.

TEXT 128 – Joseph Priestley's *Rudiments of English Grammar*, 1769

> It must be allowed, that the custom of speaking is the original, and only just standard of any language. We see, in all grammars, that this is sufficient to establish a rule, even contrary to the strongest analogies of the language with itself. Must not this custom, therefore, be allowed to have some weight, in favour of those forms of speech, to which our best writers and speakers seem evidently prone; forms which are contrary to no analogy of the language with itself, and which have been disapproved by grammarians, only from certain abstract and arbitrary considerations, and when their decisions were not prompted by the genius of the language; which discovers itself in nothing more than in the general propensity of those who use it to certain modes of construction? I think, however, that I have not, in any case, seemed to favour what our grammarians will call an irregularity, but where the genius of the language, and not only single examples, but the general practice of those who write it, and the almost universal custom of all who speak it, have obliged me to do so. I also think I have seemed to favour those irregularities, no more than the degree of the propensity I have first mentioned, when unchecked by a regard to arbitrary rules, in those who use the forms of speech I refer to, will authorize me.

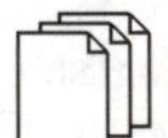

Activity 11.4

Discuss Joseph Priestley's assessment of the relative values of *custom*, *analogy*, *the genius of the language* and *the disapproval of grammarians* in deciding the forms of a standard language.

11.4 Bishop Lowth's grammar

One in particular of the many grammar books of the eighteenth century had a lasting influence on later grammars which were published for use in schools in the late eighteenth century and throughout the nineteenth century – Robert Lowth's *A Short Introduction to English Grammar*, 1762. Lowth's attitude was *prescriptive* – that is, he prescribed or laid down what he himself considered to be correct usage, as illustrated in the following:

> Grammar is the Art of rightly expressing our thoughts by Words etc ...
>
> The principal design of a Grammar of any Language is to teach us to express ourselves with propriety in that Language, and to be able to judge of every phrase and form of construction, whether it be right or not etc ...

The words *propriety* and *rightly* are important because Lowth was not describing the language in its many varieties, but prescribing what ought to be written in a standard variety of English, and pointing out 'errors' and 'solecisms' with examples from authors like Milton, Dryden and Pope. He described other varieties of usage only in order to condemn them.

The following text, which is an extract from the preface, typifies this particular attitude to language use. What people actually say and write, even though they may be socially of the highest rank, or eminent authors, is subject to Lowth's prescriptive judgement.

TEXT 129 – Robert Lowth's *A Short Introduction to English Grammar*, 1762 (i)

It is now about fifty years ſince Doctor Swift *made a public remonſtrance, addreſſed to the Earl of* Oxford, *then Lord Treaſurer, of the imperfect State of our Language; alledging in particular, " that in many inſtances it " offended againſt every part of " Grammar."* Swift *muſt be allowed to have been a good judge of this matter. He was himſelf very attentive to this part, both in his own writings, and in his remarks upon thoſe of his friends: he is one of our moſt correct, and perhaps our very beſt proſe writer. Indeed the juſtneſs of this complaint, as far as I can find, hath never been queſtioned; and yet no effectual method hath hitherto been taken to redreſs the grievance of which he complains.*

But let us conſider, how, and in what extent, we are to underſtand this charge brought againſt the Engliſh *Language. Does it mean, that the* Engliſh *Language as it is ſpoken by the politeſt part of the nation, and as it ſtands in the writings of our moſt approved authors, oftentimes offends againſt every part of Grammar? Thus far, I am afraid, the charge is true.*

The following text is an example of Lowth's prescriptive method as stated in his book, in which he is stating the use of *will* and *shall*, together with a short extract from his preface.

TEXT 130 – Robert Lowth's *A Short Introduction to English Grammar*, 1762 (ii)

Will in the firſt Perſon ſingular and plural promiſes or threatens; in the ſecond and third Perſons only foretells: *ſhall* on the contrary, in the firſt Perſon ſimply foretells; in the ſecond and third Perſons commands or threatens [7].

Do and *have* make the Preſent Time; *did*, *had*, the Paſt; *ſhall*, *will*, the Future: *let* the Imperative Mode; *may*, *might*, *could*, *would*, *ſhould*, the Subjunctive. The Prepoſition *to* placed before the Verb makes the Infinitive Mode. *Have* and *be* through their ſeveral Modes and Times are placed only before the Perfect and Paſſive Participles reſpectively; the reſt only before the Verb itſelf in its Primary Form [8].

But beſides ſhewing what is right, the matter may be further explained by pointing out what is wrong. I will not take upon me to ſay, whether we have any Grammar that ſufficiently performs the firſt part: but the latter method here called in, as ſubſervient to the former, may perhaps be found in this caſe to be of the two the more uſeful and effectual manner of inſtruction.

Activity 11.5

Identify the inconsistency between Lowth's prescription and his actual use of *will* or *shall*.

Lowth's book was intended for those who were already well educated. This can be inferred from part of the preface:

> A Grammatical Study of our own Language makes no part of the ordinary method of instruction which we pass thro' in our childhood ...

The use of the first person *we* implies that his readers, like him, will have studied Latin and Greek at school – the *ancient* or *learned languages*. This, however, did not in his opinion provide them with a knowledge of English grammar, even though they lived in *polite society* and read English literature, activities not followed by most of the population at the time.

TEXT 131 – Robert Lowth's *A Short Introduction to English Grammar,* 1762 (iii)

> Much practice in the polite world, and a general acquaintance with the best authors, are good helps, but alone will hardly be sufficient: we have writers, who have enjoyed these advantages in their full extent, and yet cannot be recommended as models of an accurate style. Much less then will what is commonly called Learning serve the purpose; that is, a critical knowledge of ancient languages, and much reading of ancient authors ...
>
> In a word, it was calculated for the use of the Learner even of the lowest class*. Those, who would enter more deeply into this Subject, will find it fully and accurately handled, with the greatest acuteness of investigation, perspicuity of explication, and elegance of method, in a Treatise inititled HERMES, by JAMES HARRIS Esq; the most beautiful and perfect example of Analysis that has been exhibited since the days of Aristotle.

**class* in this extract does not mean *social class*, but *grade* or *standard of achievement*.

11.5 Literary styles in the eighteenth century

The style of writing of Lowth and other grammarians is very 'formal'; its vocabulary and structure are unlike that of everyday language. Here are two short contrasting examples of eighteenth century writing, the first from a diary and so informal or 'ordinary' prose, and the second from a literary journal. Literary prose adopts its own fashionable choices from the language at different periods, while ordinary language in speech and writing continues generally unremarked.

TEXT 132 – Thomas Hearne's *Remarks and Collections,* 1715

> MAY 28 (Sat.) This being the Duke of Brunswick, commonly called King George's Birth-Day, some of the Bells were jambled in Oxford, by the care of some of the Whiggish, Fanatical Crew; but as I did not observe the Day in the least my self, so it was little taken notice of (unless by way of ridicule) by other honest People, who are for K. James IIId. who is the undoubted King of these Kingdoms, & 'tis heartily wish'd by them that he may be restored.
>
> This Day I saw one Ward with Dr. Charlett, who, it seems, hath printed several Things. He is a clergy Man. I must inquire about him.

TEXT 133 – Samuel Johnson, *The Rambler*, July 1750

The advantages of mediocrity

... Health and vigour, and a happy constitution of the corporeal frame, are of absolute necessity to the enjoyment of the comforts, and to the performance of the duties of life, and requisite in yet a greater measure to the accomplishment of any thing illustrious or distinguished; yet even these, if we can judge by their apparent consequences, are sometimes not very beneficial to those on whom they are most liberally bestowed. They that frequent the chambers of the sick, will generally find the sharpest pains, and most stubborn maladies among them whom confidence of the force of nature formerly betrayed to negligence and irregularity; and that superfluity of strength, which was at once their boast and their snare, has often, in the latter part of life, no other effect than than it continues them long in impotence and anguish.

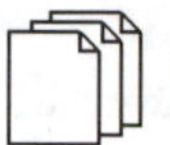

Activity 11.6

Discuss the features of vocabulary and syntax in Texts 132 and 133 which distinguish the two styles of writing.

11.6 'The depraved language of the common People'

The standard language recognised by eighteenth century grammarians was that variety used by what they called 'the Learned and Polite Persons of the Nation' (Swift) – *polite* in the sense of *polished*, *refined*, *elegant*, *well-bred*. By definition, the language of the common people was inferior. This had far-reaching social consequences, as we shall see later in the chapter. Here is some of the evidence on the language of common people, which also explains why we know much less about the regional, social and spoken varieties of eighteenth century English, except what we can infer from novels, plays, letters and other indirect sources – and they were not worth the attention of scholars.

TEXT 134 – On the language of common people

... *themselves and Families* (from the *Monthly Review*) ... a very bad Expression, though very common. It is mere **Shopkeepers cant** and will always be found contemptible in the Ears of persons of any Taste.

(*Reflections on the English Language*, Robert Baker, 1770)

(on *most an end* for *most commonly*:) ... is an expression that would almost disgrace the mouth of **a hackney-coachman**.

(*Remarks on the English Language*, Robert Baker, 1779)

... though sometimes it may be difficult, if not impossible to reduce **common speech** to rule, and indeed it is beneath a grammarian's attempt.

(*Plain and Complete Grammar*, Anselm Bayly, 1772)

No absolute monarch hath it more in his power to nobilitate a person of obscure birth, than it is in the power of good use to ennoble words of **low** or **dubious extraction**; such, for instance, as have either arisen, nobody knows how, like *fib*, *banter*, *bigot*, *fop*, *flippant*, among **the rabble**, or like *flimsy*, sprung from **the cant of the manufacturers**.

(*Philosophy of Rhetoric*, George Campbell, 1776)

cont ...

> Nor are all words which are not found in the vocabulary, to be lamented as omissions. Of **the laborious and mercantile part of the people**, the diction is in great measure casual and mutable; many of their terms are formed for some temporary or local convenience, and though current at certain times and places, are in others utterly unknown. **This fugitive cant**, which is always in a state of increase or decay, cannot be regarded as any part of the durable materials of a language, and therefore must be suffered to perish with other things unworthy of preservation.
>
> (*Dictionary*, Samuel Johnson, 1755)

> My Animadversions will extend to such Phrases only as People in decent Life inadvertently adopt ... Purity and Politeness of Expression ... is the only external Distinction which remains between a gentleman and **a valet**; a lady and **a Mantua-maker** (= *dress-maker*).
>
> (*Aristarchus*, Philip Withers, 1788)

Such comments as these clearly show that the divisions of eighteenth century society were marked by language as much as by birth, rank, wealth and education.

11.7 Language and class

The evidence of the following quotations suggests that if the language of the common people was regarded as inferior by the educated upper classes in the eighteenth century, then their ideas and thoughts would be similarly devalued.

> The best Expressions grow **low and degenrate**, when **profan'd** by **the populace**, and applied to **mean things**. The use they make of them, infecting them with **a mean and abject Idea**, causes that we cannot use them without **sullying and defiling** those things, which are signified by them.
>
> But it is no hard matter to discern between **the depraved Language of common People**, and **the noble refin'd expressions of the Gentry**, whose condition and merits have advanced them above the other.
>
> (*Art of Speaking*, rendered into English from the French of Messieurs du Port Royal 1676, 2nd edn, 1708)

Language was regarded as 'the dress of thought', or, to use another simple metaphor, 'the mirror of thought'. It was believed that there was a direct relationship between good language and good thinking. On the one hand was the dominant social class, the Gentry, whose language and way of life were variously described as *polite*, *civilized*, *elegant*, *noble*, *refined*, *tasteful* and *pure*. On the other hand were 'the laborious and mercantile part of the people', shopkeepers and hackney-coachmen, the rabble, whose language was *vulgar*, *barbarous*, *contemptible*, *low*, *degenerate*, *profane*, *mean*, *abject* and *depraved*.

This view was reinforced by a theory of language that was called 'Universal Grammar'. The following quotations illustrate a belief in the direct connection between language and the mind, or soul, and in the superior value of abstract thought over the senses. They are taken from *Hermes: or a Philosophical Inquiry Concerning Language and Universal Grammar*, published in 1751 by James Harris, the author who was commended by Bishop Lowth (see Text 131):

> 'Tis a phrase often apply'd to a man, when speaking, that *he speaks his MIND*; as much as to say, that his Speech or Discourse is *a publishing of some Energie or Motion of his Soul*.

> The VULGAR merged *in Sense* from their earliest Infancy, and never once dreaming any thing to be worthy of pursuit, but what pampers their Appetite, or fills their Purse, imagine nothing to be *real*, but what may be *tasted*, or *touched*.

For students of language today, the differences between Standard English and regional dialects are viewed as *linguistically* superficial and unimportant. The same meanings can be conveyed as easily in one as in the other, although we cannot, in everyday life, ignore the *social* connotations of regional and non-standard speech, which are still very powerful in conveying and maintaining attitudes.

In the eighteenth century, the linguistic differences between refined and common speech were held to match fundamental differences in intellect and morality. The gulf between the two was reinforced by the fact that education was in the 'learned languages' Latin and Greek. The classical Greek language and literature in particular were judged to be the most 'perfect':

> Now the Language of these Greeks was truly like themselves; 'twas conformable to their transcendent and universal Genius.
>
> 'Twere to be wished, that those amongst us, who either write or read, with a view to employ their liberal leisure ... 'twere to be wished, I say, that the liberal (if they have any relish for letters) would inspect the finished Models of *Grecian Literature* ...
>
> (*Hermes*, James Harris, 1751)

As it was believed that the contrasts between the *refined* language of the classically educated class and the *vulgar* language of the common people mirrored equal differences in intellectual capabilities, and also in virtue or morality, such beliefs had *social* and *political* consequences.

> The most devastating aspect of 18th century assessments of language was its philosophical justification of this notion of vulgarity.
>
> (*The Politics of Language 1791–1819*, Olivia Smith, OUP, 1984)

These social and political consequences can be demonstrated. The years of the long wars with France (1793–1815) following the French Revolution of 1789 were marked by the political oppression of popular movements for reform. Ideas about language were used to protect the government from criticism. For example, the notion of *vulgarity of language* became an excuse to dismiss a series of petitions to Parliament calling for the reform of the voting system. If the language of the 'labouring classes' was by definition inferior, incapable of expressing coherent thought, and also of dubious moral value, then it was impossible for them to use language properly in order to argue their own case.

> Liberty of speech and freedom of discussion in this House form an essential part of the constitution; but it is necessary that persons coming forward as petitioners, should address the House in decent and respectful language.
>
> (*Parliamentary Debates* xxx.779)

Here are short extracts from three petitions presented to Parliament. The first was presented by 'tradesmen and artificers, unpossessed of freehold land' in Sheffield in 1793 and was rejected; the second, by 'twelve freeholders' from Reading in 1810, was accepted; the third was presented by non-voters from Yorkshire in 1817. At that time, only men who owned freehold land had the vote.

TEXT 135a – Petition to Parliament, 1793

> Your petitioners are lovers of peace, of liberty, and justice. They are in general tradesmen and artificers, unpossessed of freehold land, and consequently have no voice in choosing members to sit in parliament; – but though they may not be freeholders, they are men, and do not think themselves fairly used in being excluded the rights of citizens ...

(*Parliamentary Debates* xxx.776)

TEXT 135b – Petition to Parliament, 1810

> The petitioners cannot conceive it possible that his Majesty's present incapable and arbitrary ministers should be still permitted to carry on the government of the country, after having wasted our resources in fruitless expeditions, and having shewn no vigour but in support of antiquated prejudices, and in attacks upon the liberties of the subject ...

(*Parliamentary Debates* xvi.955)

TEXT 135c – Petition to Parliament, 1817

> The petitioners have a full and immovable conviction, a conviction which they believe to be universal throughout the kingdom, that the House doth not, in any constitutional or rational sense, represent the nation; that, when the people have ceased to be represented, the constitution is subverted; that taxation without representation is slavery ...

(*Parliamentary Debates* xxxv. 81–2, quoted in Olivia Smith *op cit*)

Activity 11.7

(i) Discuss the charge that the language of the first petition was 'indecent and disrespectful', and compare it with another comment made at the time: 'I suspect that the objection to the roughness of the language was not the real cause why this petition was opposed.'
(ii) Discuss the view expressed in Parliament at the time that the language of the second petition 'though firm as it ought to be, was respectful'.
(iii) The Tory minister George Canning said of the third petition 'if such language were tolerated, there was an end of the House of Commons, and of the present system of government'. What is objectionable in the language?

The grammar and spelling of these extracts are perfectly 'correct'. In contrast, consider the following example of a letter of protest against the enclosure of common land, written anonymously by 'the Combin'd of the Parish of Cheshunt' to their local landowner. It uses non-standard spelling, punctuation and grammar, which clearly would have provided Parliament with an excuse for its dismissal.

TEXT 136 – Letter to Oliver Cromwell Esquire, of Cheshunt Park, 27 February 1799

> Whe right these lines to you who are the Combin'd of the Parish of Cheshunt in the Defence of our Parrish rights which you unlawfully are about to disinherit us of ... Resolutions is maid by the aforesaid Combind that if you intend of inclosing Our Commond Commond fields Lammas Meads Marches &c Whe Resolve before that bloudy and unlawful act is finished to have your hearts bloud if you proceede in the aforesaid bloudy act Whe like horse leaches will cry give, give until whe have split the bloud of every one that wishes to rob the Inosent unborn. It shall not be in your power to say I am safe from the hands of my Enemy for Whe like birds of pray will prively lie in wait to spil the bloud of the aforesaid Charicters whose names and places of abode are as prutrified sores in our Nostrils. Whe declair that thou shall not say I am safe when thou goest to thy bed for beware that thou liftest not thine eyes up in the most mist of flames ...

(Quoted in *The Making of the English Working Class*, E. P. Thompson, Penguin edn, 1963, p. 240.)

Activity 11.8

Rewrite the letter of the Text 136 in Standard English and compare its style and content with Text 135.

11.8 William Cobbett and the politics of language

William Cobbett (1763–1835) was the son of a farmer from Farnham, Surrey, and self-educated. From 1785 to 1791, he served in a foot regiment in Canada, and left the army after trying, and failing, to bring some officers to trial for embezzlement. He spent the rest of his life in writing, journalism and farming, and became an MP in 1832 after the passing of the Reform Act.

Cobbett began a weekly newspaper, *The Political Register*, in 1802 as a Tory, but soon became converted to the radical cause of social and Parliamentary reform, and wrote and edited *The Political Register* until his death in 1835, campaigning against social injustice and government corruption.

In Section 11.7, we saw how the concept of vulgarity of language was used to deny the value of the meaning and content of petitions to Parliament. Cobbett referred to this in an edition of *The Political Register* which was written in America, where he had gone after the suspension of *habeas corpus* in England.

TEXT 137 – William Cobbett's *The Political Register*, 29 November 1817

> The present project ... is to communicate to all uneducated Reformers, *a knowledge of Grammar*. The people, you know, were accused of presenting petitions *not grammatically correct*. And those petitions were *rejected*, the petitioners being 'ignorant': though some of them were afterwards *put into prison*, for being 'better informed'...
>
> No doubt remains in my mind, that there was more talent discovered, and more political knowledge, by the leaders amongst the Reformers, than have ever been shown, at any period of time, by the Members of the two houses of parliament.
>
> There was only one thing in which any of you were deficient, and that was in the mere art of so arranging the words in your Resolutions and Petitions as to make these compositions what is called *grammatically correct*. Hence, men of a hundredth part of the *mind* of some of the authors of the Petitions were enabled to cavil at them on this account, and to infer from this incorrectness, that the Petitioners were a set of *poor ignorant creatures*, who knew nothing of what they were talking; a set of the '*Lower Classes*', who ought never to raise their reading above that of children's books, Christmas Carrols, and the like.
>
> For my part, I have always held a mere knowledge of the rules of grammar very cheap. It is a study, which demands hardly any powers of mind. To possess a knowledge of those rules is a pitiful qualification ...
>
> Grammar is to literary composition what a linch-pin is to a waggon. It is a poor pitiful thing in itself; it bears no part of the weight; adds not in the least to the celerity; but, still the waggon cannot very well and safely go on without it ...
>
> Therefore, trifling, and even contemptible, as this branch of knowledge is *in itself*, it is of vast importance as to the means of giving to the great powers of the mind their proper effect ... The grammarian from whom a man of genius learns his rules has little more claim to a share of such a man's renown than has the goose, who yields the pens with which he writes: but, still the pens are *necessary*, and so is the grammar.

Cobbett's writings, like Tom Paine's *The Rights of Man* in 1792 and *The Age of Reason* in 1794, were practical proof that the language of men of humble class origins could be effective in argument, but both Cobbett and Paine wrote in Standard English. Cobbett was well aware of the social connotations of non-standard language and wrote an account of how he had taught himself correct grammar. He does not use use the term *standard* himself and follows the common practice of implying that only this variety of English has *grammar*. He wrote under the name *Peter Porcupine*.

TEXT 138 – William Cobbett's *The Life and Adventures of Peter Porcupine*, 1796

> One branch of learning, however, I went to the bottom with, and that the most essential branch too, the grammar of my mother tongue. I had experienced the want of a knowledge of grammar during my stay with Mr Holland; but it is very probable that I never should have thought of encountering the study of it, had not accident placed me under a man whose friendship extended beyond his interest. Writing a fair hand procured me the honour of being copyist to Colonel Debeig, the commandant of the garrison ...
>
> Being totally ignorant of the rules of grammar, I necessarily made many mistakes in copying, because no one can copy letter by letter, nor even word by word. The colonel saw my deficiency, and strongly recommended study. He enforced his advice with a sort of injunction, and with a promise of reward in case of success.
>
> I procured me a Lowth's grammar, and applied myself to the study of it with unceasing assiduity, and not without some profit; for, though it was a considerable time before I fully comprehended all that I read, still I read and studied with such unremitted attention, that, at last, I could write without falling into any very gross errors. The pains I took cannot be described: I wrote the whole grammar out two or three times; I got it by heart; I repeated it every morning and every evening, and, when on guard, I imposed on myself the task of saying it all over once every time I was posted sentinel. To this exercise of my memory I ascribe the retentiveness of which I have since found it capable, and to the success with which it was attended, I ascribe the perseverance that has led to the acquirement of the little learning of which I am the master.

Cobbett was thus convinced of the need to master standard grammar:

> Without understanding this, you can never hope to become fit for anything beyond mere trade or agriculture ... Without a knowledge of grammar, it is impossible for you to write correctly; and, it is by mere accident that you speak correctly; and, pray bear in mind, that all well-informed persons judge of a man's mind (until they have other means of judging) by his writing or speaking.
>
> (*Advice to Young Men*, William Cobbett)

and he followed up his conviction by writing a grammar book, in the form of a series of letters addressed to his son.

TEXT 139 – William Cobbett's *A Grammar of the English Language*, 1817

> ... grammar teaches us *how to make use of words* ... to the acquiring of this branch of knowledge, my dear son, there is one motive, which, though it ought, at all times, to be strongly felt, ought, at the present time, to be so felt in an extraordinary degree: I mean that desire which every man, and especially every young man, should entertain to be able to assert with effect the rights and liberties of his country.
>
> ... And when we hear a Hampshire plough-boy say, 'Poll Cherrycheek have giv'd I thick handkercher,' we know very well that he *means* to say, 'Poll Cherrycheek has given me this handkerchief:' and yet, we are but too apt to *laugh at him*, and to call him *ignorant*; which is wrong; because he has no pretensions to a knowledge of grammar, and he may be very skilful as a plough-boy.

'Cobbett considered grammar, in short, as an integral part of the class structure of England, and the act of learning grammar by one of his readers as an act of class warfare' (Olivia Smith *op cit* p. 1).

It is clear that no significant differences in the grammar of Cobbett's writing separate today's language from the English of the early nineteenth century. What we now call Standard English has been established for over 200 years as the only form of the language for writing which obtains universal acceptance.

This seems to contradict the linguistic statement that 'all living languages are in a constant state of change'. But the grammatical innovations since Cobbett's day are developments of established features, rather than fundamental changes. Once a standard form of writing becomes the norm, then the rate of change in the grammar is slowed down considerably. At the same time, additions and losses to the vocabulary, and modifications in pronunciation, inevitably continue.

12. Postscript – to the present day

The purpose of this book – to describe how present-day Standard English has developed from its origins in OE a thousand years ago – has effectively been achieved in the preceding chapters.

12.1 Some developments in the language since the eighteenth century

There is a constant change in the vocabulary of the language, and it goes without saying that there have been many losses and gains of words since the eighteenth century. English is a language that has taken in and assimilated words from many foreign languages to add to the core vocabulary of Germanic, French and Latin words.

12.1.1 Spelling

The standard orthography was fixed in the eighteenth century by the agreed practice of printers. Dr Johnson set down accepted spellings in his *Dictionary* of 1755, and also recorded some of the arbitrary choices of 'custom':

> ... thus I write, in compliance with a numberless majority, *convey* and *inveigh*, *deceit* and *receipt*, *fancy* and *phantom*.

A few words found in the original versions of eighteenth century texts have changed, for example, *cloathing*, *terrour*, *phantasy* and *publick*, but there are not many. More recently, it has become acceptable to change the <ae> spelling to <e> in a few words of Latin derivation, and to write *medieval* for *mediaeval*, and *archeology* for *archaeology*. Some American spellings have also become acceptable in Britain, such as *program* as a result of its use in computer programming. With few exceptions, it is true to say that our spelling system was fixed over 200 years ago and every attempt to reform it has failed.

12.1.2 Grammar

While the underlying rules of grammar have remained unchanged, their use in speech and writing has continued to develop into forms that distinguish the varieties of language use since the eighteenth century. This can perhaps be explained in terms of **style**, and so is the subject of a different kind of course book. In present-day English, we can observe, in some varieties of language use, a greater degree of complexity in both the noun phrase and the verb phrase.

Noun phrases

Modifiers of nouns normally precede the head of the noun phrase (NP) when they are words (usually adjectives or nouns) or short phrases, as in *a* **red** *brick*, *the* **brick** *wall* and *the* **red brick** *wall*, and follow it when they are phrases or clauses. The rule of pre-modification has developed so that much longer strings of words and phrases can now precede the head word, as in *a* **never to be forgotten** *experience*.

This style is a particular feature of newspaper headlines. For example, the news statement that might be written as:

> There has been a report on the treatment of suspects in police stations in Northern Ireland ...

can be turned into a NP as:

> A Northern Ireland police station suspect treatment report

in which a series of post-modifying prepositional phrases (PrepPs) become pre-modifying NPs within the larger NP.

Activity 12.1

State the grammatical rule for converting the clause into a NP.

The process of converting clauses with verbs into nouns is called **nominalisation**, and the word itself is an example of that process. It is a marked feature of some contemporary styles, including academic and formal writing, and tends to omit the agents or actors who actually do things; for example:

> S P C
There has been *no convincing explanation of the attempt* ...

is only the beginning of a longer sentence. It might have been written:

> X has not *convinced* us by *explaining* how Y *attempted* ...

in which main verbs are used instead of nouns or a modifying participle, and the subjects X and Y would have to be named.

This is a trend in style which depends upon the fact that the grammar of English permits nominalisation readily.

Verb phrases

If you compare the possible forms of the verb phrase (VP) in contemporary English with any OE text, you will find that OE verb phrases were generally shorter, and OE grammar lacked the forms of VP that have developed since. In MnE, it is possible to construct VPs like:

> she **has been being treated** ...
hasn't she **been being treated**?
won't she **have been being treated**?

which use **auxiliary verbs** to combine the grammatical features of **tense** (past or present), **aspect** (perfective or progressive), **voice** (active or passive) and **mood** (declarative or interrogative), to which we can add:

> She **seems to manage to be able to keep on being treated** ...

in which certain verbs, called **catenatives**, can be strung together in a chain. Such VPs are not common, perhaps, but they are possible, and have developed since the eighteenth century.

They are examples of the way in which English has become a much more **analytic** language since the OE period; that is, its structures depend on strings of separate words, and not on the inflections of words. An inflecting language is called **synthetic**.

Another development in the resources of the VP is in the increased use of **phrasal** and **prepositional verbs** like *run across* for *meet*, *put up with* for *tolerate* and *give in* for *surrender*. They are a feature of spoken and informal usage, and although the beginnings of the structure of *verb + particle* can be found in OE, they have increased in number considerably in MnE and new combinations are continually being introduced, often as slang, as in *get with it*, later to be assimilated.

12.2 The continuity of prescriptive judgements on language use

We judge others by their speech as much as by other aspects of their behaviour, but some people are much more positive in their reactions. The relationship between social class and language use in the eighteenth century, which was described in Chapter 11, has been maintained through the nineteenth century up to the present day. Here, for example, is the Dean of Canterbury, Henry Alford D.D., writing in a book called *The Queen's English: Stray Notes on Speaking and Spelling* in 1864.

TEXT 140 – Dean Alford's *The Queen's English*, 1864

> And first and foremost, let me notice that worst of all faults, the leaving out of the aspirate where it ought to be, and putting it in where it ought not to be. This is a vulgarism not confined to this or that province of England, nor especially prevalent in one county or another, but common throughout England to **persons of low breeding and inferior education**, principally to those among the inhabitants of towns. Nothing so surely stamps a man as below the mark in intelligence, self-respect, and energy, as this unfortunate habit ...
>
> As I write these lines, which I do while waiting in a refreshment-room at Reading, between a Great-Western and a South-Eastern train, I hear one of two commercial gentlemen, from a neighbouring table, telling his friend that 'his *ed* used to *hake* ready to burst.'

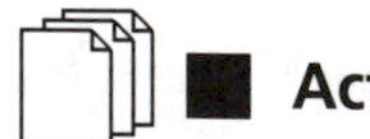

Activity 12.2

Discuss Dean Alford's comments on the pronunciation of words beginning with <h>.

Alford's attitude is no different from that of some eighteenth century grammarians in their references to 'the depraved language of the common People' (see Section 11.6).

One feature of common usage that is still taught as an error is what is called the 'split infinitive'. Here is Dean Alford on the subject:

> A correspondent states as his own usage, and defends, the insertion of an adverb between the sign of the infinitive mood and the verb. He gives as an instance, '*to scientifically illustrate*.' But surely this is a practice entirely unknown to English speakers and writers. It seems to me, that we ever regard the *to* of the infinitive as inseparable from its verb.

The Dean is wrong in his assertion that the practice is 'entirely unknown'. The idea that it is ungrammatical to put an adverb between *to* and the *verb* was an invention of prescriptive grammarians, but it has been handed on as a **solecism** (violation of the rules of grammar) by one generation of school teachers after another. It has become an easy marker of 'good English', but avoiding it can lead to ambiguity.

Activity 12.3

The following paragraph appeared in a daily newspaper in August 1989. It shows how some contemporary journalists still avoid the 'split infinitive' at all costs. Was the correction unambiguous?

TEXT 141

Correction

> Our front page report yesterday on microwave cooking mistakenly stated that in tests of 83 cook-chill and ready-cooked products, Sainsbury's found the instructions on 10 products always failed to ensure the foods were fully heated to 70C. The story should have said the instructions failed always to ensure the foods were fully heated to 70C – that is, they sometimes failed to ensure this.

(*The Guardian* 24 August 1989)

12.3 The grammar of spoken English today

The invention of sound recording, and especially of the portable tape recorder, has made it possible for us to study the spoken language in a way that students of language were formerly quite unable to do. It has always been known that spoken English differed from written English, but even an experienced shorthand writer would to some extent idealise what was said and omit features that seemed irrelevant.

Here is a transcription of some recorded informal contemporary spoken English, which uses written symbols to indicate spoken features of the language. The conventions of written punctuation are deliberately not used. The symbols represent stress patterns, contained in tone units (units of information into which we divide our speech), each having a tonic syllable marked by stress and a change of pitch.

The speaker is an educated user of Standard English, and the topic is linguistic acceptability, but the transcription, even if punctuated with capital letters, full-stops and commas as if it were written, would not be acceptable as written English.

The conventions used in the transcription are as follows:

- The end of a tone unit (or tone group) is marked (|).
- The word containing the tonic syllable (or nucleus) is printed in bold type.
- The place where two speakers overlap is marked ([).
- A micro-pause in speech is marked with a stop (.); longer breaks are marked with one or more dashes (–).

The text is part of a longer conversation between two women in their twenties. A is a secretary and B is a university lecturer.

TEXT 142 – Contemporary spoken English

A well what do they **put**| . in a . computing **programme**?| – –
B **well**| you'll hear a lot about it in due **course** |. it's what they
call [IL tests . which [stands for investigating language **accep-**
A [mm [mm
B **tability**|
A mm|
B and they've done those on groups of **undergraduates**| . we don't
know what
A [erm **battery** things|
B [erm erm **yes**| . erm sort of . **science** graduates|
[. **German** graduates| **English** graduates| [and **so** on| and **asked**
A [mm| [mm| mm|
B them| – there are various **types** of test thay give them| . they
give them a **sentence**| and there are four a. there are **three** an-
swers they can give| either it's **acceptable**| it's not **acceptable**|
A mm| – –
B it's **marginal**| . or you **know**| it's somewhere **between**| and then .
we **they**| when they mark up the **results**| have a **fourth category**|
which is their answer was **incoherent**|
A yes|
B if it was heard and they couldn't **hear** it| . if it was written
they couldn't **read** it|
A mm|
B that's **one** type| . then there's an **operation** test| they're
interested say in . well particularly seeing various **adverbs**| and
they write something like I **entirely**| dot dot **dot**| – and the
student has to complete the **sentence**| –
A mm| –
B well with **entirely**| they'll nearly all write **agree** with you|
A yes| .
B and entirely and agree [– go **together**|
A [mm| mm|
B **collate** or **something** it's called|
A **yeah**|
B [*laughs* – –] and then they in fact try **another** adverb|
and then there'll be an absolute **range** of verbs that [**go** with it|
A [mm| you know
it's quite **interesting**| the way in the **thesis**| they had a sentence
with **entirely**| . and **got** people| to er transform it into the
negative|
B mm|
A this is **very tricky**| . I should have thought there were .
B **yes**| well **quite**| they do that sort of **thing** you see| and then they
see what they've **produced**| and then they [sort of they score them
A [**yes**|
B **up**| in a certain [**way**| and they'll say have they . erm – – have
A [**yes**|
B they **done**| what they were **told** to| and if not **why** not| and then
there are various reasons why **not**| and they were **scored**| and given
a **mark**| and it's quite **in** [**credible**|
A [I think that's **one** of the most **valuable**
things| that I've thought was being **done**| in . [in .
B [mm
A in the **battery** test| because it **should** relate| quite **directly**| **to**|
the meaning of the **word**| –
B **yes**|

(Adapted from *Corpus of English Conversation*, Svartvik and Quirk, C. W. K. Gleerup Lund, S.1.5., 465–553, p. 135–7.)

Activity 12.4

(i) Edit the transcription, omitting all non-fluency features that belong to speech only (e.g., hesitations, self-corrections and repetitions), but retaining the identical vocabulary and word order.
(ii) Examine the edited version for evidence of differences between the vocabulary and grammar of informal spoken English and written English.
(iii) Rewrite B's part of the conversation in a style that conforms to the conventions of written Standard English.

(For a full analysis, see Commentary 21 in the *Text Commentary Book.*)

12.4 From OE to MnE – comparing historical texts

If you have worked through most of the book, you should now find it easier to recognise texts from different historical periods of the language, and to describe how they differ from contemporary English. Even a very short example will illustrate this, chosen virtually at random. To illustrate some of the changes in the language from OE to MnE that have been described, consider the following, which is the first verse from Chapter 3 of The Book of Genesis.

TEXT 143 – Genesis 3:1

Late tenth century OE

eac swylce seo næddre wæs geapre þonne ealle þa oðre nytenu
þe God geworhte ofer eorþan. and seo næddre cwæþ to þam
wife. hwi forbead God eow þæt ge ne æton of ælcon treowe
binnan paradisum.

Late fourteenth century ME

But the serpent was feller than alle lyuynge beestis of erthe
which the Lord God hadde maad. Which serpent seide to the
womman. Why comaundide God to ȝou that ȝe schulden not ete of
ech tre of paradis.

EMnE, 1611

Now the serpent was more subtill then any beast of the field,
which the Lord God had made, and he said vnto the woman, Yea,
hath God said, Ye shall not eat of euery tree of the garden?

MnE, 1961

The serpent was more crafty than any wild creature that the
LORD God had made. He said to the woman, 'Is it true that
God has forbidden you to eat from any tree in the garden?'.

12.4.1 Commentary on Text 143

The following detailed description of the extracts gives a pattern that can be applied to the comparison of any two or more texts.

Make a series of columns, one for each text, and an extra one to record any reflexes of the older words that have survived into MnE but are not used in later translations. Write down the equivalent words or phrases from each text.

OE	ME	EMnE, 1611	MnE, 1961	MnE reflex
eac swylce	but	now	–	such
seo nædre	the serpent	the serpent	the serpent	the adder
wæs	was	was	was	was
geapre	feller	more subtill	more crafty	subtle
þonne	than	then	than	than
ealle	alle	any	any	all
þa oðre	–	any	any	the other
–	lyuinge	–	–	living
nytenu	beestis	beast	wild creature	beast
þe	which	which	that	which/that
God	the Lord God	the Lord God	the LORD God	God
geworhte	hadde maad	had made	had made	wrought
ofer eorþan	of erthe	of the field	wild	over earth
and	–	and	–	and
seo nædre	which serpent	he	he	the adder
cwæþ	seide	said	said	quoth
to þam wife	to the woman	vnto the woman	to the woman	wife
hwi	why	–	–	why
forbead	comaundide	hath .. said	has forbidden	forbade
eow	ʒou	–	you	you
þæt	that	–	–	that
ge	ʒe	ye	you	(ye)
ne	not	not	–	–
æton	ete	eat	eat	eat
of ælcon treowe	of ech tre	of euery tree	from any tree	of each tree
binnan paradisum	of paradis	of the garden	in the garden	paradise

This can then be used to describe the linguistic features of the texts.

Vocabulary

Have any words changed meaning?

OE *nædre* meant *snake*, *serpent* and is now restricted to one type of snake, the *adder*. OE *wif* meant *woman*, but had a more restricted meaning in ME and after. OE *geworhte* (*wrought*) is the past tense of *gewyrcan* (*to work, make*). Today, *wrought* is used in a specialised sense, and the past tense of *work* is *worked*.

Have any older words been lost from the language?

OE *eac*, *geapre*, *nytenu* (plural of *nyten* = *animal*) and *binnan* are not in the vocabulary of MnE.

OE *swylce* = MnE *such*, but is used in the phrase *eac swylce* to mean *also*, *moreover*.

OE *cwæþ*, *quoth* is the past tense of *cweþan*, *to say*. We no longer use *quoth*, an archaic form, but it was used into the nineteenth century.

The present tense *quethe* was in use up to the early sixteenth century, but is now obsolete.

Orthography

Are there any unusual letter forms?

<æ>, <þ> and <ð> are not Roman letters, and are described in Section 2.2.4.

Can you tell if different spellings of the same word are due to sound changes, or simply different spelling conventions?

Some spelling conventions must have changed after the OE period, for example:

- <qu-> replaced <cw->, as in OE *cwæþ*.
- <y> and <i> were often interchangeable in ME and EMnE, as in *lyuynge*, *seide*, *sayd*, *sotyller* and *subtill*.
- <$\overset{e}{\text{y}}$> is an abbreviation in EMnE for <the>, the letter <y> standing for the OE letter <þ>, MnE <th>.
- <v> in <vnto>, letter <v>, was introduced during the ME period and written for both the consonant /v/ and the vowel /u/ at the beginning of a word (**word-initial**), for example, *verily* and *vnder*; letter <u> was used in the middle (**word-medial**) or at the end of a word (**word-final**), for example, *lyuynge*, *vndur* (= *under*), *dust* and *thou*. They were then variant forms of the same letter, just as today we use upper and lower case variants of the same letters, for example, <A>, <a> and <ɑ>.

The spelling is evidence of some sound changes that occurred after the OE period.

The word *næddre* in OE now has the form *adder*, as well as a restricted meaning. The pronunciation of the phrase *a nadder* is identical to that of *an adder*. The indefinite article *a*/*an* was not part of OE grammar, so the change of *nadder* to *adder* came later, between the fourteenth and sixteenth centuries. The dialectal form *nedder* was still in use at least into the nineteenth century.

The diphthong vowels of *ealle*, *eorþan*, *forbead* and *treowe* have smoothed to become single vowels.

It is not possible to recognise all the sound changes from the spelling alone, because MnE spelling does not reflect them; for example, the MnE pronunciation of *was* is /wɒz/ but the spelling has not changed since its earlier pronunciation as /wæs/.

Word structure

Are there changes in word suffixes (endings)?

The order of the consonants *re* and *or* of *næddre* and *geworhte* has changed to *er* and *ro*. Other examples are *bird*, *thresh* and *run*, which come from OE *brid*, *þerscan* and *yrnan*. The linguistic term for this reversal of sounds is **metathesis**.

The pronoun *oðr-e*, however, is not an example of this. It is a shortened form of *oþer-e*, from *oðer*, and *-e* is a suffix.

eall-e, *nyten-u*, *geworht-e* and *eorþ-an*: these suffixes have been lost. *beest-is* has been reduced to *beast-s*.

Grammar

Is the OE word order different from MnE?

hwi forbead god eow, *why forbade God you*: the interrogative in OE was formed by reversing the order of the subject and the verb, which is no longer grammatical for the simple present and past tenses in MnE.

þæt ge ne æton, *that ye ne eat*: the negative in OE was formed by placing *ne* before the verb. During the ME period, a reinforcing *noght* was added after the verb, which is now the only negative marker, *ne* having been dropped.

(This method of descriptive analysis can be found set out in greater detail in *The English Language: A Historical Reader*, A. G. Rigg, New York Appleton-Century-Crofts, 1968.)

12.4.2 'Your accent gives you away'

The following texts are historical translations of the story of Peter's denial, from the New Testament, St Matthew's Gospel, Chapter 26 verses 69–75. Versions in contemporary Scots and Bislama pidgin English are also provided.

TEXT 144 – Late West Saxon OE c.1050

'þyn spræc þe gesweotolað'

69 Petrus soðlice sæt ute on þam cafertune. þa com to hym an
þeowen ⁊ cwæð. ⁊ þu wære myd þam galileiscan hælende.
70 ⁊ he wyðsoc beforan eallum ⁊ cwæð. nat ic hwæt þu segst.
71 þa he ut eode of þære dura. þa geseh hyne oðer þynen. ⁊
sæde þam ðe þar wæron. ⁊ þes wæs myd þam nazareniscan
hælende. 72 ⁊ he wyðsoc eft myd aðe þæt he hys nan þyng ne
cuðe. 73 þa æfter lytlum fyrste genealæhton þa ðe þær
stodon. ⁊ cwædon to petre. Soðlice þu eart of hym. ⁊ þyn
spræc þe gesweotolað. 74 þa ætsoc he ⁊ swerede. þæt he
næfre þone man ne cuðe. ⁊ hrædlice þa creow se cocc. 75 Ða
gemunde petrus þæs hælendes word þe he cwæð. ærþam þe se cocc
crawe. þrywa ðu me wyðsæcst. ⁊ he eode ut ⁊ weop byterlice.

(*The West-Saxon Gospels*, M. Grünberg, Scheltema & Holkema, 1967)

69 Peter truly sat out(side) in the courtyard. then came to him a
servant & said. & thou wast with the galilean saviour.
70 & he denied before all & said. ne-know I what thou sayest.
71 then he out went of the door. then saw him other servant. &
said to-them that there were. & this (man) was with the nazarean
saviour. 72 & he denied again with oath that he of-him no thing ne-
knew. 73 then after little time approached them that there
stood. & said to peter. Truly thou art of him. & thy
speech thee shows. 74 then denied he & swore. that he
never the man ne knew. & immediately then crew the cock. 75 then
remembered peter the saviour's words that he spoke. before that the cock
crows thrice thou me deniest. & he went out & wept bitterly.

TEXT 145 – Fourteenth century S. Midlands dialect

'thi speche makith thee knowun'

69 And Petir sat with outen in the halle; and a damysel cam
to hym, and seide, Thou were with Jhesu of Galilee. 70 And
he denyede bifor alle men, and seide, Y woot not what thou
seist. 71 And whanne he ȝede out at the ȝate, another
damysel say hym, and seide to hem that weren there, And this
was with Jhesu of Nazareth. 72 And eftsoone he denyede with
an ooth, For I knewe not the man. 73 And a litil aftir, thei
that stooden camen, and seiden to Petir, treuli thou art of
hem; for thi speche makith thee knowun. 74 Thanne he bigan
to warie and to swere, that he knewe not the man. And anoon
the cok crewe. 75 And Petir bithouȝte on the word of Jhesu,
that he hadde seid, Bifore the cok crowe, thries thou schalt
denye me. And he ȝede out, and wepte bitterli.

(*The Wycliffite Bible*)

TEXT 146 – Early sixteenth century Scots, c.1520

(This Scots version was made from Text 145, and is of interest because it makes clear some of the dialectal differences between Scots and Wyclif's Midlands dialect.)

'thi speche makis thee knawne'

69 Ande Petir sat without in the hall: and a damycele com to
him, and said, Thou was with Jesu of Galilee. 70 And he
denyit before al men, and said, I wate nocht quhat thou sais.
71 And quhen he yede out at the yet, an vthir damycele saw
him, and said to thame that ware thar, And this was with Jesu
of Nazarethe. 72 And eftsone he denyit with ane athe, For I
knew nocht the man. 73 And a litil eftir thai that stude com
and said to Petir, treulie thou art of thame; for thi speche
makis thee knawne. 74 Than he began to warie and to suere
that he knew nocht the man. And anon the cok crew. 75 And
Petir bethouchte on the word of Jesu, that he had said,
Before the cok craw, thrijse thou sal denye me. And he yede
out, and wepit bittirlie.

(*The New Testament in Scots*, being Purvey's revision of Wycliffe's version turned into Scots by Murdoch Nisbet c.1520, Scottish Text Society 1901)

TEXT 147 – EMnE, 1582

'for euen thy speache doth bevvray thee'

69 But Peter sate vvithout in the court: and there came to him one vvenche,
saying: Thou also vvast vvith IESVS the Galilean. 70 But he denied before
them all, saying, I vvot not vvhat thou sayest. 71 And as he went out of the
gate, an other vvenche savv him, and she saith to them that vvere there, And
this felovv also vvas vvith IESVS the Nazarite. 72 And againe he denied
vvith an othe, That I knovv not the man. 73 And after a litle they came that
stoode by, and said to Peter, Surely thou also art of them: for euen thy speache
doth bevvray thee. 74 Then he began to curse and to svveare that he knevve
not the man. And incontinent the cocke crevve. 75 And Peter remembred the
vvord of IESVS vvhich he had said, before the cocke crovv, thou shalt deny me thrise.
And going forth, he vvept bitterly.

(*The New Testament of Jesus Christ* Rheims 1582, Vol. 267 of *English Recusant Literature 1558–1640*, Scolar Press, 1975 – the *Rheims New Testament*)

TEXT 148 – EMnE, 1611

'for thy speech bewrayeth thee'

69 Now Peter sate without in the palace: and a damosell came vnto him,
saying, Thou also wast with Iesus of Galilee. 70 But hee denied before
them all, saying, I know not what thou saiest. 71 And when he was gone
out into the porch, another maide saw him, and saide vnto them that were
there, This fellow was also with Iesus of Nazareth. 72 And againe hee denied
with an oath, I doe not know the man. 73 And after a while came vnto him
they that stood by, and saide to Peter, Surely thou also art one of them, for
thy speech bewrayeth thee. 74 Then beganne hee to curse and to sweare,
saying, I know not the man. And immediatly the cocke crew. 75 And Peter
remembred the words of Iesus, which said vnto him, Before the cocke crow,
thou shalt denie mee thrice. And hee went out, and wept bitterly.

(*King James Bible*)

TEXT 149 – Twentieth century Scots

'your Galilee twang outs ye'

69 Meantime, Peter wis sittin furth i the close, whan a servan-queyn cam
up an said til him, 'Ye war wi the man frae Galilee, Jesus, tae, I'm thinkin.'
70 But he denied it afore them aa: 'I kenna what ye mean,' said he; 71
and wi that he gaed out intil the pend.
Here anither servan-lass saw him an said tae the fowk staundin about,
'This chiel wis wi yon Nazarean Jesus.'
72 Again Pater wadna tak wi it, but said wi an aith, 'I kenna the man!'
73 A wee after, the staunders-by gaed up til him an said, 'Ay, but ye
war sae wi him, tae: your Galilee twang outs ye.'
74 At that he fell tae bannin an sweirin at he hed nae kennins o the man
ava. An than a cock crew, 75 an it cam back tae Peter hou Jesus hed said
til him, 'Afore the cock craws, ye will disavou me thrice'; and he gaed out
an grat a sair, sair greit.

(*The New Testament in Scots* translated by William Laughton Lorimer, Penguin Books, 1985)

TEXT 150 – MnE

'your accent gives you away!'

69 Meanwhile Peter was sitting outside in the courtyard when
a serving-maid accosted him and said, 'You were there too
with Jesus the Galilean.' 70 Peter denied it in face of them
all. 'I do not know what you mean', he said. 71 He then
went out to the gateway, where another girl, seeing him, said
to the people there, 'This fellow was with Jesus of
Nazareth.' 72 Once again he denied it, saying with an oath,
'I do not know the man.' 73 Shortly afterwards the
bystanders came up and said to Peter, 'Surely you are another
of them; your accent gives you away!' 74 At this he broke
into curses and declared with an oath: 'I do not know the
man.' 75 At that moment a cock crew; and Peter remembered
how Jesus had said, 'Before the cock crows you will disown me
three times.' He went outside, and wept bitterly.

(*New English Bible,* 1961)

Finally, here is the same Biblical extract in Bislama, a pidgin language based on English, from Vanuatu (formerly the New Hebrides) in the West Pacific. Read it aloud as if it were in phonetic script, because the spelling system is based on the spoken language, and you should be able to match the sense with the preceding texts. For example, *yad* is pronounced /ya:d/, like English *yard*, *get* is /ge:t/, like *gate*, *rusta* like *rooster*, and *save* is a two-syllable word like *savvy*, meaning *know*.

TEXT 151 – Bislama

from *Gud Nyus Bilong Jisas Krais*

'tok bilong yu i tok bilong man Galili ia'

69 Pita i stap sidaon aofsaid long yad bilong hoas ia. Nao
wan haosgel i kam long em, i talem long em, i se 'Yu tu, yu
stap wetem man Galili ia, Jisas.' 70 Be long fes bilong
olgeta evrewan, Pita i haidem samting ia. Em i ansa, i se
'Mi mi no save samting ia, we yu yu stap talem.' 71 Nao em i
goaot long get bilong yad ia. Nao wan narafala gel i lukem
em. Nao i talem long ol man we oli stap stanap long ples ia,
i se 'Man ia i wetem man Naseret ia, Jisas.' 72 Be Pita i
haidem bakegen, i mekem strong tok, nao em i talem se 'Mi mi
no save man ia.' 73 Gogo smol taem nomo, ol man ia we oli
stap stanap long ples ia, oli kam long Pita, oli talem long
em, oli se, 'Be i tru ia, yu yu wan long olgeta. Yu luk,
tok bilong yu i tok bilong man Galili ia.' 74 Nao Pita i
mekem tok we i strong moa, i se 'Sipos mi mi gyaman, bambae
God i givem panis long mi. Mi mi no save man ia.' Nao
wantaem rusta i singoat. 75 Nao Pita i tingabaot tok ia we
Jisas i bin talem long em, i se 'Taem rusta i no singaot yet,
yu, be bambae yu save haidem tri taem, se yu no save mi.'
Nao em i go aofsaid, em i kraekrae tumas.

(*The Four Gospels in New Hebrides Bislama*, The Bible Society in New Zealand, 1971)

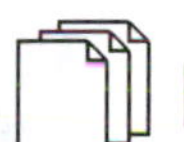 

Activity 12.5

Make a contrastive study of the language, using some or all of the texts given (Texts 144–151) as evidence of some of the principal changes that have taken place since the OE period in vocabulary, word and sentence structure, spelling and pronunciation.

Bibliography

This list is a selection of books which teachers, lecturers and advanced students will find useful for further reading and reference. Separate editions of Old, Middle and Early Modern English texts are not listed.

The history and development of the English language

Baugh, A.C. and Cable, T.
A History of the English Language, 3rd edn
(Routledge & Kegan Paul, 1978).

Pyles, T. and Algeo, J.
The Origins & Development of the English Language, 3rd edn
(Harcourt Brace Jovanovich, 1982).
(This textbook has an accompanying work-book)

Strang, Barbara
A History of English
(Methuen, 1970).

Leith, Dick
A Social History of English
(Routledge & Kegan Paul, 1983).

Scragg, D.G.
A History of English Spelling
(Manchester UP, 1974).

Partridge, A.C.
A Companion to Old & Middle English Studies
(Deutsch, 1982).

Old English

Mitchell, B. and Robinson, F.C.
A Guide to Old English, 4th edn
(Blackwell, 1986).

Quirk, R. and Wrenn, C.L.
An Old English Grammar
(Methuen, 1955).

Quirk, R., Adams, V. and Davy, D.
Old English Literature: A Practical Introduction
(Edward Arnold, 1975).

Sweet, H.
The Student's Dictionary of Anglo-Saxon
(Oxford UP, reprint 1978).

Davis, N.
Sweet's Anglo-Saxon Primer, 9th edn
(Oxford UP, 1953).

Garmonsway, G.N.
The Anglo-Saxon Chronicle (translation)
(Dent, 1972).

Swanton, M
Anglo-Saxon Prose (translation)
(Dent, 1975).

Bradley, S.A.J.
Anglo-Saxon Poetry (translation)
(Dent, 1982).

Middle English

Bennett, J.A.W. and Smithers, G.V.
Early Middle English Verse & Prose, 2nd edn (anthology)
(Oxford UP, 1968).

Sisam, K.
Fourteenth Century Verse & Prose
(Oxford UP, 1921).

Burnley, D.
A Guide to Chaucer's Language
(Macmillan, 1983).

Early Modern English

Barber, C.
Early Modern English
(Deutsch, 1976).

Blake, Norman
The Language of Shakespeare
(Macmillan, 1985).

Modern English

Quirk, R. *et al.*
A Comprehensive Grammar of the English Language
(Longman, 1985).

Barber, C.
Linguistic Change in Present-Day English
(Oliver & Boyd, 1964).

Foster, B.
The Changing English Language
(Macmillan, 1968).

Potter, S.
Changing English
(Deutsch, 1969).

Index